Voices Rising II

Cover Art: Christopher Saucedo
"Self-Portrait, In Exact Weight and Volume (New Orleans)"
© 2007 Christopher Saucedo
Acrylic and Rubber
21" x 21" x 28 ½"

Photo by Mike Smith
Used by permission

Cover Design:
Bill Lavender

Editorial Assistants:
  For Rebeca Antoine:
    Zachary J. George
  For UNO Press:
    Kelcy Wilburn
    Creighton Durant
    Erin Gendron

Printed in the USA

Library of Congress Control Number: 2009927360

ISBN: 0-9706190-8-1
ISBN 13: 978-0-9706190-8-2

University of New Orleans Publishing

Managing Editor
Bill Lavender

www.unopress.org

Voices Rising II
More Stories from
The Katrina Narrative Project

Edited by
Rebeca Antoine

Contents

Editor's Introduction
Rebeca Antoine   13

Introduction
Barb Johnson   17

Refugees in the Land of Plenty
Holly Gee   29
Interviewed by Anita Yesho

Torn Apart
Kendra Williams   53
Interviewed by Mary Sparacello

Just Piles of Houses
Glen Kirkland   56
Interviewed by Daniel McBride

Fifty and Homeless
Peter Borstell   75
Interviewed by Missy Bowen

Doing the Lord's Work
Larry and Karen Daigle   89
Interviewed by Mary Sparacello

Standing in Line and Signing My Name
Harry Sterling   93
Interviewed by Nicole Pugh

My Own Little World
Tommy   101
In His Own Words

On the Run
Jaye Woodmansee   103
In His Own Words

Everybody's Pharmacist
George Vertigell   112
Interviewed by Zachary J. George

They Brought the Spirit of Louisiana *and Gave it Back to Us*
Stefan Schmidt   129
Interviewed by Kim Guise

We Have a Job We Have to Do
Rob Callahan   155
Interviewed by Frank Lovato

The Mud Took Our Shoes
Douglas Hitt   172
In Her Own Words

We Lost Five Households
Louvin Skinner   177
In Her Own Words

Ransacked Memories
Stephanie Skinner   185
In Her Own Words

If I Had Known
Caroline Skinner   191
In Her Own Words

Can You Tell Me How We Get Saved?
Toni   204
Interviewed by Jamie Mathews

It Looked Like Mogadishu
Michael Ward Prevost   231
Interviewed by Anita Louise Hedgepeth

The Cajun Navy
Manning Billeaud   255
Interviewed by Shannon Billeaud

That's Got to be the River!
Erin Dowd 272
Interviewed by Nicole Pugh

Hubris and Two Gallons of Gas
Peter Syverson 279
In His Own Words

What the City Forgot
Lynn Morice and Robin Rodriguez 282
Interviewed by Zachary J. George

Scary, Scary, Scary
Steve Williams, Sr. 304
Interviewed by Mary Sparacello

The Lucky Thirteen
Margie Stoughton-Pyburn 306
Interviewed by Missy Bowen

Life in a Van
Benny and Millie Reine 315
Interviewed by Mary Sparacello

Seeking Refuge
Debbie Baxter 318
Interviewed by Peter Syverson

A Place Found Us
Nicole Pugh 321
In Her Own Words

Cash and Water
Mary Funti 333
Interviewed by Virginia Corinne Akins

Thought I Was Gonna Die Out There
Jesse Hampton 348
Interviewed by Zachary J. George

Blown Charts
Kirsten Stanton 360
Interviewed by Nicole Pugh

I Don't Own the Clothes I'm Wearing
Carol McCarthy 365
In Her Own Words

New Orleans is People
Niyi Osundare 369
Interviewed by Rebeca Antoine

We're Not Here to Protect You
Joel Fisher Rapp 387
Interviewed by April Martin

Editor's Introduction

Rebeca Antoine

Rebeca Antoine was born in Connecticut and holds degrees from Yale University and the Creative Writing Workshop at the University of New Orleans. Her fiction has appeared in numerous venues, most recently in Gulf Stream *and* Upstreet. *She is the editor of* Voices Rising: Stories from the Katrina Narrative Project *(2008).*

As I set about selecting the stories that would eventually make up this volume, I thought about the choices that those of us who lived in New Orleans at the time of the storm had to make. There was of course the choice of whether to evacuate— if indeed one were able to make that choice. But there was also the choice, after evacuation, of whether to come back. Many had nothing to come back to: no home, no job, no church. Some of us were able and willing to return; some of us were not.

Some chose not to evacuate because of their pets or jobs or families and stayed in New Orleans to witness what the majority of us did not. These reports from the field expose the power of the storm itself, the chaos that followed, and what none of us saw on television. In this volume, Holly Gee reports from the desolate Bywater, George Vertigell and Toni from flooded Mid-City, and Joel Fisher-Rapp from the Convention Center, as those stranded in the city did their best to fend for themselves and band together in the face of being told that no one was there to save them. At least, not yet.

I began the introduction to the first volume of *Voices Rising* with this observation:

> On my drive from Uptown New Orleans to work at the lakefront campus of the University of New Orleans, I travel down Broad Street. At the corner of Tulane Avenue and Broad Street stands Israel M. Augustine Middle School; a hulking thing, built of pale stone with a

grand double-sided staircase that leads to a boarded-up door. The sign out front reads: School starts August 18, 2005.

More than four years after the storm, that observation is still true, except now a few of the letters have fallen down. In New Orleans, and along the Gulf Coast, Katrina is not history; we live with her every day.

My gratitude goes to those brave enough to share their stories in the Katrina Narrative Project and those still submitting their stories to the archive. UNO Press Editorial Assistants Creighton Durrant, Erin Gendron, and Kelcy Wilburn worked along side Managing Editor Bill Lavender to give careful attention to this manuscript. I am grateful to Zachary George, who worked closely with me on both volumes of Voices Rising and continues to work collecting Katrina stories. Above all, I thank Fredrick Barton for envisioning this project in the days following the storm, while New Orleans was still underwater; it has been my honor to work with these stories and by doing so, those who told them.

Reading the stories so generously shared in the Katrina Narrative Project has made one thing plain for me. There were no easy choices to be made when we found out that Katrina was hurling toward New Orleans and no easy choices to be made in the aftermath of the flood. None of us knew what Katrina and the resulting levee failures and flooding would do to our city, but we also didn't know what it would do to us. This disaster brought us to our breaking points, challenged us to the core, weakened us and made us brave. As professor and poet Niyi Osundare says in his interview, "New Orleans is people," and those people are more than just survivors; they are passionate and fearless souls who continue to rise to the challenge of rebuilding this city.

Rebeca Antoine
October 2009

Introduction

Barb Johnson

Barb Johnson worked as a carpenter in New Orleans for more than twenty years before receiving her MFA from the University of New Orleans in 2008. She worked as an editorial assistant for the UNO Press on the first Voices Rising: Stories from the Katrina Narrative Project *published in 2008. In November of 2009, Harper Collins released her first book, a collection of short stories entitled* More of This World or Maybe Another.

Before the storm, I was a carpenter and had been for most of my adult life. I'd just completed my first year in the writing program at the University of New Orleans. School was starting again, and I was excited. I was forty-seven years old. I had scaled down my carpentry business by only taking jobs in the summer and during school breaks. This allowed me to make enough money to stay in school and still have time to write. I'd just completed a wall-to-wall entertainment center and been paid. That customer had another project he wanted me to do, and he'd said sure when I asked if I could do it during the break between semesters. I was set. Class met once, and then the Mayor called for a mandatory evacuation. I had never left town for a hurricane before.

First, I went to Lake Charles, to my mother's house with a friend and her brother. Lots of people evacuated in strange groupings like that because many of us, most of us, had not planned to leave. We left the day the hurricane was scheduled to come ashore. We could see the wind and the rain in our rearview mirrors.

We went to bed that night in Lake Charles. The hurricane came in. The next day, the TV said it wasn't all that bad. Later that afternoon, my friend's brother was pointing at the television, at helicopter views of a flooded city, at the shattered spine of a long, twin roadway that he kept calling the Causeway Bridge. And I kept saying, no, the hurricane didn't really hit us. That must be the one in Alabama, that twin-span. Then there were pictures of people in chest-deep water in streets that I knew to be New Orleans, streets that I drove down every day. The television flashed images of water up to rooflines. And then the endless loop of looting and people trapped on the interstate or their rooftops and helicopters and fires and the Superdome and the Convention Center. We were informed by the television that we would not be allowed to go home any time soon. CNN was implying that we'd maybe never go home, that New Orleans was over for good.

This is what we heard from our mayor:

This is what we heard from our governor:

This is what we heard from President Bush:

Nothing.

No one knew what came next.

My friends and I stayed in Lake Charles a few days, trying to track down other friends and relatives. My closest friends had landed in Lafayette. They were staying with a woman named Betty Ellison, who had gone to high school with one of them. Betty asked, "Do you know anyone else who needs a place to stay?" I went to Lafayette for a visit because the only source of comfort in that upside-down time was to be with people you knew. People you would've been sitting in the yard with back home. Once we were all together, no one wanted to leave. Being together like that was the most normal moment in the entire episode, even though we were in the home of a relative stranger. The Lafayette people brought food. And cake. I don't know why this comforted me so much, but every day I would wake up and there would be cake. We mostly didn't eat it, but every couple of days there'd be a new cake.

I snuck into New Orleans two weeks after Katrina with a friend who does mosquito research. They were only letting people in on officials business, so we posed as researchers for the CDC, a plausible disguise because of all the standing water in the city. We went to check on our houses, on our friends' houses. The smell was awful. And the heat. And the shaken-not-stirred look of the city. We drove through narrow paths on the main roads, to the left and to the right, utter chaos. A curve on the interstate was littered with the detritus of those who'd waited there for busses that never came. It was a place we knew people had died. Driving down that road made my heart tighten up, a big muscle flexed to protect itself. I couldn't stop crying. We went back to Lafayette to tell people how their houses had fared. What was lost. What was okay. What was baffling: the homeless guy who hung out at the bus stop on Broad Street in normal times was still sitting there dressed in his ten layers of clothes as though nothing had happened.

Then Hurricane Rita hit Lake Charles, where I'd initially evacuated, and my mother ended up with us in Lafayette. There were about ten people in the house by that time. After Hurricane Rita, Lake Charles residents weren't allowed back into their city, either. My mother, who was in her late seventies, drove back to the dark, obliterated city anyway. The interstate exit to her house was blocked by a couple of big orange and white striped barricades. She got out of her car, she told me, moved the barricade aside and drove on home. I mention this for two reasons. One, to illustrate the powerful drive to be home, no matter the condition of the place. And two, because it's easy to forget that Hurricane Rita struck just a few weeks after Hurricane Katrina.

If all your relatives lived along the Gulf Coast— and mine did, as did the relatives of many New Orleanians— everyone you were related to had no place to live. You couldn't stay with your relatives because your relatives had no place to stay themselves. In four years, between 2004 and 2008, there have been four devastating hurricanes that have effectively ripped up the Gulf Coast from central Florida to east Texas. I remember going to the beach near the border between Alabama and Florida for Thanksgiving of 2005, three months after our hurricane (Katrina) and a year and three months after theirs (Ivan). It was still seriously torn up over there, and my friends and I couldn't figure out why it was taking them so long to get themselves back together. We soon learned.

The day my mother went back to Lake Charles— a month after Katrina— I returned to New Orleans with another friend who lived in a neighborhood that had been okayed to visit and leave. We had no plan to leave. There was no plan for reoccupation of my neighborhood, Mid-City. It might be another month, they said, or it might be six. No one was allowed in. Never in my life had it been clearer to me that the people in charge didn't have a clue what they were doing. And that realization gave me and my fellow citizens a great deal of freedom. Once we got over the horror of watching President Bush ignore us while our Governor and Mayor locked themselves in a power struggle at our expense, we began to take care of business in the most efficient and cooperative way. Whoever was in the neighborhood cleaned up to ease the way for those who had yet to come. Neighbor by neighbor. Street by street. That didn't get a lot of press, but that's the way it was. And all of that effort was thwarted at every step because we were not even supposed to be in our neighborhoods. We were determined to stay, though, and we did.

My carpentry shop, at the high point, had water up to the ceiling. Two weeks after the storm, I still couldn't get to it because fallen branches from the giant oaks blocked the roads, which were still filled with flood water. After a month, when I returned for good, I had to go and look. I'd planned to sell my business when I graduated. It was the only thing of value I owned, and it was gone. Completely ruined. I couldn't grasp what the loss of it meant. Neither could I grasp the meaning of the Small Business Association's ruling that my business hadn't produced enough income the previous year (while I was in school) to be considered a viable business, despite all the previous years in which I had paid heavy taxes on it. I couldn't grasp the complete lack of irony in the voice of the man who explained to me that I wasn't eligible for an SBA loan because I had no collateral. He said it with a perfectly straight face. I'm sure that, as I was, he was having bad dreams at night. He was human and probably more than a little freaked out by the nightmare he'd been set down in. And that is why I could not grasp how in the world he could say what he said without acknowledging the insanity of it, which was just one tiny, tiny bit of the monstrous insanity that was swallowing all of us up.

Fortunately, my apartment was upstairs and mostly unharmed. I set up house outside on my balcony because it was cooler there. In the daytime I made trips to get food and water from a Red Cross site. It was quite a distance from my house and that meant weaving my truck through eight-foot-tall piles of debris a block long. A bathtub ring circled all the houses, showing the high point of the flood, and then the various levels as the water drained, slowly, over a period of weeks. There were X's spray-painted on the fronts of all the houses, with dates indicating when the house had been checked for gas leaks and numbers representing the number of dead bodies found inside. I had to look away from those numbers.

No stores were open. You couldn't buy ice if you wanted to, and you were rationed a bag a day at the Red Cross site. A plague of rust had come down on us. On my way to get supplies, I would toss rusted bikes in the back of my truck to fix later. People had lost their cars. Old women were walking to pick up their supplies, carrying bags of ice long distances, and I gave them rides when I saw them. Everyone rode with everyone all the time; it occurred to me what a great world it would be if we could always do that.

In the morning I would try to find a place to charge my laptop, to get an internet signal so I could download my classmates' stories. Improbably, miraculously, UNO had risen from the dead, recreating itself online. We resumed classes online a little over a month after the storm, the only university in the city to do so. There was so much heroism in that effort, such profound goodness in that reopening. And so I was able to stay with my writing workshop. All that craziness was going on, and we were writing stories— not one of them about the hurricane— and sending them to each other, a fact I still find unbelievable.

In the afternoons I worked to unfreeze the rusted gears of the bikes I had picked up. Gallons of naval jelly and a toothbrush. I put the marginally functional bikes in the back of my truck and dropped them off at the Red Cross. People rode off on them if they needed one. Everything worked like that. Nobody locked anything. Everyone shared. It was what kept us from losing our minds. It was what reassured us that, contrary to what CNN was suggesting to the world, we had not all devolved into animals.

We all knew plenty about the bad stuff. What didn't get reported all that much was the good stuff. The ordinary, daily acts of kindness. I remember once, standing in line for something (we were always in line for things) and making eye contact with the guy behind me.

He said, "How's your recovery going today?" I will never ever forget that. We were all broken and half a click from a postal moment, and people were tender with each other. "How's your recovery going today?" It was an acknowledgement that we were living moment-to-moment in profound uncertainty, but we were in it together. Signs popped up in yards, not sponsored signs, just little reminders that people thought would be helpful: "Recovery is a marathon, not a sprint. Pace yourself." And there was humor: "Waterfront property for sale."

When we got where we were going in whatever line we were in, there was always someone who would ask: What's your address? No one knew the answer to that; an address meant you needed to receive mail to get your life back. There was no mail delivery. No P.O. boxes to be had. People would bust out crying when they heard that question. And often a complete stranger would put his arm around the crier and just stand with him until he stopped. We all knew. And we were mostly tender with one another.

I worked to clear a path up to my apartment because there were giant tree branches— a twisting, waist-high blanket of branches— covering my entire yard, blocking the bottom flight of my stairs so that I had to climb up a fallen tree to the landing. Up the next flight, I had to climb over the fallen pipe that contained the building's power feed. I showered in the unheated water that we'd been told not to shower in. It was so hot outside, and it didn't rain one time. I decided if I had to die because of the toxic water then so be it. I already had to carry my drinking water and the ice and whatever food I had up a tree and then over the pole and then up the rest of the stairs. Not having to carry up more water to bathe in was worth dying for.

On my balcony, at night, I would read my classmates' stories. I would write stories. I had a headlamp. Other than the glow of that headlamp and my laptop's screen, there was no other light in the whole neighborhood. No other person. Months of this. Most of my friends were still out of town. Nobody had a real plan for the future because the future of New Orleans was still up for grabs. Sometimes I worried the whole place would burn down. Fires started and burned unattended. I could see them in the dark, quiet distance, no siren going to the rescue. Complete silence except for the clickety-clack of my typing, a comforting sound.

I was isolated from my loved ones. Everyone was bouncing from place to place. Cell phones didn't work very well. Horrific conversations got broken up every minute or so, and you'd have to redial the call and tell the story over. "They found the dog, but they couldn't find her mother…" "They were left on the interstate for three days in the hot sun…" "The hospital told them that if they stayed, they could bring their families and their pets. A week into it, rescue finally came but said they'd have to euthanize their dogs…" "They ended up at the Convention Center…" "They ended up in New Jersey…" "…in Austin…" "…in Atlanta…" "…in Baton Rouge…" "They finally gave up and moved to Canada…."

Every car trip was a slow evisceration, the bizarre landscape ripping my insides up. The crashed helicopter on the bayou a few blocks from my apartment. The boats and cars in the middle of the street or on end, leaning against a tree, or a front tire through the window of a classroom. The refrigerators, with their rotting food stinking of death, their carcasses covered in angry graffiti. The animals that didn't make it through the storm. The long lines of sad, scared people at the Red Cross, whose volunteers must've received in their training the advice to touch people on their shoulders. The Red Cross, as an organization, got a lot of bad press at that time, a lot of criticism for the way they handled donations. On the street, as individuals, they were our lifeline. Kind, kind people, squeezing shoulders quietly until the crying stopped.

And good soldiers of the National Guard. Around dusk, they did their patrols in a golf cart. Teenaged boys carrying M-16's. I wasn't supposed to be in my neighborhood. No one was. These boys weren't supposed to allow me to stay. It was their duty to tell me to leave, and they did. Every day they did. But that's as far as it went. They never got out of the golf cart because we had an understanding, and you can't ask for more in a situation like that.

In that fall semester, in addition to the writing workshop, the creative writing program offered a course called the Katrina Narrative Project. Rick Barton, who was our teacher and also Provost for the University, thought it might be a good idea for students to interview people who'd been through the storm and to document their experiences. Some of us were given the task of editing these early documents. We'd go through and copy edit or make suggestions for future drafts. All of this as though there weren't utter chaos going on right outside. Like Blackhawk helicopters weren't flying back and forth, so low they made our ribs vibrate. Like people weren't living with relatives far away or sleeping under a stranger's dining room table. Or hiding out on their balconies in a pitch-dark city. No. We sent one another documents. We edited. We sent them back. That was my earliest involvement with the stories that, along with those from the Writing Katrina Project implemented by UNO's sociology department, were the basis for this book.

It wasn't until November 2005 that the electricity was restored in my apartment building. My neighborhood and most of the city remained dark. It would be almost a year before there were stoplights in my neighborhood.

A year and a half later, I was working at the UNO Press, helping prepare the manuscripts that had been gathered together by Rebeca Antoine and the staff, who had the difficult task of going through hundreds of accounts to decide which ones would appear in the first book. Every day, I would read through those narratives. I would leave the office and go to read them in an empty classroom.

One day, sitting in that empty classroom, reading for the sixth or seventh time an essay about a classmate's grandfather who died soon after the storm, I found that it still brought me to tears. I knew it by heart. I knew what was coming, and yet it brought me to tears. I had expected to become numb to these stories, but I never did. They contained the kind of truth that is hard to know. They illustrated that now and then, in life, the person you are going to be disappears, and in a second, you are on a road to being, not a more refined version of yourself, but a new, somewhat unrecognizable self. And you might be galvanized by this experience, or you might be broken by it. Tough people got angry and their anger caused them to sink. Meek people were emboldened and rose. There was no way to tell ahead of time which it would be.

When we look back at the devastation caused by war or natural disasters or man-made financial disasters, it is tempting to look for causes, to record statistics, projected rates of recurrence, and then to believe we have an understanding of what happened. In more sanguine times, numbers comfort us. We build our houses on higher ground. We design a color-coded system for terrorist threats. We impose regulations. But the changes that issue from a disaster are geometric in their increase; people are changed, and they pass along the change in a million different configurations, not to one person but to everyone they meet. And so these stories, these accounts of what happened to the people of New Orleans, during and after Hurricane

Katrina, provide a first-hand source of how we were changed and why and when and, a little, to what degree.

This book contains not just the story of a few people in a specific place and time. It is actually the story of us all. It is the story of how we are battered by being in this world and about how sometimes we sink. But, more importantly, it is the story of how, having been battered, having sunk, we then rise. These are the voices of the storm. Rising.

Refugees in the Land of Plenty

Holly Gee
Interviewed by Anita Yesho

Holly Gee was one of many Bywater neighborhood residents who did not evacuate and used the Country Club, a gay bar on Louisa Street, as a community center.

So tell me— you've been in New Orleans how long?

This Mardi Gras it will be 20 years.

So you've been through a bunch of hurricanes before.

I've been through hurricanes before, but they've always veered away. You know, it didn't really hit us smack-dab-on before. And even though it seemed like a serious one this time, and we should really leave, and I was boarding up my windows the day before— it's easy for me to be in denial and hope for the best anyway. When Harold, my ex-husband, went out looking for gas, we couldn't find enough. We couldn't find enough gas to fill up the tank and leave, so we just looked at each other and said "Let's just stay." We both wanted to.

When was that?

It was August 28th, which was my birthday, the day before Katrina. So on my birthday I was boarding up windows. We just decided to stay, and I thought, "Oh, it will probably veer away like it always does, and it won't hit us smack-on with the eye." So there we were; it was storming away. He stayed with me.

What was it like during the storm?

It was very noisy. Very, very noisy. You could hear things banging against the side of the house, things flapping, and the wind was really loud. It was more exciting than scary, really. I don't worry about things that haven't happened that much— I try not to. So I was hoping for the best.

Were you in this house?

Yeah. This house has been here since the mid-to-late 1800s. It's been through many storms. It's solid. I mean, it's kind of raggedy— it's got holes in it, but it's basically solid, and I didn't think anything would happen to me.

We're about a block from the levee here....

Yeah, about a block from the river. So that night was just a noisy night, just a normal night. I cooked dinner, I drank wine, the TV was on, and we were watching the weather report. We went to bed listening to the storm, and then early, early in the morning it just kept going on. During the day, when it was still storming, it was kind of cool to look out the window and watch. Everything was boarded up, but there were little slivers between the plywood so we could look out at different places. At one point I opened the kitchen door; we stood there and watched, and the rain was kind of going uphill.

So the storm ends, the storm kind of petered out. It was Monday afternoon, still raining, but it was kind of sunny, and I think everyone who was here was antsy to get out and see what happened. Everyone wanted to get out and look around and see what happened. Finally, it let up enough, and we took a little walk and looked at my brother's house. There was standing water in the road over there [on Piety Street]. And it was "Oh, look at that house; it's completely fallen in." It was just interesting to see what kind of damage had happened, what kind of trees made it through, what kind of trees didn't. Pecan trees fared very poorly.

But the amazing thing about it— walking around— was that everyone who was out— it was like we'd gone through this enormous thing and we were all connected. From then on, everyone talked to everyone else. You wouldn't just pass by someone. For weeks and months afterwards, you talked to people. So we were hugging and talking, and there was a closeness with people afterwards that was really, really nice.

There was one little old man on the block, and me and Harold were here. And we didn't know what would happen. We had the radio on a little bit and people were talking about looting and things like that. So it was the typical fear— the fear of the unknown— that everyone felt. Those first couple of days you could see people walking around with guns hanging out of their pockets. Everyone who had a gun was walking around with a gun. That's just the way it was. Because there was no authority; it was just us, left to our own devices.

I noticed that right away all the corner stores had been broken into. Bars had been broken into. You know, people needed stuff. They needed food, they needed liquor, they needed cigarettes— that kind of stuff especially. Cigarette machines got broken into. I'm sure pharmacies got broken into. Nothing was really around me like that.

How do I explain... it was... I had plenty of food. I had water so I knew I would be okay. Suddenly there was no electricity or gas. No TV. No newspapers. No police. No fire. We were just on our own. It was just anarchy. And anarchy was very interesting. I didn't know what anarchy would be like, but for us, in this little corner of the world, our anarchy was people banding together and hanging out together for safety and just for community— sharing food, sharing information. Because all we had was each other, and that was the really beautiful thing about it. That's all we had; we had each other.

And then we were refugees in the land of plenty. The produce warehouse, A.J.'s, down the street half a block, rolled open their doors the day after Katrina and said "Spread the word throughout the neighborhood. Come get all the fruits and vegetables you want." They just gave everything away. People were going over there with shopping carts and hand carts, filling them up with cases of all kinds of fruits and vegetables. I had tomatoes. Luckily I took practical things like potatoes and onions and stuff that lasted a long time. But also we had avocados and mushrooms and wonderful fruit. We had all kinds of stuff. And then it was just the people [who] started gathering around. People called it "Gilligan's Island," and in a strange way it was.

There was a lot of stress involved in our lives because of the drudgery of living with no electricity, no running water. I heard some splashing in the pool next door the next day, so I walked over there, and there were some naked people swimming in the pool at the Country Club. I walked over, and they had cocktails by the side of the pool; and they were swimming, and they looked up at me and said "We're members!"

I just said "That's okay! I don't care— I don't think anything like that matters right now."

[Laughter]

They had ice in their drinks, and I looked at them, and they said "Well, the bar is open. Somebody broke into the back of the bar, so you can walk right in the back of the house." So I said "Oh, okay," and I walked in there. I had a glass of orange juice, and I was thinking I'd better hurry up and drink this orange juice because it's going to go bad. And then all of a sudden there was this ice machine and full bar, so I thought "Well, I can make this into a screwdriver." And from then on it was just drinkin' and eatin'. It was partying; it was hanging out by the pool, chit-chatting with people, fixing food. That was our life. Everyone in the neighborhood hung out there. It became this community center. There must have been 75 or 100 people a day coming there and eating at the height of it. And I have pictures of that. But what happened was more and more people started coming around. People heard that the Country Club was open.

First of all, every morning you'd see people coming with buckets. They'd carry a couple buckets and they'd dip them into the pool and walk back home, so they could flush their toilets. So we all had the pool water for keeping our toilets flushed. We didn't need to use any of our bottled water for that sort of thing. We put chemicals in the pool every day and swam every day, so we didn't have to take a bath. So that was covered.

And we had not only all those fresh fruits and vegetables— there was another warehouse across the street [that was used by] a steamboat cruise line— I can't remember what it was called exactly— but they had a big walk-in cooler with milk and cheese and eggs and cream and bread— all kinds of stuff. And you could walk in another door, and it was a walk-in freezer that had big boxes of shrimp and steaks and chicken and ham. Just all this stuff, frozen solid. So we had all this food. That's why I say we were refugees in the land of plenty because we had all these people [eating] all around the pool.

All the people who were here, the survivors, the people who stayed— there were a lot of what I call the "gay caterers:" people who hung out at the Country Club before the storm. They had all the tables set up; they had tablecloths on the tables; they had chafing dishes out. We rounded up every neighbor's barbeque we could find with either briquettes or propane. And I had an outside kitchen set up behind my house, so I could just hand stuff over the fence.

My job became that I cooked breakfast every morning— a big pan of some kind of eggs with stuff in it; then I would fix coffee. I boiled water, and we had cream from the warehouse over there, so we had fresh cream and fresh coffee and breakfast and [other neighbors] cooked the rest of the day. After a couple of days of that, I thought, "I don't want to be a slave to just cooking, cooking, cooking all day, so I said "Forget it. I will wash the big pans and dishes." I did that because I was boiling water [anyway]. That was plenty to do because I did the breakfast thing, and that was it. But it was really nice.

One day I kind of choked up; I kind of teared up. Maybe it was day four or day five. I walked over there, and Kevin, the guy who was coordinating everything, had so many people— somebody peeling garlic, somebody peeling shrimp, somebody chopping onions. All these people were working together to create these big meals, and they would just cook and cook and cook. It was just wonderful because it was young, old, black, white, gay, straight. It was everybody— the dregs of the neighborhood that didn't leave. It was everybody together. There were children there. It was this really nice gathering of people.

So that was the whole first week. And it was very interesting. Strange things had happened during the week, but we were just on our own. We had this giant fire about on the third day when Dennis Sheen Transfer Company, over by the A.J.'s warehouse, caught on fire. I think they might have had fireworks stored in there because it was a sight to be seen as things went BOOM BOOM BOOM— the sky was just lit up. Like fireworks. And there were thousands of some kinds of tanks, like the propane tanks that are on barbeques, but I don't think they had propane in them. They had some other kind of gas. And those things started exploding, and it just went BOOM BOOM BOOM. It was the scariest thing.

Someone had knocked on the door at three in the morning and said, "Hurry, hurry! Get up! There's a giant fire down the street." So we got up, and there we were in the dark, trying to get dressed, and we ran outside, and sure enough there was this giant fire just burning away. Luckily the wind was blowing it towards the river. I thought "My God, now what? We survive the hurricane, and now the whole neighborhood is going to be burned down." We had no fire department to call. We had no people to help us.

So there we were watching this, just standing in the street in the middle of the night watching the fire burn for hours. And it just got louder and louder. At one point a giant BOOM went up in the sky. It was like a giant mushroom cloud of fire and light and the sky was lit up for what seemed like many seconds— many seconds of bright, bright light. Brighter than the middle of the day. And I ran for my life. It was like a movie, and I was running away from the fire as fast as I could. [Gestures running as if in a slow-motion movie scene].

I didn't know if Harold was alive or dead. He and another guy had gone closer to the fire, and they were crouching behind a dumpster watching the thing when the big boom happened. That was one of our many instances, too, of realizing how much information and a lack of information the world had about what was going on in New Orleans.

See, we didn't see any news. We didn't see television or read anything. We had no knowledge of how the rest of the world saw us. We could see how we were living, and that was plenty to deal with to get us through our daily lives. The only help I was doing was cleaning and cooking. Some people I knew, like my friends Richie and Emily, they had a canoe, and they took the canoe over to the wet across St. Claude Avenue, and every day they rescued people out of attic windows, pulled people out, rode them to land, went back and got more people. That's what their life was like that week. But my life was on dry land, taking care of myself, and helping the people around me.

We were watching that fire and someone went and got a transistor radio, and we were listening to it. It was a call-in show, and someone said "I live in the Marigny. I'm worried about that fire. I can see it over by the river. What's going on with that big fire?" And some official, I can't remember who it was, said "Oh, yes, we're aware of that fire. We're containing it right now."

They were not containing it! He said "That's an abandoned warehouse." That was not an abandoned warehouse! It was a full warehouse! The things that guy said we knew [were wrong]. That was typical. We knew people were not telling [us] what was really going on.

[The fire] died down, well, it didn't really die down. It kept burning for days and days and days. But luckily it never spread over to the other side. So that was good. But we had that to deal with. We had all these different things. We had helicopters, too, from about the second day. Helicopters. One after the other. Non-stop. Flying over us, flying over us. To the point where I was thinking, "They must be over here trying to look at the naked people by the pool." You know, because the first couple days, that's what it was. And then after more people in the neighborhood found out about it, then it was just more of a big family scene and there was no more naked swimming, but at first there was. So at first I just thought, "Oh, that's just George W. Bush flying over looking down at whatever."

We were just on our own and everything was fine. We had everything we needed. Lots of water. We realized that all the water tanks were full of water too, and we never got around to tapping them because we didn't run out of bottled water. The Country Club was just stocked to the rafters with everything they thought they needed for Southern Decadence weekend, which was coming up, which was going to be a big week of business for them— or so they thought. So they had cases of beer stacked up to the ceiling, cases of bottled water stacked up, so we had everything. Everything we needed. So that was that. That was week one. That was hurricane week.

And then came day eight.

Now, by the eighth day, even though I'd been swimming in the pool every day, my hair was getting really dirty, and I couldn't stand it anymore. I had to wash my hair. So what am I going to do? I don't want to contaminate the pool more, so I figure I'll just wet my hair then lean it over the side and shampoo it and then pour a bucket of water over my head, kind of rinse it out that way. That was my plan.

I put my bathing suit on and walked out the door with towel and bucket and shampoo, and here came, to my complete surprise, about eight military vehicles. Humvees and whatnot, driving up the street, all filled with soldiers. They all jumped out and positioned themselves all over the block. All over the sidewalk. Down by Markey's Bar on the corner. Everywhere. And they all had rifles. And I know... well, they all pointed guns at me. Because they had the scopes on top, like a flashlight, and it was just almost dark and after they talked to me a few minutes I could see all the lights pointing at me in the dark. So I know the rifles were pointing at me too.

What happened was there was this little old black man walking down the street too, leaving the Country Club for the night, and they stopped me when I was close to him, and they told us both to drop what we had in our hands and put our hands up, and we stood there. They interrogated us for over ten minutes. They asked us all these questions, and I was just trying to explain what was going on, that we were just a bunch of neighbors hanging out, that we're the people who didn't leave. That some people didn't leave because they have animals and they weren't able to evacuate with them, and that for whatever reason people were still here.

They were very worried about what was going on back in the Country Club, these soldiers were. You could tell these soldiers were very scared about what was going on in our neighborhood. And they didn't know our neighborhood. They'd been told all kinds of stories about the dangers of New Orleans.

And this is [the Upper] Ninth Ward.

Right, and this is the Ninth Ward. So I stood there for ten minutes in my bathing suit, hands up, all these soldiers pointing their guns on me while I was trying to explain that there wasn't anything to worry about back there. That the people back there were just neighbors hanging out, and all we're doing is using stuff as we need it, from places that have already been broken into. The breaking and entering, that all happened in the first day or two. We were looting— that was true— as we needed to. We weren't stealing VCRs and things. We were taking food and something to drink. There was no reason to worry about what was going on back there. The criminals came and went. But they didn't want me to take them back there and show them the situation. They were very serious. Everything was extremely serious.

With guns pointed at me, there was only so much I could do. So they made us sit on the curb, so I'm sitting there on the curb, and half a dozen soldiers walked back to the Country Club and rounded everybody up— children and everything. There were a couple moms with kids. Everyone walked out with their hands up. And they said to us all, "Don't you know there's a curfew? You're out past dark."

And I said, "Well, you know, all we know is what we tell each other. We hear things and we tell each other things. We don't know what to believe or not. People did tell us there was a curfew a couple of days ago, but we haven't seen any officials; no one's really put up a notice or anything. No signs on the corner or anything." So we'll obey the curfew if we have to, but nobody told us anything before then.

They sternly let us go home and told us not to be out after dark. It was very weird once the soldiers came. Until they got used to things, they were very strict about things like that. Once it got dark you couldn't sit out on your front porch and have a glass of wine. And it was dark; we didn't have electricity, and what were we going to do? Go in and watch TV? No. We couldn't go in and turn on a light, it was hot, it was summer, people didn't have their air conditioning. Of course we were sitting out on the porch, maybe with a glass of wine or something. But oh no, we couldn't do that. We had to go inside after dark. It was ridiculous.

But after a while, after a couple of days, they realized there really wasn't anything to be afraid of, and they relaxed, and they saw us taking the hand truck over to get more food, and then we'd come back and cook it. They were fine with all that. In fact, most of the soldiers were thrilled to find out I was boiling water and actually making real coffee (and I had real cream) because all they had was instant coffee. So soldiers would line up at my gate every morning that whole second week and come over and have coffee. And that was really good. They knew we were taking cream out of the cooler. They didn't care. They knew it was going to go bad if we didn't use it.

The catering guys, they got smart. They would take a couple of cases of beer out of the bar, take it over to the deep freeze, stick it in there, go back a couple hours later, and then they'd yell out "Cold beer!" and then everybody would go, "Oh! Cold beer!" So that was our little life of eatin' and drinkin'. It was pretty nice. And the soldiers, they didn't take part in the drinking, but they palled around with us after a while. They borrowed guitars and dartboards; they had nothing to do. But when they first got here, I think they were fresh from Iraq or whatever. To them, this was a war zone.

I said to them, "Why are you making us hold our hands up? Aren't you here to help us?" I couldn't stand it. Their mentality was like they were occupying this strange land. And it was a strange land, but there was no reason for them to worry or be afraid, and they realized it after a while.

That whole second week— "Military Week," I call it— they co-existed with us fine, for the most part, after day eight with me holding my hands up. From then on there wasn't anything like that where people pointed guns at me— until the day I left.

The day I left was two weeks after Katrina. Every day the soldiers would come around and say, "Are you ready to leave? We're not going to make you leave, but we really want you to leave." And I said, "Why do you want me to leave?" Well, they didn't really explain things except to say that "it wasn't healthy," that there was fecal matter in the water and blah blah blah. I said, "Well, I don't go over where the water is. I'm on the dry land. Why would I go there? I don't have a boat. I'm not going to slog through that." But I think they just wanted to make things easier for themselves.

When did [Hurricane] Rita come?

That happened right after I left, because that was when they really started pushing. They knew Rita was coming and they started getting insistent. The people who stayed when I left hid out.

I got back the beginning of week five. I went around to visit people I knew who were here when I was here. The ones who stayed said they hid out in their houses— they made sure their lights weren't seen— no candles were by the window. They were very careful to be "underground." That's the way they were able to stay.

I wouldn't have liked that. That wasn't my style at all. I was like, "Hey! Why don't you come over for coffee?" [Laughter as she pretends to wave enthusiastically to a neighbor.] So that wouldn't have been good. I was very upset, really, that they made me leave.

The soldier came around, and he pointed a gun at me and said, "I'm not going to ask you anymore. You have to go. It's martial law." And I said, "Well, what does martial law mean?" He said, "It means you have no rights, and we tell you what to do."

I said. "Well, what if I don't want to go? Look, I have everything I need here. I'm taking care of my house. I feel like it's safer for my house if I'm here. I have food; I have water. Why should I leave? If I leave I'm going to have to put gas on my credit card, stay in motels on my credit card, buy fast food. Why are you going to make me do that when I have everything I need here? I don't need to go out into that world and spend all that money."

They said, "Ma'am, you can't work here. It's going to be months before they open up again." I said "What do I need to work for? No mailman is putting bills in my mailbox either."

Anyway, they didn't agree. They insisted that I leave. And I thought, "Well, it wouldn't be so bad to take a nice shower in a motel room and clean up." And Harold said, "Well, we probably won't have to stay away very long. We'll probably get to come back soon." Luckily, a couple days before that we'd been given some cans of gas by some German reporters who came around and interviewed us.

[The Germans] were on the way to the airport when they left, and they said, "Why don't you take our extra gas?" which I was thrilled about because that's why I didn't get to leave to begin with. I didn't put it in the car right away. I kept it in the living room until we wanted to go.

People were puncturing gas tanks like crazy; people were in a panic to leave those first few days. People's gas got siphoned, and then when they couldn't do that they punctured holes and drained gas out. I knew my car was okay, so I kept the gas, and when they made me leave I took Harold and a couple of the guys from the Country Club I didn't know before that night the four of us took off.

That was a strange scene, just trying to drive out of New Orleans. We kept driving for a while. Then we'd come to water. Then we'd have to turn around. We finally went the wrong way across Interstate 10 and went across the Crescent City Connection on the wrong side and got out that way.

One thing I saw when I got back in late September was city buses abandoned all over this neighborhood.

The streets were covered with city buses. People were stealing buses and hot-wiring them. Some, to try to escape from the city, and some, I don't know what their reason was. But there were buses all over the place. Abandoned vehicles. And people just didn't know how to drive [the city buses]. They turned the corners [and wrecked], and there were many corners with buses. There were a lot of obstructions in the road.

The "old hippie survivalists," were the ones that were hot-wiring skip loaders and tractors and stuff, and they were going around clearing streets of limbs and debris as much as they could so we could get around. But there was so much obstruction in the road, and many abandoned vehicles, buses, that sort of thing. And there were tractors and forklifts and that kind of stuff because people were stealing things; they were moving things so we could use them and get around.

All the signs were down or pointing in crazy directions from Katrina. Once the soldiers came there were military in every kind of uniform you can think of. You saw everyone here. There were Royal Mounted Canadian Police here, I think. Everyone was here. But they didn't know the one-way streets, so it was a strange world where you could go anywhere you wanted in any direction and nobody cared. That was really kind of cool. There weren't many people on the street. There were military vehicles, mostly, but they went slow. There were bicycles and pedestrians and everybody [traveled in whatever direction] they could. It was really kind of nice, and for months afterwards there was that.

There were many changes, but slowly and surely things got back to normal. But the abnormality of the world was so sort of surreal and kind of cool and interesting for me that I feel kind of bad that I talk about it like this. Because of all the destruction and loss of life and property that people experienced. But my particular life just wasn't that.

I mean, I lost my roof and a lot of fence and some trees and have some carpentry damage on the side. The electrical line for one side of my house pulled off, so I didn't have electricity on one side of my house for months. I had a couple of things to deal with, but no tragedy. I had no loss, really. I had gains.

I had gains of stuff because trash-picking was so excellent after Katrina, between landlords putting people's stuff out and people just leaving with only one carload. There was furniture and clothes and kitchen items on every block. It was all over the place. For people who like to scrounge around and pick the trash it was fantastic around here. I know people who drove around Mid-City and found paintings and antiques and all kinds of stuff. I didn't go out looking for it, but when it crossed my path I would stop and look at stuff. So now I have all this stuff. It's ridiculous how much stuff I have. And I have a cat now that I didn't have. I didn't have a pet, but when I came back from being evacuated, there was a cat living under the house, and clearly she just moved in and lived here. So we're roommates now. So that was another gain I had. There have been many gains and changes from Katrina.

Where did you evacuate to when they made you leave?

We didn't know where to go. We didn't know what to do. But this one guy, Kevin, who we took with us, one of the "gay caterers," said he had some friends who have a plantation house in Natchez, Mississippi. So he said, "Let's go there." He said they have this gorgeous old plantation home on a thousand acres, and the whole place is just filled with antiques, and he went on and on about it.

And I thought, "Yeah, right." Because this guy had started out being really, really efficient in what he was doing and really kind of organizing things and giving everybody focus and hope. But as time went on, he— along with many other people— was finding it harder and harder to cope emotionally with the stresses of life. For one thing, I never realized how many people take medications. And you couldn't just go to the pharmacy and get your medications, so a lot of people were trying to cope however they could, with whatever they could, which was a lot of drinking. I don't know where people got their drugs, but people had... whatever they had. People were coping as best they could. And this guy was taking maybe thirty Valiums a day toward the end, so he was super-loopy.

It was just the last few dregs of us who the soldiers hadn't talked into leaving yet. I talked him into leaving with us and another guy. But he could not remember where this plantation house was, so it took us nine hours to get somewhere that's only two and a half hours away.

The soldiers told us to leave by eight in the morning. I asked, "What are you going to do if I don't?" [A soldier] said he would kick my door down and grab me up and put me on a bus, and then I'd be on a one-way trip to who-knows-where. So if I didn't want that I should get myself out of town. So that's the way it was explained to me. Those were my two choices. I thought, "Do I really want to push it and challenge this martial law thing? Do I want to take a chance on a bus? Or do I just want to drive to some motel?"

We left and we finally found this place in Natchez. I thought for sure he was dreaming it. We finally pulled up to it, and sure enough, it was this fantastic plantation home on a thousand acres. The place was filled with beautiful antiques. Every bedroom had a giant, amazing bed. The whole place was just gorgeous, and it was filled with refugees from New Orleans. There must have been about twenty-five people there. Mostly people from the Marigny and the Bywater, several people I knew. And everybody was gay, pretty much, there. Well, almost exclusively. When we got there it was kind of magical. When we pulled up around five we were all dirty from the road and driving around all stressed out, and the people said, "Come on in! You're friends of Kevin? Yeah, you can stay. We're having a party tonight. Why don't you go clean up?"

So I went and got the closest thing I had to party clothes and got all cleaned up. I was all happy and showered, and here was this beautiful party with hors d'oeuvres and cocktails with ice— which we hadn't seen for over a week and a half. It was wonderful, and there were many people in glittery dresses and drag. Because it was supposed to have been Southern Decadence, and the people who would have been King and Queen or Grand Marshall of the Southern Decadence parade had taken refuge at this house. So there were lots of people there all dressed up. It was really funny. At one point I was talking to this guy, and he stopped and looked at me and said, "Why, you're a *real* girl!"

I said, "Yeah, I'm the only real girl at this party!"

So we stayed there a couple nights. They put us up, gave us a mattress in a hall upstairs. There were other people sleeping up there. But we had to get out of there. I didn't know them, and didn't want to impose on them too long. So I started calling friends and family because I [now] had a phone I could use.

I arranged to go to Daytona Beach where my mother's cousin had a mobile home in a little trailer park for old people. There were only old people there. They live on a farm in the Midwest, and they go to Florida every winter. They spend their winters there, so it was empty. I had a shower there and a little kitchen and bedroom and computer and everything. It was really nice. I felt like I was on a little vacation. But that was also the first time I saw television. I saw all the scenes of the Superdome. I just sat there and cried.

This was two and a half weeks after Katrina, and it was all on the news still at this point. I saw what the rest of the world saw— the aerial shots, the devastation, the people all hot and starving and needing care and the Superdome and crying babies— all that mess. All I knew about it when I was here was that people would walk through the neighborhood every once in a while and say, "Don't go to the Superdome; it's bad over there." Why was it bad? I don't know, we were just not supposed to go to the Superdome.

So that was kind of rough. I spent a couple of weeks recuperating. I started a quilt; I started sewing and sat and watched cable news. I went to thrift stores and went to the beach every once in a while. It was kind of like a little vacation. I went to the grocery store; I cooked. It was a little bit of normal life, playing house in that trailer. But I was so antsy to get home. I couldn't wait to get home.

We would be watching TV, and as soon as Nagin came on [we'd jump] and say, "Mayor Nagin! What's he saying?" Then they finally opened up our zipcode— remember everything was by zipcode and even though we're the Bywater, Upper Ninth Ward, we should be considered along with the Marigny and the French Quarter. We're a little sliver of dry land by the river, but we weren't considered that at all by the people taking care of New Orleans, or trying to. We were considered 70117, which they didn't want to open up because of the Lower Ninth Ward. So finally it looked like it was going to be time soon, so we came home a few days early, before they really announced that we could.

We drove on in. It was good to be home. It was interesting to see what had happened and not happened. Things were still strange and surreal around here. Sometimes things were a surprise, what got damaged and what didn't. Pecan trees really fell a lot. There was a house I used to own on Burgundy Street that just got squashed like a pancake. A little tiny house with a great big tree behind it that fell over, and it was like a fly under a flyswatter. Just smashed. That was a sight to see because the two houses beside it were just fine, and it was completely gone.

There were so many people here supposedly trying to help us. The animal rescue people— they caused all kinds of problems. They broke into people's houses and caused the houses to have things stolen from them. What they didn't realize is how many neighbors were taking care of their neighbors' animals. People know each other here. There were big bags of dog food ripped open on the sidewalk with piles of dog food and cat food on every block. [Local] people, of course, were worried about rats.

There were piles of garbage. The Country Club garbage was insane because we kept cooking all this food, all this food, and the neighborhood was dwindling down and there weren't as many people to eat it. Each day there were fewer people. Well, Kevin and those guys— I already told you about thirty Valiums a day— he was getting loopier and loopier, and he was just going over there and cooking more food, cooking more food.

I kept saying, "Kevin, don't cook so much food. We don't need it anymore. There aren't as many people." We had all this excess food, and it was just stinking like crazy. Across the street here we had a giant mound of garbage. There was nowhere to move our garbage even if we could move it with a bulldozer and take it somewhere. No one really wanted to help us do that, and it was just a big ol' stinky mess. So [the soldiers] agreed that we should burn it. So from that day on we got to sit out at night and tend the fire. We would burn our garbage every night.

We had a great big bonfire every night, for maybe five days. We would just burn the garbage, and sit out there late at night, as late as we had to. We'd start in the afternoon, and it would still burn into the evening. Suddenly it was okay we were out a night because we had the fire. They didn't make us go in as soon as it got dark, and that was kind of nice. The stars were so beautiful. It was like camping in the middle of nowhere because without the electricity in the city the stars were visible and sky was so beautiful every night. It was kind of magical.

Some people were so paranoid. I told you about so many people carrying guns. It was craziness, all kinds of stuff. But one thing I remember when I got home— it was week five— I bumped into a friend that I hadn't seen for months. She came over to visit, and she said there was a guy down on Dauphine Street— Dauphine and France— who had a generator, and he was having a block party every night, sort of a potluck dinner every night, and he was playing movies. I thought, "That sounds fun." So I went down there, and they didn't have enough chairs, but some other neighbor was throwing away a bunch of plastic chairs, so I took a big truckload of chairs over.

He had a great big sheet that he tacked onto the front of this Creole cottage, which is a big, flat house, so we had this giant movie screen. He had the generator going; he had a digital fancy movie projector. He played a movie every night, and we had these parties, and there were people around. It was the only place lit up at night. The scary thing was going home every night on my bicycle because you couldn't avoid the potholes— there were no streetlights. It was a bumpy ride going home.

I went to this party every night, and after about the third or fourth night during that week, people were sitting around and talking about how our zipcode was going to be officially open the Saturday coming up. This one girl said, "Let's stand on the street corner and welcome people back on that day. We'll stop people. Let's give them a sheet of information about where they can get medical care, where you can get cleaning supplies, where you can get food. Because people don't know you can live here and stay here. We need to tell people."

They compiled this nice handy list of things about how you could cope with life here, what you could do, and I joined them. There were four of us, and we stood out on a street corner. Now, all these girls I was with are all very colorful-looking girls, you know, dreds and crazy haircuts and tattoos and piercing and crazy outfits. They're kind of circusy people, and I was just ordinary looking. We were standing there talking to people, handing out sheets. It was fun. I was doing what I like to do best— walking around talking to people and being friendly. So we were doing that, and here came this reporter from the New York Times. She wanted to interview us; she had a photographer with her, too. So she interviewed us all, and she talked to me quite a while. She took a group shot of us all. And wouldn't you know it— even though I was quoted on that article and my name was on the front page of the New York Times, they got the quotes wrong; everything was taken out of context. I remembered saying the phrases, but the way it was edited, it really didn't go together. I wasn't really talking about what it sounded like I was talking about. So that was very annoying. You think the New York Times would have the ability to get the story straight. That was kind of interesting. And to top it off, I was cropped out of the picture. It was just these crazy-looking girls. And the reporter even came over to me and took me aside and said, "So, why are they dressed like that?" I said, "Well, that's just the way they always dress."

Helicopters did start landing in Mickey Markey Park to bring us cases of water. They would land and dump all this water out. See, that was another thing…. All these people came to help. The Red Cross came, and they were giving us meals in these styrofoam containers. All these church groups would come and give us boxes of all kinds of stuff. We had so much stuff, the people that were here. I'm sure it was very helpful to people who didn't have a lot, but me— you look at my pantry, and it looks like I'm the mother of ten kids, like I'm a Mormon or something. Everything's stacked up because I buy in massive quantities when it's on sale. That's basically what I do.

I'm trying to break myself of that habit now that I live alone. I had plenty, but some really needed help, and they did get it.

The amount of help and the people who needed help was so uneven it was ridiculous. I, for instance, was denied the $2,000 aid from FEMA because they said I applied too late. They said I was two days too late, but I told them I couldn't get out of town until I was given that gas. Anyway, I called Dallas, and they told me to write a letter of appeal, so I wrote a letter of appeal. They didn't respond to it for months— they said they couldn't find it. I wrote another one, and they finally denied me after making me go through all this stuff.

When I got back, Washington Square Park had that kitchen set up, the Welcome Home Kitchen. It was wonderful. I loved that place. I went there every day. It was like my little Country Club scene had been a few weeks earlier, but it was a much bigger group.

It was a Rainbow Family kitchen…

They were used to doing it. All of a sudden there was breakfast, lunch, and dinner. I would go over there because I like to get up early in the morning, and I would go there and have coffee and breakfast. I saw many people there, kind of caught up with people. That was when I started seeing people whose houses had flooded, people who were living in other parts of the city. It really started hitting me what happened. Well, it hit me when I saw it on the news. My reality was just a little different than most people's.

How has the neighborhood changed since Katrina?

Well, my particular neighborhood, in some ways hasn't changed as much as others. We didn't flood. But on the other hand, many people have moved, and there are many different people living here instead. My particular block used to have three old ladies living alone. Each didn't have a car, lived in her own house that she'd been in probably since the '40s or '50s. They lived here all their lives and they're all gone now.

They got out before the storm?

In one case she moved away before the storm, and her family wasn't about to let her come back; they sold the house. That's happened throughout the neighborhood.

A lot of people who rent have had their rent doubled or tripled. There's a lot of turmoil and trouble that people have had regarding housing. It's hard for people to find places to live. And another giant change, just visually, looking around— it used to be when you saw people walking on the street they used to be black people, mostly. And now it's Hispanic people. We have so many Mexicans and people from Central America here roofing and drywalling and whatever. Those guys— I talked to a few of them— they like it here, but they're living with many people in one apartment because it's so hard to find apartments and the rents are so high. That's one of the definite changes. I really am sorry I don't speak Spanish. We have so many new people, and the catering trucks on the corners, selling tacos and tamales and things, we never had before. So I feel like I'm back in California again. Over at Lowe's you see guys lining up for day labor....

You have so many people coming here looking for work, from all over America, looking to make a little money— either by hard work or scamming or some combination. The sad thing is all the people who used to be here, if they had a place to live, they could come back and work. They had that one-way ticket to who-knows-where, and they're stuck there. Nobody's paying for them to come back. The government took people out of here, but after that you're on your own. I'm worried about the long-term effects on New Orleans because we've lost so many of the people who created the culture.

Torn Apart

Kendra Williams
Interviewed by Mary Sparacello

Kendra Williams, a teenager, was four months pregnant and staying in a New Orleans hotel when Katrina hit. She waded through chest-deep water trying to get to her cousin's house on the West Bank. For three months after the storm she stayed in different cities and states.

Me and my mama was split up. We were all by my grandmother's house in the East, in New Orleans East. But my mama went back to Kenner to see about her husband, I guess because they was sick. Me, my grandmother, my sister, my aunt and her two kids, we went to a hotel where we stayed for the storm. The hotel is right down the street from the Superdome. We were about to stay at the Superdome. It was a long, long line. They had babies out there, and it was raining. I wondered, "Why aren't they letting those people in?" My grandmother always cries [now], "That would have been us."

During the hurricane, the TV kept blinking on and off. Stuff constantly kept throwing against the windows. If you looked out of the windows, you'd see broken windows everywhere. We had about 90 or 98 relatives at that hotel. We kept running from floor to floor to see if everyone was all right. We didn't have no power, a little bit of food. The room was so hot. We slept in the hallway. We had babies. The babies needed milk. They just had diapers on. Everybody was getting frustrated, hollering at each other. I was itching and irritated.

We left on Wednesday. When we got out the streets was clear. The windows were all broken around us. We only had a little bit of gas. We headed to my cousin's house on the West Bank. Some of the streets were flooded, so we had to ride on the sidewalk. I was in the car that got flooded. So we had to get out and swim. The water was about this [chest] high. We barely knew where we was going. We swam to the house. We stayed there for a day. The backyard didn't look like a backyard because the fence was gone.

We fought over where to go. We were going to go to Tennessee. People said, "I don't want to go to Tennessee." I got in the car with the rest of my family. I went to sleep, and the next thing I knew I was in Atlanta. People were still frustrated. I was wanting to know where my mama was. I didn't know where my daddy was. They took our picture, and I think they put them in the newspaper, so we could find our mama. That was too bad because I was also wondering where was she at; was she okay? After almost three weeks, my mama came to get us. I was just ready to go home. I didn't care about the damage.

But when I got back down here, no schools were open; no hospitals were open. I'm pregnant. It will be seven months on December eleventh. I was tired of being here with only a generator. I talked to my daddy the day of the storm. He was leaving. He went to Alabama because we already had family up there. The hardest part was my mama taking us to the bus to Alabama. I had never been on a bus, and I didn't think I would be on a bus leaving my mama. When we got there, they treated us nice. I didn't have to pay for no school supplies. They were handing out money. In Alabama, [my mother] came and visited us. She was crying. She missed us. I didn't really want her to leave. My dad was fussing. He said, "take them back with you," and she did. Atlanta was only two hours away, so we visited there. We had a great time. Mama got a birthday cake because her birthday was October 3rd. We was away from her on her birthday. My sister, she's sixteen. Her birthday was the day after the storm. She had really nobody to celebrate with but me. She was supposed to have a sweet sixteen party. She prepared this party the most. Still to this day, I still can't give her a party. I had a wonderful sweet sixteen party— I had boys, I had girls, I had a hotel. She said, "I want a party like yours." She didn't even get a birthday card. I tried getting her a little cupcake and putting a candle on it. I don't think that still made her happy. I guess she wished all her friends were there. We came back to Kenner. I work at McDonald's up there on Loyola [Drive]. It will help a lot with me and the baby. I want my own house.

All my stuff was by my grandmother's. It made me really wake up. How did my grandma's house survive that? I got all my pictures back, all my certificates, my baby's first ultrasound. Katrina took a whole lot of things away from me. My baby's father is far away from me. In Abbeville somewhere. He's acting all crazy. It's stressing me out. Now, everybody's split up. I have family in Arkansas; I have family in Alabama, Atlanta, Wisconsin. They spread out all over. I mean we traveled. To the [New Orleans] East by my grandmother, to the hotel, to the West Bank to Atlanta to Kenner to Alabama to Kenner. We was traveling everywhere. I've never been to Alabama. I've never been that far before. All I can say, this Christmas will be wonderful. Everyone will appreciate it more.

Just Piles of Houses

Glen Kirkland
Interviewed by Daniel McBride

Glen Kirkland lived in Port Sulphur, LA, and was unprepared for the destruction he found when he returned to his home after Katrina .

What was your childhood like, growing up in New Orleans?

Ah, it was pretty good. Lived off of Magazine Street. Lived there probably 'til I was about five or six years old. From what I remember it was pretty good, streetcar riding, you know, Audubon Park, pretty good. Moved over to the Westbank at probably six years old and lived there ever since.

What was your life like immediately prior to Hurricane Katrina?

It was pretty good. I lived in Port Sulphur, Louisiana, approximately forty miles south of New Orleans. A fishing community, you know. Outdoors. Not a lot of people, probably 6,000 residents before the storm. Pretty small, tight-knit place.

What is it like growing up in a small town like that. Or not growing up rather, but living?

Uh, pretty good. Everybody knows everybody, you know. You can get things done, accomplished, because everybody knows everybody. The parish works with you well, and it's just a totally different thing from living up in the city.

When did you first hear about the storm?

When it first hit the, I guess, the Caribbean, you know when it first started to get into the Gulf is when I started paying a little bit of attention to it. People that live down there by us, we tend to pay attention to storms once they hit the Gulf of Mexico because [the gulf is] fifty miles, forty to fifty miles from New Orleans. We get tropical storms down there that will give us a lot of weather and not really give New Orleans a lot of weather. People know a couple miles, thirty miles makes a big difference when you're dealing with hurricanes. When they come in, you could be thirty miles to the west of it and really not get too much. Be thirty miles to the east and get knocked out. So, we watch them pretty extensively down there. It was probably a week before the storm ever hit that I really started paying attention to it.

Through what medium did you hear about the storm?

I mostly checked out the internet, the weather stuff off the internet. Because when I get home from work the news is over, so I really didn't have that opportunity. But it was mostly the internet, and it was, uh, I started watching it, like I said, about a week before. And as it progressed I didn't, still didn't really take it too seriously because it was still way away, and it was projected for Florida and this and that. And I didn't pay a whole lot of attention to it.

Did you stay or leave? And how was that decision made?

We stayed up 'til the day before the storm actually came. They wanted everybody to evacuate, and the way the storm came in, I don't think the whole city took it real serious until three days out, four days out, when they started making arrangements to evacuate people. And the contraflow plan that they had in place evacuated my area first, and once they evacuated everyone, they didn't make it mandatory. Me and my son stayed. Like I said, we didn't take— I think it was blinded. [This] generation is blind; we've never seen, [we] don't remember the bad storms. So, we've been… We've always had these near misses. New Orleans, Louisiana, been getting these near misses for the last couple years. Bad storms, they miss us. And

I think we got comfortable with that. And I didn't ever think it was gonna hit. And then I, even in the back of my mind, if it was, I didn't think it was gonna do what it did. The house that I bought and what I lived in was— it's a seventy-five-year-old house, and it's been through Betsy, and it's been through Camille, some of the bad storms. And, it's still there. Never really flooded too much. But like I said, a couple clicks of that storm to the west or to the east makes a big difference, and this one just came in right over Port Sulphur. The eye crossed right, it turned right over the boot of Louisiana and came right over Port Sulphur. And it really, really did a job.

But we stayed 'til the day before the storm, the morning. The weather started getting bad, and it started really…. I was in a trailer, a mobile home. I had bought the house, and we wasn't finished with it yet; we were renovating it. And I lived in a mobile home. I put a mobile home on the property in the back. I had two acres of land. And I put the mobile home in the back and lived in that and worked on the house. So, we was in the trailer when all the weather started, and it was rocking that trailer pretty serious. And once it got to that point I was spooked, and I said, you know, "We gotta roll." So we left probably about fifteen hours, twenty hours before the storm actually got onto the coast of Louisiana. And there was nobody on the road. We were like the only nuts out there leaving at this time.

Where did you and your family go for the storm?

My wife left way before. She left like two days— when they told us to evacuate— she took my kids and went to Baton Rouge to her sister's. Me and my son, like I said, we left too late. And when we did leave we couldn't get fuel. We had like half a tank of gas, and we weren't getting far on that. So, we left from my house in Port Sulphur, and we went to Marrero, to my mother's house, which is about forty miles up the river, and that's where we stayed for the storm.

How was the storm as it passed?

It was pretty hairy; it was pretty hairy. It rocked some trees around, knocked down the power lines, and flooded the street. My mom got about three or four inches of water in her house, which ain't a lot, but it was spooky. It was probably the worst, the worst I've ever seen that I can remember, and I've been through Betsy and Camille. I was young, and I don't remember— I vaguely remember them storms,— but this one really, it was something.

What do you remember about those prior storms?

I remember being in our attic on Magazine Street as the water was coming up. It didn't really get real high there. My dad was in the National Guard, and they actually had to go to Chalmette to go…. Chalmette got really flooded, St. Bernard [Parish]. And they had to leave us during the storm and told us to get in our attic. Because they were hearing all the water levels down in St. Bernard and all, and they were getting scared because the water was coming up in New Orleans, but it never did get really bad. But I remember my dad and the news reports… Same thing with them going, getting people off the rooftops. People having to bust holes through their attics to get out and get on the roof.

How long was it before you were able to return to your home?

It was a good three weeks, four weeks before— almost a month, before they let us back in. And they were escorting people through; they really weren't letting you just go in on your own. They were convoying a couple of cars at a time through, and the reason was because everybody knew everybody down there, and the devastation was massive. They didn't want people just going in on their own and wandering around. The logistics wasn't there, you couldn't— you didn't know where your property was or your house wasn't where your house was no more or broke all up, and there's just nothing on your property. So they didn't want people wandering around. So they'd bring us in five, six cars at a time. It was pretty crazy.

What was that experience like? What were you thinking as the convoy was driving?

When you're heading down to Port Sulphur, you come through some cow pastures that are there. And you got Highway 23, and you have a little bit of land, and then you have the Mississippi River. Well, as we were going, we could see the holes in the levee that the water— when the water came over the levee, it was hitting the side of the levee. It looked like a bucket scoop had dug holes all along the levee and it was just, it was really freaky looking to see that the water had done so much destruction to the levee. There was driftwood all over Belle Chasse Highway, all over Highway 23. Big pieces. I mean, Oak trees of driftwood that came from the river over the tops of the levee. And it was just a lake. I mean, the water was still, after a month, the water was still up to the road. And as far as the eye could see, the cow pastures looked like the Gulf of Mexico after a month.

After I saw my property— I have a friend of mine who lives not too far down, probably another mile down the road, and I wanted to go see his property, check out his place. And we couldn't get to his place. It still had water through and through. So, there was only— we could only go another mile down the highway from my house, and then there was still water. And they were having to airboat people out from that point.

When you finally did see your house, what did you see?

Oh, it was totally destroyed. Washed, washed away. Part of the house was still on the property. It had moved it about 200-250 feet and actually set it on the highway. And the other section of the house— the house actually broke in half— the other section we really never did find or couldn't find. It just must've broke up into debris. When they let us go through, there was debris— they bulldozed the highway to allow people to come through. So, most of the debris settled on the highway. Just splinters of houses. The highway's the highest point. So when the water went down everything settled up on the highway, and they bulldozed it, pushed it all to the side. So you really couldn't determine what was yours, what was somebody else's. It was just piles of stuff on the side of the road. Houses. Piles of houses.

You put a lot into this house. How did you feel when you saw it? When did it set in?

It took a little while. It took a couple days, maybe two days after I went down there the first time and went back again. I brought my mom down and my kids. My kids were looking— that's, that's when it hit home. You know, I worked on the house for five years, and we were about three weeks away from moving into the house. We never did actually move into the house. We were putting light fixtures up the morning we evacuated, the morning we left. We were hanging up the hall light fixtures and all the stuff. But it really didn't hit me 'til I brought the kids down. The kids, they kept— I got a seven-year-old; he just didn't understand. They were staying in a hotel room in Baton Rouge, and it was just you know, "Are we on vacation?" And I'm like, "No." I'm talking to him on the phone saying, "No, y'all are not on vacation." "When can I come home, Dad?" And I said, Maybe in a while." And once they were able to come back here to Marrero, to my mother's house, we still couldn't go back down there. So he's still wondering what's going on, you know. "Where's my toys?" He wanted his Legos. He was crazy about Legos, and he had tons and tons of Legos. He wanted his Legos. And it started getting to me, the questions, and then I didn't have any answers. I was explaining to him about the hurricane. He knew the hurricane; he knew all of that. But he couldn't grasp the concept that our house isn't there no more.

We tried to make this place— because it was so far down— we tried to make it home. So that once we got home we had every amenity that the kids could want. We put a pool, we had swing sets, they would camp out. We really had a good time there. And I had to bring him down and show him the property and the devastation. He just wouldn't believe that this hurricane took our house and took all of the stuff with it. He said, "Okay, the hurricane took the house, but did it leave the dogs?" And I'm like, "No, dude, they took everything. It's all gone." And once they saw it— and he was shocked. And when I saw my kids crying, that... They realized that they lost everything. But then it made me realize that we lost, that all of our worldly possessions were gone. And you sit back, and you look at it and go, you know, at least nobody got hurt. Everybody says, "You got your health. You got your kids and all," but, it still ain't the same, it still beats you down because there's just nothing there. And your kids just don't understand what happened, and the magnitude, and the aftermath. It was like, so quick. We were standing out on the property crying, and then when we left, I'm telling him, "Things are gonna be cool. We're going to get us another house and all." And he says, "Okay, we're moving in tomorrow?" Like, so quick. They snap their fingers. They don't understand the concept of what's happening and the aftermath of it and the rebuilding process that you have to do with your life. I don't think nobody had. None of these younger generations, including myself, people my age just didn't realize that this could happen. And once it did, it was just total chaos. And you just didn't know where to go or what to do. What's the next move? You got kids and a family, what do you do with them? You got three pairs of pants, some shoes, and whatever you could jam in garbage bags when you left, and that's it.

Everybody thought we was coming back, you know? We would've took a lot more stock and packed up my house and took computers and everything, but we really, really thought we was coming back. And to come back to what was there was just, it was mind boggling.

In some cases, as on the West Bank, the damage to homes was random. It seemed like one house might have been totally devastated and the next house, maybe a shingle was gone.

How was the damage in your neighborhood?

It was across the board. From where I lived… There's an area called Diamond, which is closer to New Orleans than me, a couple miles up. From Diamond on down to the Gulf of Mexico, it's probably sixty miles. It's a little strip of land; it's not that wide. But it's probably sixty miles. And from Diamond down, there might have been five structures standing out of everything. There was a high school in Boothville; Venice High School was still standing. It had been washed completely through. Nothing inside. A skeleton of a high school, skeleton of a building. Three stories, completely washed through. But the structure was still there. There's a church down in Port Sulphur that's still standing. It had been washed through. And a couple other buildings, but nothing, no houses, there were no houses that made it— slab houses— my house was an above ground house; it was on pillars.

My neighbor's house was a 4,000 square-foot brick home, and it was like it didn't even exist. There was not a brick. I mean, we couldn't find one brick from the whole house. It washed the slab away. Slab home, washed the slab out. The slab was in the middle of the street; it had gotten bulldozed when they...I mean it totally devastated everything. Except, they had camps. That's the real weird, weird thing. A place called Happy Jack got camps that are on sticks. Which, they're all twenty feet in the air, but they, they made it. Everything underneath them washed, but they made it. And that tells you it wasn't a real bad wind event. I mean, the winds got bad, but it wasn't devastation from the winds, from the strong winds of the storm. It was a storm surge. It was the water that came through. And they estimated about 32 foot of water. When you get a wall of water 32 feet high coming through, it's washing things away. And it, it really did a job. There's a carcass of a horse 25 feet in a tree. Just settled in there after the water went down. I had a television out of my trailer that's 25, 30 foot in a tree. Looks like you could plug it in and play the thing. And debris hanging in the trees, people's clothing. It looks like they decorated it with clothes. But it's all in the tops of the trees. So, all the stuff was floating around, and then when the water settled it all got hung up in the tops of the trees, and it was just clothes, coffee tables, doors, shutters. Just all kinds of debris in the tops of the trees.

There was a saying going around in New Orleans, spray painted on many of the homes: "You loot, we shoot." Did you have any encounters with looters or any similar experiences?

Yes, I had one experience with a gentleman, I don't know if he was a looter or what. A friend of mine, a Gretna policeman, he said, "Dude, they're looting houses... It's chaotic." He said, "There's no power. We're maintaining our own is basically what we're doing. You're on your own. If you got any weapons, arm yourself."

Well, the night when we came to my mother's house, when we left it had gotten dark on us. It was probably midnight when we came to my mom's. My mother lives right off of Lapalco and Ames [Blvds.].

Between Ames and Barataria, not too far off Lapalco. Well, we always enter the back of my mother's house. No one ever uses the front door. So, naturally, when we got there, me and my son walked down the alley between the houses and went to go in the back door. When I turned the corner, a guy was coming out of the yard in between the houses. And I had a shotgun with me, and I jammed him up against the wall, and I was screaming at him, "What are you doing? What are you doing?" He's hollering, "Please don't shoot me!" My son's hollering, "Please don't shoot him!" I'm hollering, "I'm gonna shoot him!" It was just— and it's pitch black; I can't even see this guy. I couldn't tell you what this gentleman looked like. It was the scariest thing I ever been through in my life. I don't get scared very easily. This was spooky. 'Cause everyone was screaming. It's black, pitch black. No street lights, no lights in the houses. Nothing.

You hear all these rumors of what was happening, and then you walk up on somebody. I was so nervous. I was so scared that I was gonna shoot him just by being nervous (and shoot him). And we had a... We had passed a National Guard truck or military vehicle when we came into the neighborhood, and my son ran down to the corner and flagged them down. They came down and confronted the guy and talked to him and took him off. The guy said he was lost, he was wandering, you know. But yes, there was, there was rampant looting. The scene at the Oakwood Mall— all the people coming over the bridge. That was the situation that, you know, we was hearing all on the television and the radios. That there was such massive looting going on— that when these people started coming over and going into Oakwood, bashing up the mall and starting fires— it was pretty, pretty hairy. From what we seen... Me and my son actually got on with a company called Base Logistics once the storm had settled, two days after the storm, three days after. And they had us bringing food and drinks to emergency areas where the politicians were and emergency people and all the police heads and all. And we were driving a big refrigerating truck, and we talked to a lot of lot of people and I would say the Riverwalk [Marketplace] got no water. No flooding damage. But it was looted. The whole place was looted. Food, jewelry, clothes, every tennis shoe in the city was stolen. You know, every jersey. Thirty, forty cars, a hundred cars from Sewell Cadillac. I mean, it was just out of control.

And a lot of people say the city wouldn't be in such bad shape if it weren't for the looting that went on. That a lot of businesses would have been able to come back right after the storm with a little cleanup and open. And actually provide some type of, you know, normalcy about what was happening at the time. But the looting was so massive that it was, it was just— it was the Wild West. It was something I've never experienced before in my life. And hopefully I never have to experience it again.

How did it make you feel seeing New Orleans' inhabitants looting one another?

I was upset. But I was shocked at first. This city had a lot of problems before the storm. We had one of the highest murder rates in the country. The education system was a total joke. It had a lot of problems and a lot of criminal element in this city. And I think that a lot of these guys hung around knowing that the city would be eighty percent evacuated, the police would be in disarray, and that they could almost come in and [have] free reign in the city. That's basically what it was. These groups of thugs were going around, and they would steal the cars, go ride around in cars. They broke into the Wal-Mart and stole every weapon and every bit of ammunition. It was the Wild West. And it upset me, but it didn't surprise me. And it upset me to see that the city could've came back a lot quicker. We could've been a lot better off if these knuckleheads wouldn't have done what they did. You know, I can understand people looting for food because if my children were here, and I had to feed them, I'd break in somewhere and take some food and some water and blankets, you know, whatever, flashlights, batteries, whatever you can get. But to go and pull from the scenes on TV, and from what I personally seen, baskets, grocery baskets filled with Nike tennis shoes, you know? Filled with VCRs and DVD players and big screen TVs. Pushing it through waist-deep water. It didn't make sense. It shows the country what element was in this city before the storm. You know what I mean? And it really upset me.

I heard rumors of looters or suspected looters just being shot. Have you heard any similar stories?

Yeah, we heard a bunch of stories. We actually ran across a gentleman when we were driving the trucks through. We seen a couple bodies floating in the water. Pretty shocking, to drive up and see someone floating in downtown New Orleans where you used to walk around, and now there's a body floating around. We tried to give these people respect. But what do you do with them? We kind of pushed a couple of them, pushed that one body away and drove the truck by. This one guy we found, he was definitely shot. He wasn't drowned, he didn't drown, he was definitely shot. I don't know if he was a looter or what, but we had talked to a couple of guys that we delivered food to, and they were talking about their escapades over the nights. We'd roll in with breakfast in the morning for these guys. They would be out and in this at night. They had night vision. It was the National Guard, the military. Once they came in, they took control. They took a day or two to get in, and these guys were still going crazy in the streets. One officer told us that they confronted, that morning, some guys coming down the street in a stolen Cadillac, from Sewell Cadillac, with rifles sticking out of the windows of the car, coming at a police barricade. He said they were on the bullhorn telling them to stop, and these guys kept rolling, so they opened fire on the car. The car backed up, turned around. He said the car was full of people, they don't know…. They were told at one point that if they couldn't get control, if they ran up on looters, to shoot them and tag them. Tag them a looter. It was very widespread. A lot more than the media let on.

If you were on the ground seeing it happen, it was a lot more than what the nation seen. You know these antique shops in the Quarter, some of the jewelry shops. Every business downtown was looted. Every, every one. I now… I've been working for a glass company for twenty years, Zinsel Glass. We're in there now doing window repairs on every store on Canal Street, every place in the Riverwalk. The hotels were looted; it was just unbelievable. And I think they had to take control. You know, these guys had weapons. I would've shot them.

So you feel that policy of shoot and tag was a correct one at the time?

I think at the time it was. Because it was out of control. It wasn't Mom and Pop looting to stay alive. It was thugs looting to benefit. They were looting to take this stuff, go somewhere, and sell it. And they had weapons. And if you confronted them, there was no law. It was lawless; the streets were lawless. They could shoot you. So, it turned out, survival of the fittest. If you had a weapon and you rolled up on somebody, you better use it and talk about it later.

Was your property insured and if so, how did the insurance company handle your claim?

I had insurance. I had flood and homeowners. I had minimum flood, which was my fault. I was one of these people that you'd hear about who were underinsured. I didn't know this at the time, but I do now.

My flood insurance— wonderful. Paid off the claim very quick. The rest of the damage to the house was... Because I had minimum flood insurance, it didn't cover the whole cost of my house. My homeowners wouldn't pay anything. I was very angry; I was very upset about...everybody's been going through this...it's been seven months, and we're fighting our homeowners.

But in reality, in my case, I look back and say, "We had thirty feet of water." I mean how much will the homeowner's policy cover? They cover from the flood line up. We had thirty feet of water; there was nothing over the flood line. Everything was underwater. So, looking back at it now, I'm kinda kicking myself because I think I beat these people up for no reason on the phone. And I think a lot of people were beating them up, beating up their homeowner's policies and insurance companies because they feel that they're owed money. I think that a lot of people were underinsured because we didn't think this would happen. We didn't think that thirty foot of water would ever rush through. No one ever thought there would be twelve feet of water throughout the city of New Orleans. Through and through the city of New Orleans. It's pretty shocking to ride by it today and see the water lines on Claiborne Avenue over the doors, over the top of the doors. You just go, "Jeezum Petes, the whole city was underwater." The insurance companies are taking a beating; I mean they're really taking a beating. We are fortunate that we live in a state that is crazy with the insurance— that they provide a vessel for these insurance companies to come in, and they give them a cushion to try and keep these companies here because we are in a storm area.

They have taken so many hits between Louisiana, Mississippi, Alabama, Florida that, you know, a lot of insurance companies don't want to write policies in Louisiana. Louisiana has to have a buffer for these insurance companies to operate or they probably wouldn't be able to operate, and that's where I think I look back, and I think that I shouldn't have beaten these people up as much as I did because I was trying to get something that I really didn't deserve because my house did go under thirty foot of water, or floated, or whatever happened was due to water. It wasn't due to wind.

What kind of impact has this storm had on your family life every day?

It's major. We're dealing with it as we speak. I got phone calls today; we're applying for SBA assistance. It's seven months, seven months; we're staying in a rented house. I got a few…little bit of furniture, some clothes. I have no idea up to this point what my family's going to do for the future, if we're going to buy a house; we obviously can't build where we're at. The levee system's not up to par; it's not going to be up to par. The funding probably won't… They need, they're talking 2.9 billion dollars to get the levee system up to FEMA's standards or they won't insure anyone. Well, there was only 6,000 residents who lived down in that area before the storm. There probably won't be half of them coming back. I doubt we'll get the funding to do what we gotta do. So, moving back to where I was from is out of the picture, because I was underinsured, I don't have enough money to actually just go out and purchase another house.

We applied for SBA assistance right after the storm. I mean, like a week; soon as they said, "Apply," we applied. It's been seven months. I got contacted today; they lost all of my files. So I have to start over. So, it's like, where do you go from here? They keep talking, like, "We're giving 6.8 billion dollars to the state, housing grants." No money has trickled down to the people yet. It's been seven months. It's a hit everyday to try and go to work and do your job and deal with the insurance people, deal with the SBA people, deal with the FEMA people. Dealing with everyone to try and get this assistance is almost a job in itself, to deal with the government to try and get this assistance. And I've worked my whole life. Since I was 16 years old I've worked and never once drawn on unemployment or been a burden to the system or tried to— have to have assistance. Never been in that position before, luckily. But now that I am, I see the bureaucratic red tape and the bull that it takes to get any assistance at all, for anyone. So, at this point we really don't know what we're going to do.

How do you feel about the way FEMA has handled the aftermath of the storm?

I think it could've been done differently. I think the finances, you know, the storm itself, I think the military should've been brought in a lot quicker; it would have halted a lot of the looting problems. Because once the military was here, it stopped. Them guys don't play. When they got here they took control. They took back the city. And it was a godsend once they were here. As far as FEMA and the rest of the— the financial part of it is the thing. FEMA needs to cut the red tape. I think the federal government really needs to get the money to the people as soon as they can get it to them. Whatever vessels or venues they need to do so.

My life is in limbo. My future is in limbo. My family is in limbo. We just don't know where to go from here. We are totally dependent on the federal government now for assistance. It's just… It's an everyday battle. The emotional rollercoaster… You know, you get a phone call, and they're telling you, "Okay, you've been assigned to a unit… Your papers have been assigned to a person." Well, the magnitude of this is so big. The workload of that one person is probably 5,000 cases. So, I'm at the back of a line of five-to-ten-thousand other people that this one person has to deal with. You know, it's just a never- ending rotation of the roller coaster ride. No matter what entity or who you deal with, you get the ups and downs constantly.

I think FEMA needs— either FEMA or the government needs to— in the future, get assistance to the people as soon as possible. If the moneys are coming, all the red tape and all the arguing and the bickering and the, "who wants this, this one should get this...." And now I'm hearing Houston, Texas, wants grant money because of the influx of people over there. Their infrastructure is busting at the seams, and they need money to run their police forces that need the overtime now because there is 100,000 [more] people there, which is understandable, but we need the money here. The sooner they can get money into people's hands, the sooner people will have an urgency. There's no urgency no more. Right after the storm, it was all hoopla, the government's coming in, Bush is like, "Yeah, we're going to do whatever it takes," and all this— well you get that feeling they're going to take care of us or try to help us.

And then seven months later, there's still nothing. It's hard to comprehend that something like this could be going on within the United States. We have a tsunami over in Japan or whatever and within 24 hours the United States has two billion dollars worth of equipment and everything over there to help these people, but right here in its own country, it can't seem to grasp and get the help down here, or even want to. It's bickering, arguing, you know, all the odds, everybody's against everybody, but we're Americans, and we're human, and we need help. And we need it quick. They still have their houses. They still have whatever, they still have their three or four houses. They get their vacation house on the coast devastated and blown away, they got two or three other ones to go... But it's the area we live in, I know that. I know we should... People say, "Well, you live down... And you build a house on the coast, what do you expect?" You got these people that build on cliffs out in California, you get the mudslide comes wipe their house out, and they stand there looking at it like, "We'll rebuild, we'll be back for the sixth time." We're funding this, the government is funding this; they need to help us, too.

Knowing what you know now, would you have done anything differently for the past five or six years of your life?

Oh, yeah. I would've, for one thing, insured my house a lot better. That would've been the first, that's the first thing I think of. It's an eye opener, makes you think about your kids. [Makes you think] that life is nothing. That you're just a small, little piece of the puzzle down here. That material things don't mean a lot. I was never a real materialistic person, to have really nice, fancy stuff. I've always had old cars in my yard, tinkering with things all the time. But in retrospect, I was a materialistic person because I did thrive on my house. My house was my thing. And I put five years of my life into this house; my whole family did. I wish I wouldn't have put the five years of my life in the house and maybe more time to my children and doing other things now. It makes you see that it's not all about the materials. It's about people, and you gotta be as good as you can to your people while you got them because at the stroke of a hand, it could all be gone.

What are your plans for the next five years?

Ah, I'm not leaving the area, I'm gonna stay. Like I said, I'm a New Orleanian, and I'm going to stay here. I'm going to try and buy me a house again. Find me a place and make it mine and hopefully the government comes through with the money, which I'm sure they will. I'm sure we're going to get some assistance and get some help. I'm one of the fortunate that my job was there right after the storm. A lot of people didn't have that opportunity to start working right… A lot of people are still out of a job. My industry, the glass business, thanks to the looters, is booming. You know, that's one positive thing for me, that I do have a job that's going to be plentiful and be there a long time.

I'm just gonna hang in here and try and make the best of it. Hurricane season's rolling up on us real quick. It's a couple… About a month away now. And they're predicting a lot, just like last year. These storms are getting worse, they're getting more frequent. We had a record year last year. They foresee the same thing again. All I'm going to do is insure my property as much as possible, and this time when it comes, I'm leaving. I'm not going to hang in, I'm not going to stay. I'm not going to take that chance. Because, like I said, these things, a couple clicks on that map to the west and the area where I'm at, where we're at right now, might not be here. It might look like where I'm from, down in Port Sulphur. So, there's no staying around no more. I'll definitely run from them.

Fifty and Homeless

Peter Borstell
Interviewed by Missy Bowen

Before Katrina, Pete Borstell, his wife Joan, and their 16-year-old son Billy lived in Gentilly. Though the storm destroyed their home and most of their neighborhood, their family relationship bloomed in the quiet that followed.

So at what point did you know you were going to go?

Well, what happened with me was— I'm an attorney, and I've been working up in Aiken, South Carolina, on a train derailment case. I came back Friday before the storm; I drove back from Aiken by myself in this little Paseo because I got left up there, and the last car they could get me was this little Paseo. So, I'm driving back here (about eleven o'clock) Friday night, and my wife calls to tell me there's a storm out there, and I didn't really think much of it.

The next day I came into town and was working in my office because I'm working like two weeks here, two weeks up there, and my son calls me up (about six o'clock) that evening and says, "Aunt Kathy's evacuating at three in the morning!"

So I'm like, "What? I'm not going to do any of that; that's insane. I've never left before." I've always stayed. I've never evacuated before. So, I turned on the news, and it was a Category Five and all that...

What did you think when you saw the TV?

Well, what really saved— what made a big difference was that the year before (we always go see Duke play Florida State in Tallahassee, and it was a Saturday night game, so on the way home) we stopped off at Pensacola Beach. This was February, and we saw what Ivan had done to Pensacola Beach. So once I heard [Katrina] was a four or a five, I said okay.

Billy had already left with my sister so it was just Joan and I. So I said, "Okay, but we're not leaving right away because I got to get some rest because I'd just driven some 600 miles all Friday in a Paseo, okay?"

So [Sunday morning] I sobered up after Saturday night, and we found a place to get some gas around 9:30 a.m., and then we take my wife's car to her parking lot [in the state building behind City Hall]. But instead of putting anything in it that might have been valuable— now in hindsight, we could have put our wedding pictures, our World's Fair posters, our Jazzfest posters, Billy pictures, all that up, but not knowing any better...

So around 10:30, 11 o'clock [a.m.] we're figuring all the sane people have already left, so we should pretty much zip right through. Well, right at that point was when Nagin declares the mandatory evacuation. So we're right in the middle of everybody getting out of town who had any kind of car that could run. In fact, it was already blocked up from the Interstate. Elysian Fields was already bumper to bumper from there. I hate any kind of traffic, so I'm driving down the service roads and everything else. I tried to get into St. Bernard [Parish], but it was already blocked off— they wouldn't let you in, and this was like twelve-thirty Sunday, so I had to go all the way back around, and I took a service road, and got to [I-] 510.

And we were with everybody. You know how they say about how they should have used buses? If they'd used buses they'd have gotten everybody out, because anybody who had any wheels was on that road. You saw cars you could tell... I mean, there were cars breaking down as you were going along. We saw one truck, a flatbed truck that had to have had 25 people in the back, okay? So that's why I think it's ridiculous; they should have used those buses. If people wouldn't have used those cars, if they could have caught a bus, there's no way they would have gotten out as quickly as they did. They could have gotten out.

It took us eighteen and a half hours to get to my father's house, which is Milledgeville, Georgia, which is usually an eight-to-nine-hour drive. It's about an hour from Atlanta. We got there just as the storm was starting to hit New Orleans.

Were you listening to the radio on the way up?

That's when we heard Nagin…like, somebody came on and said the prisoners would be okay, and it turned out the prisoners flooded out and were on the ramp. It was all kinds of weird stuff like that. And that's what he was saying, too. Nagin was saying if you can't get out, the 'Dome is your last chance, but it's not going to be nice. The electricity is going to go out, it's going to be hell to be there, so if you can get a way out…and a lot of people heeded his words, and that's why we saw all those cars when we were out there on the road.

But it was so deceiving, too, because you'd be in all this traffic, and I'm in a stick shift. And we're just about to Hattiesburg [Mississippi] and thinking, "Let's find an alternate route through Alabama to get out of this mess, and then the traffic would go." And then we'd say, "Well, maybe it'll be okay." The one place it was really bad was where I-20 and 59 come together. Normally that's not a problem but it was down to one lane, and you had all these people from Jackson that were evacuating…We had really big traffic all the way to the other side of Birmingham, and by that time it was three in the morning.

Was it raining?

We hit some bands in Hattiesburg, but once we got north of there it wasn't.

It was weird; everyone had their pets. You'd stop at one of these rest areas and everybody'd have their pets. We'd let them out and do their thing, and then you'd be pulling out of your parking spot and people'd pull right in behind you.

So, we finally made it to my Dad's house, and my sister was already up there with her two Great Danes, and I had my two dogs, so we're kinda doing that traffic stuff with the dogs; let the other ones out, and let the two go in, that kind of thing.

At that point in time we were just trying to get in touch with people. I luckily had an 803 cell phone, but anyone with a 504 [area code] you couldn't get in touch with, so that was scary, wondering what happened to good friends and all that. And then we started to hear...people'd call me...Patrick who works in my office, he was stuck in St. Bernard and told horrible stories about what went on down there.

When did you find him?

Had to be after Labor Day. 'Cause I heard from Douglas on Labor Day, that's when his phone came on, on Labor Day. In the meantime, we had this big-time case in Lake Charles where they were trying to screw us out of this big attorney's fee, and I'm trying to get in touch with the judge out there, so all that was kinda going on, and we had no idea what we were really going to do.

It really became apparent that we weren't going to go back when they said they weren't going to let anybody in. When they finally said they weren't going to let anybody back in for a week or ten days or whatever, that's when my wife and I finally decided to take my son— we left my dogs with my dad— to Aiken, where I had my temporary office. And that's when we tried to find an apartment and all that.

The main thing was to get my kid in school. He's a junior in high school, and he'd already, by that point, missed almost two weeks. So I asked around and finally got him into the best school we could get to, and that was weird, because they've got these really weird things for busing, quota things, so one area could be one school and then the next block would be different. So, finally, I went down to the School Board and said, "Look, he's been out of school all this time. We got to get him into school. I'll make sure he's in the right district for the school. Can he at least start classes?" And they were pretty good about it.

And the Red Cross was pretty good; they gave us a thousand-dollar voucher for Wal-Mart.

You had nothing. What had you packed? You'd never left before.

I expected to come right back. I had a couple of thousand-dollar suits that were dirty, and I thought, well, I'm not going to smell up my suit bag, so I left them there. I brought rinky-dink clothes, clothes that didn't make any difference, because we were just really in a hurry. Like I said, I'd just gotten back. I'd been up in South Carolina already. I was kind of looking forward to relaxing, staying in New Orleans that week through Labor Day, and then going back up. And then all of a sudden, here we are, rushing out of town, you know?

Were you getting reports about your house?

My wife and my dad, they were just focused on it, but my brother-in-law…this is weird, his best friend is, like, the chief investigator for the DA's office, and he just happened to go to Macon, Georgia [a few miles southwest of Milledgeville] to get out of the thing, so he was over all the time, and he was getting these reports from fresh on the street.

How'd they hook up?

They just kind of found each other on the cell phones. So he was getting all this information, and that's what we were hearing, too, about all the looting and stuff, and that was pretty bizarre, but after a while we knew we weren't going to be going back for a while. And when they were talking about the canals and all that, we had a good idea that that was going to be our house, that it was going to be flooded.

And then they had that thing where you can look on the aerial thing on the computer, and it said nine feet. And then my sister went down later on and told me it was pretty much kaput but that was after we'd gotten an apartment and everything.

But there were some funny things that happened. We went down to the Salvation Army and there was a lady there from Hattiesburg who'd lost her house too, and so Joan hadn't even been there three, four days and was already on the front page— these two ladies, one white, one black, hugging each other from the storm, and then they did interviews of both of them, so she was on the front page of the Aiken paper on her fourth day there!

Billy, my son, was trying to act like we weren't refugees, you know. I'm like, use your vouchers, and he didn't want to do that.

Luckily, my wife has a brother in Atlanta and a sister in Charlotte, and they brought some stuff together, brought us some furniture and stuff for this apartment.

You didn't have a thing.

Nothing. Joan had maybe three shirts and two pairs of shorts, and that was about it. But we left in such a hurry. I had some friends of mine tell me that they packed a bag for their dog, but didn't pack anything for themselves, so they got where they were at, and the dog had tons of stuff, and they had nothing! Dog was doing great, all kinds of bones and toys and everything.

This town is very friendly. Everyone's been very nice to us. My dad's church gave us, like, three hundred bucks, which was nice. [Joan's] family came with all kinds of furniture and stuff, and that really helped out a lot.

Billy's been trying to make the best of it in school, but it's hard because he would have been a big man on campus and all that.

Did he get extra attention at first, singled out as the Katrina kid?

Well, yeah, but he was trying to play that down. He didn't really want that. That really wasn't what was going on. They really tried to help him scholastically; I've got to say that. The administration was really cool. They were really pretty good. And I was really proud of him. That first week he went, it was that Friday of the first week, and I said, I'm going to go to the office and do a little work. And he said, "Drop me off at the football game." Football's big up there, I mean, they get like 15,000 people to go see a high school game, okay? What does Tulane get? So he went. I dropped him off, and he went.

How has it changed him?

He was really down in the dumps until he started hearing from some of his friends. He was trying to get them on his own cell phone, and when he started hearing from some of them and finding out that they had some of the same problems that made him feel a lot better.

So the New Orleans kids started comparing their new schools?

He's got a friend over in Dallas who says, "There's all gangs here, Billy. I'm not tough! They all want me to join gangs, and I'm doing homework just to get away from them. And all the girls are pregnant!" And he's a big kid, like six-two, and he says, "I'm just a big teddy bear, and they want me to join gangs." So when he heard his friends talking like that that made him feel a lot better. That got him laughing.

But we had all these weird things we had to go through, like all this trouble with our Bank One account. We couldn't get anything done by phone, so we had to get up really, really early in the morning and drive all the way up to West Virginia where there was a Bank One branch. That was the closest one. So we got up at like five in the morning and drove about three hundred miles to get to a Bank One…

Three hundred miles so you could talk to a real person?

So we could get all this money that we had. We had maybe three or four thousand dollars, and we couldn't get at the money. So it was weird things like that.

My wife and I, we've been on pins and needles because she has a good job with the state, and we've been waiting for her to get the call that she has to come back, and she's told them February 1, so she's been in limbo.

Have they continued to pay her?

They did through October, and now she's been getting unemployment, but that's been a battle trying to get those funds. Right now, if she comes back we don't know where she's going to stay, but she doesn't want to lose that job.

Well, that brings up the house. What happened when you first went back [to your house]? You'd had warning?

Well, I had my sister telling me it was bad, but first off, I left [South Carolina], and I thought I could get a hotel room at two in the morning in Evergreen, Alabama, and they were all booked up. So I said, well, if they're all booked up here, the hell with it. That was before the I-10 was fixed, so I'm on the [Highway 11] bridge going through Slidell and was…amazed. Boats in the trees still, whole houses slid over…this was in October.

You were up in Georgia and South Carolina not seeing your house or getting at your stuff that whole time?

Right. That was when I first went back. It was right before the deadline to file for bankruptcy under the old laws, and I had a couple cases, and so I had to do that. So I worked the first day and stayed with some clients' parents across the lake that night, and then the next morning came across the lake to my house…

I couldn't believe Slidell. These clients put me up and that was real nice of them. But just driving in, looking through East New Orleans, and the sun was kind of coming up, and it looked like a ghost town.

So I worked that first day and didn't see my house until the next day, and I'm kinda glad I didn't, because I would have freaked out if I'd gone there immediately…I realized it was all kind of gone, you know? [Becomes teary] I couldn't believe the trees were all gone…

Did you have any trouble getting into Gentilly?

No. I started seeing all these people with masks on, so I knew that was bad. Once I saw it…

Someone had written on it: "We love you, Pete." And that was kind of cool. One of the neighbors wrote something on all the houses. There was one for everybody, like, don't worry, it'll get better for one house, you know, little sayings.

But I walked in and all these flies hit me, and the smell was unbelievable. I just had shorts on, and I didn't want to catch anything, any of the mold, and I just turned around and walked out and called Joan and said, "There's nothing here." They still don't really believe me because they haven't been down here yet. They're coming after Christmas and then they'll really see it.

Did you try to get anything out?

I looked at it, and it was all moldy, and God knows…all the pictures were moldy. I had a baker's table, and all the legs were broken off. That thing weighs a ton; it took three of us to get it in the house, and the legs were broken, so the water must have dropped out all at once or something, or knocked it around. My grandmother's dining room set's all ruined. We had a lot of junk anyway, but… I haven't even opened up the back. It looks like water's still leaking out of the back. The water was up, well, I stood on the stoop, and the line was at least a foot and a half over my head. [Borstell is about five-foot five, and the stoop is approximately three feet off the ground.]

Was there water left in the bathtub and stuff like that?

I didn't even get that far in it because there was so much junk in there and I wasn't insured, so I was really afraid to walk in there, in case I got cut or something like that. I mean, I knew a little bit about mold because a couple of years ago when they said it wasn't going to be covered under homeowner's [insurance] there were going to be a lot of cases, so I took a class on it. So I knew I didn't want to catch any of that.

So now I'm trying to get the mortgage paid off. It really gives us a new freedom. My kid going to college is my only real concern. He can go to Tulane for free as part of my wife's severance package from when she worked there back when he was three or four years old. That was the deal: five years of undergraduate education. So that's why we never really worried about college for him. And now it's a shell of what it's supposed to be, and I don't know what I'm going to do. I really want him to enjoy college because it was the best four years I had.

I promised him he would have his senior year at De La Salle, so if [Joan] comes back here we're going to have to find us a place to live.

Has FEMA given you anything? What about a trailer?

Well, they've given us some stuff, but you're dealing with the flood people. I had flood insurance, so I'm trying to get that all done.

How are you going to deal with where to live?

I don't know yet. I have no idea. And then you hear these horror stories. I was coming back from Baton Rouge yesterday and the announcer was saying his little apartment that was six hundred and fifty dollars a month before the storm is now sixteen fifty. So I don't know what's going to happen.

Have you applied for a trailer?

We did…It's kind of weird. On one hand, I was tired of the house anyway. We want to move to a condo anyway after Billy's out of the house, and we've been thinking about that anyway, because I hate fixing things up, I hate yard work and all that, so if it's just the two of us it makes sense. But having it forced on you… And I love this city. When you go somewhere else you realize how much you do love this city, and even though the people in Aiken were very nice to us, it's still not the same.

The only thing that bothers me are the posters. And I had all these cassettes of recorded music I'd recorded through the years, all kinds of stuff. That gets me. And the photos. The rest of it, the furniture and that kind of thing, I could care less. I'm not a materialistic person. And for years I've been telling Billy and Joan that I'm going to put a dumpster in front of the house and whatever they didn't pick in two days was going in it. We had a lot of junk. It's just I didn't want it all wiped out at once.

How do you feel about rebuilding on that same lot?

Oh, I don't want to rebuild. I really don't. I don't want to live in a house anymore. So in a way, that's cool. But if I have to, I may get an SBA loan, and build it, and turn around and sell it to pay for [Billy] to go to college, I don't know. If Tulane turns out to be really not what it was supposed to be...I mean, they fired two hundred and fifty professors. They're getting rid of the Engineering Department. So I don't know.

There's silver linings to everything. My wife and I will be twenty-five years that we've been married, and I strung her along for seven years before that, and we realized we still care about each other. This has forced us to spend all this time together. Before that, we'd both been so busy, and I've been up in South Carolina, and when you've got a teenager you're running him back and forth to wrestling matches and that kind of stuff, and we never really had time for us, so that's good.

And I got an extra year with him, because if we were here we'd just be picking him up and dropping him off, and that'd be about it, and so now he's basically stuck with us. I felt bad for him on his birthday because he called all these people and no one called him back, so I ended up hanging out with him, so that's kind of good.

And another thing is that both of our parents live within three hours of that area, so we've seen her parents and mine a bunch more times than we normally would have, and my dad's seventy-five, you know? So that's been an advantage. So there's been certain things. And we did land in a town where the people have been very friendly.

Here's what I'm really hoping. I'm hoping my train case and Billy's school all merge together and end at the same time, and [Joan] through the state, is going to get some help finding an apartment where we can all live eventually, and then we'll be back here for next year.

I mean, this is the best city in the world to live in. And when you're away you miss it. I've been to Atlanta. Atlanta's great. But Atlanta's so big. Up there, it's eighteen miles to Augusta, and people say, "I'm running to Augusta. I'll be right back." Distances don't mean anything. Here, to me, working in Gretna and living in Gentilly, that's too far to work and drive! But there it's like nothing. It doesn't mean anything. Columbia is fifty miles away and that's no big deal; it's less than an hour.

Where is home?

Home is here. It's here. All my friends are here. Every time I come back, that's proven. Memories are here. It's temporary up there, no doubt about it.

But then again, you come back, and, like this weekend, it's so hard to get anywhere, the driving is bad, and you wonder how long is it really gonna take? When I was in Pensacola Beach, and there were all those big hotels, and they were nowhere near being completed eight months after Ivan. How are they going to do that in a town that's destroyed? Here they're talking about twenty-to-fifty-thousand homes destroyed and having to be bulldozed, you know?

How long is it gonna take? And will the character change? Are they gonna build all these little pre-fab houses? That was the nice thing about New Orleans, the neighborhoods were all different. Is it all gonna be the same now?

I turned fifty three weeks ago.

Fifty and homeless.

Doing the Lord's Work

Larry and Karen Daigle
Interviewed by Mary Sparacello

Larry Daigle couldn't imagine evacuating without his wife, Karen. And Karen couldn't imagine leaving her pets behind, despite her family's pleas to evacuate.

Larry Daigle

Her mom and dad called and said we've got to leave. They called a little bit later and said now it's a [Category] 5. Her brother called. They wanted us to leave. Everything was packed. I had our will. I came back inside. Karen was sitting at the table with one of the cats in her lap. She said, "I can't leave my animals." I said, "If you're staying, we're going to die together. When I said 'til death do us part that was it. If we die, we die."

We had food and drinks, candles, flashlights.

It sounded like a freight train coming through here. Transformers were coming up. Whoo. Shutters were peeling, things flying. After the hurricane, we went outside. I said, "Karen, come see. That water's rising to the street, to the sidewalk, to the driveway, to the house. Are the pumps on or not?" I moved my old-time jukebox— I bought it for $4,000 before the storm— from the front room, to the hall, to the kitchen to the den. Good thing it was on rollers.

[Our neighbor] Ruth called on the landline. She said, "The water's coming." We invited over Ruth, her husband Robert, and their two children. We listened to the radio, shared stories. We ate sandwiches before the meat went bad. The next morning, Robert and I took the boat and went to his house to rescue his cats. The man across the street left his speedboat. He said, "If you need it, take it." I took my gun and put it on the end table. I told Karen, "If anybody comes in shoot them." We saw a black family down the street, a man, his wife and their three-year-old girl and infant girl and a puppy German Shepherd. He was going down the road with his truck and hit a low spot. The engine stalled. His wife started hollering. She was hysterical, that woman. "Help, help. How are we going to get out of here?" We drove them back to their house. He took out his wallet, "How much do I owe you?" He asked. I said, "Nothing, I'm doing the Lord's work." We stayed that night, but as soon as it got daylight we were leaving.

A black boy and a white boy came walking down the street. They asked, "Can you bring us to the front of the street?"

I said, "We don't have a car."

They pointed to our packed car. "What about that?"

I said, "That car flooded. That's why we can't leave."

We only saw one police car. He stopped us on the way out. He said, "You've got ID? We've got a lot of looters. They took every bullet, every gun." We didn't know anything that happened until we got to Karen's relatives in Lafayette. When we got back, about a month later, we joined Vineyard Church and handed out food, water, ice, cold drinks. We'd go up and down the street distributing it.

I think for everything you do there's a reason for it, and I think the Lord wanted us to stay just to help people.

Karen Daigle

[My sister and her husband] had all left. They called us and wanted us to go with them. I told them we couldn't because of the animals. They called back and told us it was really going to be bad. It was my sister's husband, John. We packed the car and we were going to go. But then I told them I couldn't go. I think in my mind I thought it would be like any other year. They passed us in the past. I didn't think anything would happen. We called down to some of our neighbors. "Ruth, if anything happens, you can call us." The couple down the street stayed too.

It looked like a river. White caps just flowing down the street. The hurricane took the carport. We heard it. It just lifted the whole thing. You couldn't even get down the street with the trees and the debris. After the hurricane, our landline telephone still worked. As people were leaving they came by trying to use our phone. Before the storm, we all exchanged phone numbers. They were all calling us. "How high is the water? How is our house?"

On Monday we lost electricity. We ate on a Boy Scout grill. We left three days after the hurricane because we had no electricity. We weren't going to have electricity for a while... Plus the water. We were pretty much here on our own. All the neighbors had pretty much left. Looters were breaking into the Academy [Sports, about one mile away]. [Larry] said, "They have guns. They're looting everything." Everyone was leaving, and we were the only ones here. Going out that day that we rode out of here, on the way out, it was unbelievable. Just to see people's lives, the houses. Everything. I never thought I would live to be in something like this. I cried the whole way out.

We drove back and forth from Lafayette, where we evacuated, to feed my animals and leave food for strays. We returned to Kenner, permanently, about a month later. When we did come back, we were the first ones to come back. We had a mess to clean up. I missed my pets. You could tell they missed me. They don't know what's going on inside. We had to push everything in two rooms because the front of the house, which is built on a slight hill, flooded. I have to keep them locked up in the back because they don't understand. They don't understand the trailer. It's different, and they're kind of nervous in the trailer.

When mail started no one was here, so I kept all the mail. Everyone had their box. They'd call and we'd report to them. They would come every now and then. We took care of the animals around here. There were dogs sleeping on tables. We fed stray animals until their owners returned.

"If I had to do it over again, I would," Larry said.

"We both would," Karen added.

Standing in Line and Signing My Name

Harry Sterling
Interviewed by Nicole Pugh

Harry Sterling once aspired to be a meteorologist, so when the news declared Katrina a Category 5 hurricane, he knew it was time to leave New Orleans. In addition to being an amateur weather man, he also plays a very mean guitar.

Right before the hurricane hit, what was going on for you?

I was performing at the Funky Pirate that Saturday before. Everybody was watching the hurricane for the last three or four days. Nobody knew what it wanted to do. I was watching the hurricane from time to time and I was saying, "This is a strange thing." It was doing this little Gulf loop like it doesn't know what it wants to do. Everybody was asking me, "What's it going to do? What's it going to do?" And I was saying, "I don't know!"

Why were they asking you?

Back when Betsy hit, I was a young child and it amazed me what a storm could do to a city or a neighborhood. It rocked my mother's house from side to side. As much danger as everyone was in, I still felt that it was an amazing thing. So weather attracted my attention as well as the stars and space. I was going to be a meteorologist long before I thought about becoming a musician. I still look at it because I did a lot of dabbling in it when I was in junior high school and elementary school. All of that kind of went out the window when I met Danny Barker. I still am fascinated by the way weather patterns are. And just be watching the local news and reading up about this and that...

You have gotten pretty good at predicting them, huh?

Yeah, I'm pretty good, I guess. It was hard to call Katrina. I said, "I don't know exactly where she [is] going." When the two ridges began to combine, which was about that Friday night, and it didn't look good— you needed at least one of those ridges to turn east in order to turn Katrina back towards the Atlantic. It was moving slow. It caught on to the ridge and came straight up but it didn't start moving until that Saturday. And while she was moving slow, she was gaining strength. So playing the Funky Pirate— we finished at one a.m.— I went to Johnny White's and had a drink with a couple of folks and then I went home. When I got home, it was still a Category 3. I went to bed at 3:00. I got up at about 6:30 to go use the bathroom and take a walk through the house to check on my roommate and her children— everybody was snoring. Then I looked at the television. I said, "Wow, she's gotten larger. She's gotten bigger than she was three hours ago." I turned up the volume. It said, "Hurricane Katrina is now a Category 5." I said, "You have got to be kidding me! It was a Category 3 three hours ago!" I started yelling, "Let's go! Get up! Get up! We've got to get out of New Orleans!" "Why?" my roommate said, "The storm is a category five. This city can only withstand a category three, not a four or a five. Anything above a Category 3, we have to go. We have to get out of here!"

I was going to go to church that morning. My sister was getting ready to leave with her friends, and she said, "Why don't you come with us?" I said, "No, give me your car." And she came and picked me up. I gassed her car up and brought her home. She went down the street to her friend's, and then I went Uptown to board up a friend of mine's apartment. He called me all the way from Japan. He said, "Bro, please go board up my house." I said, "No problem. I'm on my way over there now." I came back, and everything was packed. We stuffed everybody in the car, and we got out on two o'clock Sunday.

After nine hours of driving, we made it to Baton Rouge, Louisiana, which is only 87 miles away. It is an hour drive with regular traffic. And that is where we stayed. We watched the news. Katrina hit that Monday. It was an amazing thing because we were in Baton Rouge and I was standing outside when Katrina hit New Orleans. And the wind was terrible. I saw trees in Baton Rouge uproot themselves and fall— that is a sight.

So we are watching all this rain and wind in Baton Rouge. Naturally, we didn't know what was going on in New Orleans. There was no news coverage from New Orleans because there was no power. There was a news crew from CNN saying, "We're in New Orleans, in the middle of Hurricane Katrina, and I think we are going to go inside." I was like, "I think you better go inside alright."

The next day was when we saw what was actually going on. Really, there wasn't that much footage. After the levees broke was when we saw the devastation of the city. Monday night at about three in the morning: "News Flash. New Orleans East. I-10 East highway bridge across Lake Ponchartrain has been demolished by the hurricane." And when they showed the first pictures that Tuesday morning at about 7:30, I said, "Oh my God. Look at the Twin Span. It is terrible." I said, "This storm blew the bridge down."

Then we saw where the levees broke in the Ninth Ward, in New Orleans East, and [at] the 17th Street Canal. I was like, "My God, the city is literally under water." But it wasn't from the storm. It was from the breach in the levees. I was like, "I thought those levees were impenetrable."

Then we saw pictures of the area where we live on Claiborne Avenue, right between St. Phillip and Dumaine. It looked like we had lost everything. From the aerial shot, it looked like the water was up to the roofs. We actually had six and half inches of water. It came about three feet into the house. It actually would not have gone in there, but by the house sitting in that water for two weeks, a couple of the pilings broke and the house leaned and let the water in just a little bit.

The Wednesday after the storm is when I went into survival mode. I had not had time to actually sit down and grieve over what has happened to my city. It was— get in touch with FEMA, get in touch with the Red Cross, get in touch with this and that. Also, before we left I stopped at an ATM machine and cleaned my account out. I actually had to go to several ATM's to clean it out. I didn't know what was actually going to happen. I took the money that I had, almost a year of savings, and I said, "Okay, I need to get my people out of here. I have to survive."

I went in to the mode of learning Baton Rouge. I just knew that as soon as I became familiar with how to get there [to the Radio Shack where his roommate got work right away], I would use that route to get to other points of the city… So, Baton Rouge became New Orleans. I started standing in line and signing my name. I wasn't able to get in touch with FEMA right away. FEMA was very hard to get in touch with. Matter of fact, Red Cross wasn't even in Baton Rouge.

They didn't even open a Red Cross until a month ago!

About that. It just so happened that we passed it one day and we said, "Let's go see." We went right in and came right out. They were opening centers for three hours and they had thousands of people over there. They didn't have enough workers. Finally they had enough workers. They were saying that you have to be out there at four in the morning. I was saying, "That ain't happening. No, not after being out all day, seven and a half hours." I stood seven-and-a- half hours in a food stamp line to get a card. We filled out the application the day before, and at three o'clock we had to be in line. So at three, we were in line. And we stayed in that line until about nine-thirty that night. When I got that card, I said, "I ain't goin' to the store. I'm going home, and I'm goin' to bed." After standing in 90 degree heat for six hours— it was insane.

Then there were all the different stories. You know, people are going to be people. Some people, their survival mode is different than others. Mine is, "stand there, chill out, get some water, talk to people and hear their stories." While other people are, "Blah, blah, blah..." For me, I am going to stand right here and not move a muscle. Standing in line and signing my name was the course of the next three weeks.

It took you that long to get everything?

Yes, and then going around to all the music stores and registering, letting them know that I do teach kids, that I am trying to find a job. We didn't know what was going to happen here or when the Funky Pirate was going to open back up. If the Funky Pirate wasn't going to be open by November 1st, I was headed for Houston. I was going to go to Houston and find music work there.

Did you have contacts there?

Plenty. We couldn't get in touch with each other, but we were text messaging. I couldn't get in touch with no one, and that was scary. So I just got on my cell phone and printed, "WHERE ARE YOU?" I just started getting everybody's cell phone. And at about 3:30am Tuesday morning (after the storm), my cell phone went, "Bleep, bleep, bleep!" I had twenty-five messages. I answered every one. It took me two hours, but I answered every one and let them know where I was.

I was really worried about a drummer friend of mine, Corey Walters. I had talked to her briefly before the storm. She was in Hattiesburg, Mississippi. Then I didn't hear from her for two weeks. I think I was standing in the food stamp line when she finally called. I was so happy. I was almost in tears. I was so worried about her.

From that point on, everything began to run smoothly. I got in touch with FEMA one morning at about one o'clock. I said, "Well, good morning," to the lady from FEMA. She said, "Good morning— and who am I talking to?" I said, "I'm Harry Sterling. And you might as well start taking down all of my information. But you are going to wait a minute. I am in the process of making a sandwich and I just finished brewing coffee. Would you like a cup?" She said, "Honey, if I could reach though the phone, I would come and have a sandwich with you." I said, "You have such a wonderful attitude." She said, "Just take your time. I'll just ask you some questions. What kind of sandwich are you making?" I said, "It's turkey. I'm using the type of bread that Subway uses— a French roll. And I am putting on there turkey, lettuce, tomato, baby spinach, some white American cheese, a couple of pickles, mayonnaise, mustard." She said, "How thick are you putting your mayonnaise?" I said, "Baby, its got to be sloppy." Then I said, "Now I am sitting down." She said, "Now, Mr. Sterling. I said, "No, ma'am. Call me Harry." She said, "Well, Harry. My name is Tiffany. It is a pleasure to meet you." We started talking, and she got the information.

It was one-thirty in the morning when I talked to FEMA after being on hold for two and a half hours. But it was good because I wasn't leaving. As soon as I heard, "You have just reached the Federal Emergency blah, blah, blah…" I said, "Good." I put my earpiece in. I put the phone in my pocket, and I walked around the house listening to crappy piano music. It was terrible.

Then it came to the point where we weren't feeling comfortable where we were. My first cousin has a house that was behind hers. I told her that I would get my people in there. I paid her rent for a couple of months while I was there. My roommate is still there. She is getting ready to leave Radio Shack to get back to drafting and construction. That was what she was doing in college. After her kids get out of school she is going to move back to New Orleans.

When were you able to go back into New Orleans and look at your house?

Almost a month later. We pulled up to the house and our mouths dropped. We didn't get any water. Driving back through New Orleans, we didn't know what to expect. What had us actually prepared is when we started crossing the spillway. There were these two houses. The one house was standing. The other was on its side. That was the main reality check. Just as we got into Jefferson Parish, we saw whole sides gone. Whole office buildings— gone. There were people pulling over and crying. I was like, "I don't have time for this. I have to get to my house." That was the only thing on my mind.

Like I said, we saw all the debris outside of the house and it was terrible. Then we went inside and we were like, "We didn't get any water! Yippee!" But then I looked down and realized that we had some water. When we walked around the front, we saw that the house had started leaning. But the only place we had mold was right underneath the air-conditioning!

Oh, but honey— it smelled to high heaven. I didn't open the fridge. I ain't that good. I couldn't handle it. I knew that that refrigerator was going out. We were excited because everything that we had there in the house was saved. Everything else was in storage— but that's another story.

Then I said, "My babies aren't here."

Tell us who your babies are.

Three Gibson guitars. Two Fender guitars. Two Yamaha guitars. They were stolen. I lost things through looters the first time. They took the guitars, and I said, "My God." We are talking about guitars from maybe 1974 up until the year 2000. I had a Gibson L6S that my mother bought me when I was in high school. It was worth about $20,000. It's history. I had a Les Paul that I had recently got, and I was going to give to Al [Carson]. I was going to will it to my good friend upon my death. I had a collector's Fender guitar— a Wayne's World guitar— that I only paid a hundred dollars for. Now it is worth about twelve hundred. I had nine guitars. I have one left. It was custom-made for a friend of mine and he didn't want it so he sold it to me. After I got the bugs out of it, it plays better than anything new. That was the one I took with me. That was the only one I could take with me because the rest of them couldn't fit.

I tell you, it was such a shock. I never believed that someone would steal guitars. But it happened. I said, "Okay, forget about it. These are material things. Think about it. No one can replace you. You can replace that wood and those strings. With all this relief help that is getting ready to come to you, you can go anywhere and buy any guitar you want. So chill out. That mindset kicked in. And then the grief was gone. It was just gone.

My Own Little World

Tommy
In His Own Words

Tommy, a methamphetamine addict, found an oasis in the middle of chaos complete with his own swimming pool, hiding only when the National Guard came by in their Humvees.

I spent most of my time on Chestnut and Philip [Streets]. Down in the Garden District. Big mother of a house. Found it when I was on my bike riding downtown on about the third day after the storm. I stunk, and it was hot. Really hot, man. It's like with no power and nothing, no ice. You can't even begin to believe. So I find this place with a pool. Gate wasn't even locked. I had it all to myself. These people, they had everything back there— a barbecue set, umbrellas— and it was all out, looked untouched, except for all the junk in the pool. But back there in the yard there was a shed, also not locked. Man, it's like some people just left, like time stopped and everybody just straight up disappeared. Yeah, but… So, there I was, back in this yard, all fenced in. Felt protected. Like my own little world. But the pool is all busted, and so I go to the shed to look for, well, I don't really know what I was looking for. Bleach? Hell, I didn't know what to do to clean a pool. But I get into the shed and it's just packed with pool toys, paddles, soccer and basketballs. Tons of shit. But also they've got chlorine for the pool. Bottles and bottles of it. And so I just took one look at the directions, skimmed the leaves and garbage off the top of the pool, and dumped the bottles in. And I'd just chill out there, day after day, you know. I never went into the house. Didn't need to. I had stuff back at my place on Prytania. Figured this life wasn't so bad at all. And I was alone most of the time. Had to keep out of sight of the cops and soldiers in the Hummers.

For the most part, though, everything was cool, kinda like it is now, with Uptown being this island, where not much has changed. I mean there were the rumors, and I don't know what you were all hearing on CNN and FOX and those guys, but the rumors here were crazy, like cops having a hit list of drug dealers and criminals to kill. What was worse, for me anyway, was all the stories about looters up by me, was afraid I'd get shot or arrested or something. It's like the end of the world, and I had my own pool and just hung out. Wouldn't it have been something if I'd had a blender and could've made some margaritas and daiquiris with those little umbrellas in them?

You know the best part about all this though? I don't want you to think I'm a bad guy or anything, 'cause I'm not really. I just have my proclivities. Some people like to smoke or drink or screw. I do meth. Crank, whatever people call it. But because of the storm, there wasn't any to get, couldn't buy none of it. Everyone had left. And so I guess I just went cold turkey. I smoked a lot and drank too much, but at least I got off the bad shit.

Anyway, I stayed at that pool, did my whole routine for about three straight weeks. I never left. And then the people started coming back— Uptowners first, business owners mainly. I have to say, I kind of like the way it was when I had my pool. I know it wasn't so great for everybody, especially those stuck on the bridges and at the Convention Center, though I never even knew about any of that for the first few weeks. But I had it pretty good. A nice, quiet city all to myself. And now people are coming back and talking about how things are going to change and be different and better, and I don't really know if that's true. But they weren't here. I had this city to myself. Had that pool. It was an amazing thing, like an oasis in the middle of chaos. In some ways I miss it.

On the Run

Jaye Woodmansee
In His Own Words

Jaye and his wife got out of New Orleans in time to avoid Katrina, but Hurricane Rita put them on the road again. Jaye compares the city to a snow globe shaken by god-sized hands, and so, with New Orleans always in his heart, Jaye relocated to Florida.

The first inkling I had of the storm that would change so much in my life was a news report about a Category 1 hurricane named Katrina. It was passing by the Florida Keys and seemed like any other midsummer storm, 75 mph winds and moving from the Atlantic into the Gulf of Mexico. Having grown up in the coastal South, I'd seen many storms of this size and type and thought very little at the time about any danger it might pose.

The next time I took notice of the storm was some hours later when I saw a news report telling me that Katrina had grown in strength to a Category 4 hurricane. Now, a storm that grows that quickly and is still that far south in the Gulf is something to take notice of. It could go anywhere along the coast and do a lot of damage. I'll ride out Category 1 or 2 storms— I'll even sit in my home in the French Quarter if I am going to be on the "clean" side of a big storm that makes landfall more than fifty miles away— I did that with Hurricane Andrew back in the nineties— but a Category 4 storm anywhere in my area is nothing to fool with.

The following morning, Friday, August 26th, I learned that Katrina was growing in strength and would be a Category 5 hurricane very soon, and that the storm path looked like a dead-on strike for New Orleans. I knew then that we weren't going to ride this one out in our living room. Watching the news reports all the rest of that day, I noticed that the city and state authorities seemed very on edge, more so than I have seen in some time. After all, here it was, the disaster that they had been warned about for years, a strong Category 4 or 5 bearing down on a city that was below sea level. I remember seeing the first news conference with Mayor Nagin talking about the possibility of Katrina coming into New Orleans for a landfall. What caught my eye was that Governor Blanco was standing right there beside him. Wow, I thought. They are worried about this one. By nightfall I had made up my mind that my wife and I would be pulled out of town to wait this storm out somewhere else. With memories of the last New Orleans evacuation in mind (a friend took 10 hours to get to Baton Rouge last time) I planned to get out ahead of the bulk of the traffic.

Saturday, the 27th, started early for me. Filling the car with gas was the first order of business. I thought that we would be away from home for five to seven days— ten days tops— and then come right back. I started to pack and prepare the house for us to be away for that amount of time. My wife's family owns a home in Galveston, Texas, that we have used for short vacations and visits in the past. I thought that would be perfect to hole up in until the storm passed and we returned home.

My wife, Mary, didn't seem to be that worried about the whole thing and thought that we should wait twenty-four more hours and see what Katrina was going to do, but waiting just ran so contrary to all my gut feelings. For whatever reason, I knew this was going to be a bad one, so evacuation was not something I wanted to leave until the last moment. My heightened anxiety over this storm convinced Mary that waiting was not an option, so by midday we were both busy buttoning up our townhouse on Burgundy Street and getting ready for what was supposed to be a few days vacation.

Mary and I taped windows, cleared the courtyard of items that might fly about, locked our house shutters, and most importantly, cleared out our refrigerator of any food that would spoil. We turned off the utilities, all the basic storm readiness steps one should take before an evacuation. By 5 p.m. on Saturday, and just as Mayor Nagin was calling for a voluntary evacuation of the city, we were pulling out of our courtyard, locking the gate, and heading west.

One thing I have learned living in New Orleans is that the I-10 is not the fastest evacuation route. It can back up, becoming bumper-to-bumper traffic quicker than any other highway I know. Bearing this in mind, I crossed the Crescent City Connection and headed out of town on Highway 90. The trip to Galveston, on any normal day, takes about six hours. Even with the other evacuees on the road, we arrived with only a few delays in nine hours.

We arranged for two close friends of ours, a couple by the names of Niesa and Jason, to join us in Galveston. They both worked in the service industry on Bourbon Street, so they were not able to leave town until late Saturday evening. The two of them drove out just ahead of the real traffic nightmare and made the trip to Galveston in roughly twelve hours, arriving very tired and wrung out.

The four of us spent the next day watching the television news reports as Katrina made landfall. It was very hard to believe what I was seeing. Winds and rains that were tearing it apart at the seams were pounding the city that I have called home for close to fifteen years. The cover on the Superdome roof flapping like an old tarp, the windows of the CBD high-rises blowing out and smashing to the ground, all the people huddled in their homes with no power or help. It was like watching a Hollywood disaster movie. It didn't seem real. How could it be real? I had been through bad storms before, but this was the huge, biblical, wrath of God stuff I was seeing on the screen. What was my Big Easy going to do in the face of this? Then, we heard that the levees failed and that the metro area was flooding. Katrina was a massive blow to the City of New Orleans, but it was the breeched levee system that allowed Lake Pontchartrain to destroy it.

The anxiety level in the Galveston house rose sharply. Watching reports of flooding, looting, and people trapped in the Superdome and Convention Center was too much to take. Niesa was so upset that she ended up in a terrible state of agitation that caused her to vomit small amounts of blood. Jason was coping by blocking it all out, drinking beer after beer. After a few days of stress, Niesa informed us that they were leaving and heading for the West Coast where they had family. The next morning we wished them a safe trip. (We learned later that they had their own adventures on the way to California. I still don't have all the details about what happened to them, but it seems that the combination of an emotionally upset girl, a stressed out boy, two cats in a car, and a big rock in the middle of the road resulted in a damaged undercarriage and a two-week delay from being jerked around by a shifty mechanic in the middle of New Mexico. It made for a very long road trip to San Francisco.)

Mary and I now had a chance to talk about what all this meant and what we would do next. We are both computer people so we kept our laptops with us the whole trip. They became our main source of information. I did all our registration with FEMA online, and we monitored the condition of the city by satellite photos on the web. I was amazed at how the Internet was used by people after the storm to organize and pass information better and faster than the government. The French Quarter e-boards activity helped us find out where people from the Quarter scattered to in the evacuation long before the phone or other means of communication were working in the city. Mary and I found posts about us on the boards asking what happened to us, where were we, and were we all right? We posted messages telling folks that we were fine and safe in Galveston. We both felt better knowing that this information was passed along to those who care about us and for them not to worry.

Following the news for the next few days, I was stunned by what I saw was happening in New Orleans. Days passed and no aid arrived for the people trapped in a crippled city. The more I watched, the sadder and madder I got. Mary just stopped watching it all together. It was too much for her to process at one time. I can't blame her one bit. It was overwhelming. I'm still very angry with my government leaders on all levels for how they behaved during this epic disaster.

By the weekend after the storm, I knew that we would need to make a permanent change. We'd talked about moving out of the French Quarter for sometime, two years in fact, but it had only been talk up until this point. The Quarter is a hard place to leave once it has a hold of you, and it had both of us good and tight. Another week or so went by with more news about home, about who was safe, who was still missing, and what damage was done to our home. Then I heard about another storm out in the Atlantic called Rita. The weather reports said that it was a fast-growing storm and could make landfall in Galveston, Texas, as a Category 5. It was like living a rerun. Watching a storm grow bigger and stronger in no time at all heading straight at us. Damn! Didn't I just do this three weeks ago?

Strangely enough, this same week was the 105th anniversary of the 1900 Galveston hurricane that claimed 1,200 lives and destroyed 95% of the city. With that in mind, the people of Galveston were now looking down the barrel of a Category 5 storm after having seen what Katrina did to the coastal cities, and they were scared. You could feel it. Again, my plan was to get out of the area before an evacuation call would clog the roads. Mary and I started to prepare the house for a storm. I wanted to leave early. "The sooner the better," I thought. We had friends in Dallas who just had a new baby, and they very much wanted us to come for a visit. Perfect, I thought. Dallas is far enough north to be safe from the effects of Rita, and we can catch up with old friends.

It was Tuesday morning, and I was hoping to be on the road for Dallas before sunset. To my surprise, Mary let me know that she felt that since the storm was not due for landfall for five more days that we were jumping the gun on leaving town. Katrina fever she called it. Before too long we were in the midst of a very angry shouting match. A lot of emotions triggered screaming back and forth, but in hindsight, it seems a release was needed. We were both stressed to the limit and vented at each other. In the end, we called a truce and finished packing up the car, and closing down the house for a storm that, for all we knew, could completely wipe the whole island out. With the picture in my mind of coming back to find nothing but a slab where a house use to be, we left Galveston for Dallas. There was a subdued mood in the car on the drive north.

We made the four-hour trip to Dallas in six hours, again with only minor delays, arriving at our friend's, Katy and Andrew's, home. Katy and Andrew have known us for years and are very dear to us. We both stood at their wedding five years ago and hadn't been back for a visit since. There was some talk that Rita could come into Texas in such a way that Dallas might feel hurricane force winds over the weekend. That had the Dallas folks scared and on edge. At the very last moment, Rita turned and made landfall on the Texas and Louisiana border. A great deal of damage along the coast, but Galveston and Houston were spared any real destruction. Texas got very lucky on this one.

We stayed a week with Katy, Andrew, and little Nick, their new baby boy. It was the best visit with friends I have had in years. I caught myself, once or twice during the visit, feeling guilty for having such a good time when so many people's lives were disrupted; some had lost loved ones, and many had lost everything they owned. Could it be some form of survivor's guilt? It was hard to say. When Mary and I returned to Galveston, we found the house there just fine. There was little to no damage, and town life returned to normal quickly.

It was very early October when we decided to make a trip back to New Orleans to see for ourselves what was left. For weeks we heard horror stories about looting and shootouts between armed thugs and militia. We didn't know what to expect. We decided upon October sixth as our returning day to the French Quarter. This was our first time back since leaving on the twenty-seventh of August. The trip was only for one day. A quick in and out, to collect valuables and assess any damage to our townhouse. Driving back into New Orleans was a true shock. The whole place looked like a war zone. Trash and debris everywhere, homes and cars coated in slime and sludge, boats sitting high and dry in the neutral ground [median] where the receding flood waters had left them. All the vegetation was brown and dead from the pollution in the floodwater. It was truly a sad sight to behold. It was as if the entire city was one enormous snow globe that had been shaken by some god-sized hand and all the bits were flown about. The general feeling in the air lacked vitality. Little life was to be found. I've felt this before in hospitals and in the presence of a very ill person who did not have long to live, but never at this magnitude. The city was gravely wounded and it showed. I realized that the place I had driven out of on the twenty-seventh of August didn't exist anymore. The city I knew was gone and would never return to what it had been. For all the complaints and problems I had with New Orleans, I would miss it very much.

We arrived in the Quarter and found it in a shambles, but better off than most of the city. Rounding the corner of our block, we pulled into our courtyard to find the place more or less fine. Some scattered bits of trash and roofing tiles from the adjoining building lying about, but on the whole, all as we had left it weeks ago. Once inside, we discovered no water or wind damage to our things and no looters had made their way in. It was like returning home after a long vacation. The only damage at all was a pair of storm shutters on the front of our second floor balcony that had been blown off by the high winds due to wood rot and termite damage in the doorframe. They were both laid out neatly, one on top of the other on the balcony deck, as if they were waiting to be painted and put right back up by some handyman. Our old Norge refrigerator was still working and didn't take too much effort to clean the musty smell out of it and put it back in use. At the time, I think we were the only people in a ten-block radius that didn't have a duct-taped refrigerator in front of their house. Mary and I retrieved some important papers, photos, and other items to take back to Texas with us for safe keeping and then locked the house until our final return in a few days time. Driving back to Galveston, we talked about what we wanted to do and both agreed that it was time to leave New Orleans and move on with our lives. We very much wanted to buy a home, rather then rent as we have done for the last eight years, but after Katrina what hope did we have of finding a place that we could afford? There was little or no chance of that happening with the city the way it was, and it would be that way for a very long time to come.

Within a week, on the twevlth, we returned to the French Quarter and informed our landlady that we would be leaving the townhouse and moving away. We had thirty days to pack the whole place and put it in storage. The fact that we could find a storage unit to rent at all in the city was a surprise, but we lucked out again and were able to rent a space only one block from our house. Again, in the midst of so much tragedy, we had the way smoothed for us by some unseen force. That had been a kind of recurring theme for us throughout the whole ordeal, trouble and disaster all around us, but not happening to us. I can only attribute it to some form of karma watching over us. I'm not one to talk about guardian angels, but amidst the worst natural disaster in United States history, we came through remarkably unscathed. In some ways it has been a blessing for us by allowing us to move ahead in our lives and find new horizons and challenges that we have both needed for sometime now.

Mary and I moved out of New Orleans and relocated to a home in central Florida. I will never forget my time in the Big Easy. I have great hope that it will rise again as the unique Southern treasure of style and culture that I grew to love so well. When the good times roll again in the Big Easy I'll be back to drink to the city's health and pass a good time, but for now I weep for the Old Girl with all her faults. My heart is still with her.

Everybody's Pharmacist

George Vertigell
Interviewed by Zachary J. George

During Katrina, George Vertigell stayed in his Mid-City neighborhood, eventually raiding the local grocery store pharmacies and distributing medications to his neighbors.

How old are you George?

Thirty-five, brother.

How long have you lived in New Orleans?

Really too long here and there. Probably about twenty five years, I imagine.

So, you came with your family?

No, I grew up here in the beginning, moved around, year to year, off and on.

What's your occupation?

Construction, painting, drywall.

When did you first hear about the storm?

Basically like three days, when it was first coming up around Florida. I wasn't even watching the news really. I didn't really hear it was going to hit until Saturday. We were at a bar, watching it come in. I was with my ex-girlfriend. She was flipped out. And I'm thinking, I'd like to check this out.

So you wanted to stay?

Yeah. And then I basically, I was sent to do that because people I know were going to be staying. I'm used to risking my life doing what I do. Just painting houses and whatnot. So, I figured I could handle whatever happens.

Where were you when the storm hit? Where were you staying?

I was staying at my friend's apartment where I lived. Dumaine and Carrollton.

How was it right after the storm… Before the levees broke?

It seemed okay. There was a lot of litter and everything around. See, the way it started. My ex-girlfriend came to pick me up the Sunday. She was basically scaring me into leaving; I mean we're not going to have electricity or anything. So, I said okay. Let me get a few days worth of clothes into this bag. And we took off. And I was asking her to look for some people I knew from here. I guess everybody split. We finally get on the highway and get on I-10 to go to Slidell. From there I was thinking, "You know what? I need to get out here. You need to let me out." And she was like, "No. I'm not letting you out." Finally we got to the Slidell exit. We're going down toward Esplanade. I just see all the traffic stopping. I figure we're about 250 yards from the Esplanade exit. I said, "You better take this exit, or I swear to God I'm gonna jump out of the fucking car." Sorry.

You can curse.

All right.

This is your story.

I'm just telling you what I said. She said, "Are you sure?" I said, "Yeah, goddamn it. Let me out now. I'm not kidding. First of all, I'm not dealing with this traffic. Second of all, I'm not riding ten hours in a car with you. I think I'll deal with the hurricane, thank you very much. It's either like this, either I get a life sentence for killing you, or maybe I survive this hurricane." She dropped me off by the only place in the city that was open it seemed. She dropped me off at Sidney's on Decatur Street.

Sidney's?

Sidney's. They sell liquor and beer.

Then what'd you do?

I said, "See you later;" gave her some money for gas. I told her, "Good luck. Thanks for thinking of me." So, I went inside, and thank God, they had my favorite. They had my sake. They had my Buki Sake and they had the Pearl Sake. I bought two bottles of each, so I had four bottles of sake. I knew I had to stock up on that. Cigarettes, food, candy, shit to live on for a few days, whatever. From there I popped a pain pill, drank a beer. I bought us some beer. And I walked to Canal Street. I had a heavy load now, but at least I'm set. A little piece of mind. When I got to Canal Street, the buses we're still running, all the way to Carrollton. Walking down Carrolton, I saw this lady. She was a little offset. She had head trauma a long time ago, so she gets a check. She was walking around aimlessly, so I ran up to her. I said, "What the hell are you doing?" She said, "I was looking for a place to stay." I was like, "Ah Jesus." I brought her over to where we were at because our house is up on piers and that. That freaked me out. Thank god I got off and came down because she'd have been screwed. We just met right at the right time. Anyway, after the hurricane hit, a friend of mine had given me some Ecstasy, so I took that. So, when the hurricane started to kick around one in the morning—

While the hurricane was hitting?

Yeah, right when it started to kick off.

What did it look like to you?

It looked insane, man. Plus a bottle of sake on top of that. I actually ended up staying on my friend's porch, on Dumaine, watching it all go by. 'Cause he has a good porch to watch it all. Actually the guy whose porch I was on is a Creole, country, sausage guy. I'm just watching all these garbage cans, everything flying by. Around two-thirty, it's really starting to kick. By three, it's really starting to kick. I'm just sitting there, enjoying myself. Right around four o'clock I decided. I think I might. I was thinking all kinds of weird thoughts, like, "I wish I had a kite. Especially one of those parachute kites like you have on the beach. I'd go down by the bayou, dress up like Benjamin Franklin, with a camcorder. If I had a camcorder, a Benjamin Franklin outfit, and a kite, it'd been on, baby." I just said, "Fuck yeah."

That's Monday you're talking about, right. When it hit?

Or Sunday. Whenever the hell it was. Actually, Monday morning.

And then after it hit, shit was cool, or shit was...

Well, this is the hurricane. I'm watching it inside the house. Around six or seven it's really kicking. I'm watching ceramic ceiling tile flying everywhere. When a gust of wind would come in at 150. It's flying, flying, flying like Frisbees off the roof. And I tried walking out in the middle of it. But the rain when it was gusting out at you. It would almost knock you down. And then it felt like bb's or something.

Like riding a motorcycle in the rain?

Right. Like riding a motorcycle in the rain doing 120 miles an hour. Smacking you in the face. I was like, "Fuck this, I'm going back inside." So, I just watched it through the window, drinking another bottle of sake, still buzzed out. In awe of everything that was going on. Finally I decided to go to bed. Maybe ten o'clock or something. I was like, I've had it. I'm fucking wasted. I finally go to bed. I wake up, and it was still windy, strong and windy.

What time was that?

It was about two in the afternoon. It came over and kept on going. It's just cruising. I go outside, meet up with some friends of mine, see them out there. I walked through City Park. It looked like a war zone. It looked like they had a war there. Like when you break a toothpick off and twist it in half, that's what all these pine trees looked like. Everywhere. All these old pine trees I'd been seeing there ever since I was a little kid. So we went up to our friends. Of course it was raining so much it'd flooded a little bit. Figured the sewers were backing up. So we were just hanging out, having a beer, probably three-thirty. We're all just hanging out. I said, "Well, we made it. We made it through it, man." And we noticed along Orleans and Carrollton. We noticed water coming across the street, kind of inching away. By the next hour it was already across the other side of the street and it was already crossing over. So we thought, "Well. Looks like the gutters are all backing up, the water's rising. It'll probably settle down later." Nobody's radio was working or something. So we went on drinking. We finally went home. Turn on the generator and watch TV or a movie or something 'cause I think the cable was out. Yeah, cable was out. We just went on from there. Next day it's nine o'clock. We're all hung over. We hear like a [knocks four times on the table] knockin' at the door. We say what's up, 'cause we were living upstairs. The guy goes, the shit's hit the fan, buddy. We're fucked. I'm kinda lookin' at him, then I look outside and go, "Oh, Jesus." All the water was like about three feet high. Down the street where we were at. He goes, "Man, it's just beginning. The shit's just beginning. We're in for it now." I go, "Shit, man, no kidding. We're going to have to be watching out for all kinds a crazy sons a bitches now." People are gonna get restless. People are gonna be pissed off. People are gonna be scared. People are gonna be freaked the fuck out. So I'm going home, and I'm getting to my... Well, I'm going to see if the chick's all right. Sure, she's okay. I said, "I gotta go get a canoe, man." I knew that my friend had one about a mile away.

You were still at that place on Carrollton?

I was at my friend's house. Yeah, on Carrollton. So, I cruised down and trudged through it. Thank god it was...

Just walking through the water?

Yeah, and then I got to the safe street, where the bridge is right before. So I took a right and borrowed this life jacket from a guy that was scooping water out of his boat. Then I went down the neutral ground and I backstroked it down Giuseppe because it was pretty high. Found the canoe tied up to my friend's. His neighbor's truck. Got the cat out of their house. Canned foods. Brought it back and everybody was like, "Where the hell did you get this shit? God damn, you the man, bro." I was like, "Let's go shopping," because I stopped at the firemen's house. They said, "They already busted in the Winn Dixie." So, I was like, "It's time to go shopping, dude. Get the stuff that we need." So we shot on down there. Got the whiskey, cigarettes, water and whatnots we could. That's what we were headed for because we had a shitload of food anyway. And it just started from there. Found out where my other friends were living on St. Ann. So we just started shopping, playing Robin Hood because all these people would be screaming at you. "Hey, hey, can you help us over here?" 'Cause the cops weren't helping fucking nobody. When you see them passing in the swamp boats they're like, they just cruise on by, and there are people yelling at them.

What were they doing? What was their purpose there?

I don't know what they were doing. I guess they were handling up on whatever they had to deal with. They probably figured that we can't do nothing for every-fucking-body here. Just keep going. People were probably asking more than likely, just take us wherever the fuck we need to go, whatever shelter you have. Just asking questions. A lot of older folk wondering too. So what we did? We were living not too far from Delgado. So we'd go over there and tell them exactly what needed to be done. After that, I sliced my ankle on a piece of glass. I guess it was Wednesday or something. Or maybe Tuesday. The Sav-A-Center was open, though.

Open for business or just…

It got broken into. They weren't selling nothing. There were no cashiers. I said, "Well, let's do this." We went canoeing right over the gate. Right into that place. It was all really surreal. It's like one minute everything's great and all of the sudden it's a camping trip. On the bayou. Lucky we had that canoe, man. 'Cause it would have been hell. So we went in shopping. In the liquor aisle somebody broke some glass so I gashed my leg and I just knew that I fucked myself up. So I put my foot up. I propped it on the… I was like, I knew it. I needed stitches. I showed it to you. I thought fuck it; I'm going to find a pharmacy no matter what. I'm not going to die in this filth. God knows when we're gonna get the hell out of here. I don't want to get gangrene or whatever. Plus, everybody else is probably getting sick. I went back to the house, got the saw. Battery operated. Cut through the pharmacy. There was a cage and I'm like fuck this. All these people were like, "We've got people that need insulin. We've got diabetics." Three or four people said they needed insulin. And I didn't know. I didn't know it had to be refrigerated. I cut through it, and some other dudes came and said, 'Dude, you getting through there? Mind if we go in there with you?" I don't give a shit. Be your own pharmacist. So, we're going through there. Tagging it. Ting. Tingggg. Hitting each bolt. I said, "Let's open it up some more." Tingggg, tingggg. People's like, "What that is? What's all that noise?" [...] We got in there, and the young lady I was with, her friend was a nurse, so she knew what to get. I was looking for insulin and shit. Whatnots. 'Cause God knows it was going to be a long stay, you know. And people were going to need to be calmed down. Not to mention, it made life a lot easier. So, we went in there. The guys went in there. I saw this guy from California. All of a sudden this guy was like, "Dude, I found it." "Dude, what'd you find?" Later on I chased him down, and he's like, "THC pills for cancer patients." "Hey, I got some people that need some of those." I got some of that from them. Whatever else they got. We got everything that we needed. We accommodated. We passed out antibiotics for about an hour to people. Giving 'em handfuls of 'em so they could pass it out to other people. You know, 'cause probably a lot of people were ill. Basically we got a bunch of bleach, bunch of cleaning products so that we could wash our feet off. The muck, the nastiness. So, we went on from there. Cleaned it out as much as we could. Or she did. And whatever we could accommodate other people with. We got all the antibiotics we could. I knew I was going to end up dead. So, I wrapped myself up and just kept going, was like, "I can't stay on the porch, man. These people are counting on us to get shit for 'em. And I don't need to be sitting around complaining, fuck." And so, Malibu Rum and pain pills is what kept me going for awhile. And Glenlivet as well."

Were other people aware that you had all these pills?

Yeah. They were passed out here and there. Old people that needed fucking valium. People are like, "You guys got any cigarettes?" and I'm like, "You guys need any valium by any chance?" Yeah, man. 'Cause they were rattled. Those people stuck out. So people. We couldn't get any insulin. All we could do was grab all the Ensure we could. For diabetics. Ensure for diabetics is what it said. So we'd say, "Look, this is all we can accommodate you for. Well, help you along."

So, you were like this head pharmacist helping out all these people?

Yeah. I was the pharmacist for the neighborhood. Taking orders. Writing out prescriptions and stuff.

Where'd you go after this, after you broke in there and got all that stuff?

We went to home base. And we kept. We didn't know how long we were going to be there so we just stocked up every day. Half the time we were stocking up for ourselves, and then we're passing things out to other people so they could stock up. In their buildings, their houses. People that were up. They were very grateful, because they're like, "No cops are stopping to help." And actually we were accommodating the firemen as well because we were going down Orleans and our backyard goes that way. And he comes up and he goes, "Y'all have any cigarettes by any chance?" 'Cause he'd seen us canoeing around. I'm like, "Yeah, man." We gave 'em a whole bunch of cartons of cigarettes. I said, "Hey man, what brand you need?" "Marlboro's if you got 'em.'" "Yeah we got 'em Marlboro Light's, Hundred's. Y'all smoke menthol?"

Was it like a black market thing? Were there other people as well? Were people selling stuff or was…

Oh no, no, no.

Were they out there helping each other out?

Everybody was actually being accommodating to each other. Of course, you always wanted to watch out for your canoe 'cause you never know when some idiot's going to come by and jack you.

Everybody was pretty cool man. At first I was carrying a gun, but then I figured everything was pretty calm after two days, so I thought, I'm not gonna carry this piece anymore. I don't need to. Yeah, man. Just kept meeting people, here and there. Hanging out at the house. Going back out. The only thing I feel real fucked up about… There's an old guy down the street. I told him I'd be back in two hours. And when I came back his front door was locked. With a padlock on it. Nobody would answer. I went around for like ten minutes trying to— I told him, you know, I'd be right back. And he didn't answer. The front door was locked. 'Cause it was open before. If he didn't answer, somebody must a came by and picked him up or something. Nobody would answer. So I said, "Guy, maybe you lucked out," 'cause I'd seen some boats passing down that street. Maybe he lucked out and somebody seen him. Man, I fucking left after ten minutes or so. I was fooling around with my friend. Bang, banging on the door. Banging around on the back of the house and shit. Come to find out later he had a heart attack in front of his front door. I couldn't understand why the door was padlocked. You have to go outside to padlock it and then go back in.

Maybe somebody came by and found his body and…

But it was only two hours later, man. And I found out two months later they found his body. They found him, dead. I was like, fuck, man. I should have busted in the window or something. That fucked me up for a good bit. He was a very cool old dude.

How old was he?

He was like eighty, but still.

You knew him from the neighborhood?

I knew him because my friend lived two doors down from him. And right when I was almost to the end of the block I heard somebody screaming, so I went back. And, fuck, I wasn't able to help him. I went back to help him. Fuck. I don't know. I don't know why his front door was padlocked. Because you have to come outside to put on the padlock and then you have to waddle out back through the water or something.

What was it like at night?

It was just kind of eerie sometimes. It was just quiet. Just listening to it. It sounded like the swamp around. Here and there. Mosquitoes were fucking nuts. After a few days the waters getting hot and stagnant. Funky, and you're like, "Ah, shit." Luckily, there was a swimming pool around the corner that didn't get flooded. 'Cause City Park didn't get flooded in all areas. So we were able to wash. It was pretty fucking....

In the swimming pool?

We didn't get in the pool. We didn't want to contaminate it. We just panned out water and poured it over ourselves. We didn't know if we were gonna be there for two weeks, three weeks. We just had the camping thing situated. After awhile, we're just doing the same old thing every day.

What was the routine like? What was your daily routine like?

We went shopping every day. Drinking every day, basically.

Same Sav-A-Center and Winn Dixie on Carrollton?

Yeah, basically.

How long did the stash last that you got from the pharmacies?

Well. I gave most, probably at least half of that stuff away to people around, and then I kind of felt weird about having some on the plane. Finally, after all the platoon came by Saturday and I guess Sunday, the National Guard came up. I'm thinking, we had been doing guard duty because we didn't want people coming around. We had guns, rifles. 'Cause you don't know how desperate people are going to be. You're hearing about these other people. You're hearing this fucker's car alarm going off, people trying to break in. We were on higher ground. Woo-woo. Look up and he fires a couple warning shots into the water. When I was in front of our house— like the first day after it flooded, and the night came— here were these dudes in canoes, looking with a flashlight trying to look into houses, and I can hear them coming down. They couldn't see me yet. And I was like, "No, no, I'm gonna let 'em know there's somebody in this fucking house. They're not gonna come around here." So, when they coming up, they flashed the light right in my face. I had the gun and was like, "How's it going fellas? What's up guys? How you doin'?" They said, "Not much. We good. We good." I said, "All right, man, y'all take care." And they just kept on going, turned the corner and... Just to let them know, hey, this ain't the place to go. 'Cause they had that lady in the house. I didn't want some idiots going in there, some bad seeds coming around, thinking that... having this poor woman get victimized or whatever. So, then we eventually brought her over to our house where other people were staying 'cause it was a two story.

Cool. Water only came half way up to the steps. It was two blocks from City Park. After that the National Guard came in, I heard whish, whish, going through the water, so I just grab a gun. I'm just holding it next to me. He goes, "Everybody keep it cool. It's just the National Guard. We just want to talk to you." 'Cause at night they would go around looking. Whatever lights were on, whatever generators were hitting. They wanted to know who's still around. They're doing a mandatory evacuation. I immediately put the rifle down. They were national guard. They were cool. "We just want to let you know we're coming to pick up people. It's mandatory.

So get whatever's most important to you. Forget food and stuff, because you'll be accommodated. And whatever's most important, bring it with you because we're gonna pick you up and we're gonna helicopter you there. So we talked with them. Of course, we're all freaking hung over. In the morning. When they come [knocks on table three times], "Hey, it's time to go." We're like, "Jesus Christ." We didn't really get our shit together. Some of us didn't want to go. When the generator got kicking, we were watching some TV, seen the national news. Jesus. They're talking about all kind of craziness that's going on, shipping people to Houston.

Why not just stay here? Insanity. Crowded in like sardines. But we had to go. It was just mandatory. They brought us to City Park. We helicopered from there to the airport. All stoned out of our minds. So we ended up on a plane and went up to Charlotte, North Carolina. I was taking a lot of vitamins. Silver Centrum. 'Cause I didn't want to eat much and then have to use the bathroom while you're canoeing. Went to Charlotte, North Carolina, at a civic center.

Did they tell you beforehand where you were going?

No, we weren't sure, but then afterwards they told us where we were going. We all hung out together. There were four of us. We got there. I don't really even remember getting there. We got a shuttle bus. They gave us cots and stuff like that. Seen a lot of older people and stuff like that. Got to talking. Been knowing people for about five days now. Everybody was extremely, extremely nice. Something I wasn't used to [In NC accent] "If there's anything we can do for you, just let us know."

They were so nice it was freaking you out?

Yeah, I was like damn. I'm used to being in New Orleans and getting pissed off at somebody every two days, being on the road 'cause nobody knows how to use a fucking blinker in this town. Just idiots you see on the street.

What'd you do while you were in North Carolina?

Luckily, I was just kind of depressed, bummed out, tired.

Where were you staying?

At the civic center.

How many people they have there?

Oh, a shitload. They had everything all around us with cots everywhere. A lot of people just set up to help out. The Red Cross. So I stuck around until I heard somebody talking about FEMA being able to give you some money, for to help to get by. I said, "Well, I gotta stay. I needed to know if I was gonna be able to get help. I only had a few hundred bucks on me. Luckily there was a sports bar down the street, like a quarter mile down the road. Thank god, at least finally some sanity in this whole situation. Everybody was calm. A lot of them were calmer because they were like, "I don't think I wanna leave Charlotte. Everybody's nice here. Fuck New Orleans." A lot of people from the projects were there and whatnot, you know. All walks of life. After I found myself some sanity at the sports bar for four days I could not buy myself a drink. Everybody's real.

How long were you in North Carolina?

I'd say about six days. I would've been there five, but I met this guy from California. He was really cool. He was working in North Charlotte. He got me drunk on Wild Turkey. I missed my bus. So I had to wait another day to actually catch a Greyhound. They gave me a voucher. Made me realize why I hate fucking Greyhound man. God, it was horrible. I ended up in Panama City around nine in the morning. It was about an eighteen-hour ride. All the way through, Charlotte to Panama City. With stops and all.

These were the people you knew from here still?

Yeah, they were in Panama City. They told me where they were going and I remember calling them when I was at the civic center. So, yeah. From there on I had some sand between my toes for about six weeks. They set us up at one of those ma and pop hotels they were about to mow down later because of the condos that are coming up. They let us stay there, man. Just. Our backyard was the beach. But I was so depressed and freaked out by everything. I didn't even go to the beach for like a week. I was just like... This isn't even like a vacation.

Cause you don't know what's going on back here.

I was just freaked out by everything. It was just a bum situation. But they were trying to make the best of it, and I started to finally come around. Just like you and me, we need to fucking work. We need to do something. Feel constructive. Yeah. When you're working your ass off you feel like, God, I fucking hate work. When it comes down to it, if you're not working you feel like a lazy piece of shit. I'm unproductive. I'm not making any money. What the hell, man? I need to do something. I tell you what, I had some money in the bank. And I was going around trying to get a job, and they're like, "No, that's okay." Sometimes you're looking around, and they want to pay you a bullshit wage, like ten dollars an hour. Come on, man. I can't make that kind of money. Then I decided to a little bit. Then I thought, "To hell with this." So, after getting some money from FEMA and having money in the bank, I was like, "I'm a take another couple of weeks off." It was between hanging out at the beach, drinking. I started getting lazy. I'll tell you that. Hanging out at the beach, drinking sake. Everything was free. Free clothes, free food. Only thing that wasn't free was booze. And you're like, "Yeah, whatever. I'll get that."

Your Red Cross card says, "No tobacco, alcohol, or firearms, yet you could use it on an ATM in a bar."

Yeah, yeah, yeah. Exactly, man. So, that's how that happened. And it just kept going. And I was like, "You know what, I gotta get the hell out of here." Finally. And it was great because then I met these girls. They were like in the same place. One was a nice blonde, the other a pretty brunette that finally came in that I've always wanted to… I've always took a liking to. So everything started getting real copasetic 'cause the other one would go out of town for a couple weeks. I'd be with her, the other chick. Then she'd go out of town, and I'd be with her. Very accommodating, man. I had a really good summer. Then we ended up coming back to New Orleans to get the rest of the stash that I had. Well, I met, I made a lot of friends is how I should put it.

You were the pharmacist.

Everybody liked George.

Was there a point when you thought, "Well, I'll just stay here in Florida?"

Well, there was because one of the chicks wanted me to stay with her. I was like, "Hey, if you're looking for a relationship, I got a lot of responsibilities to deal with. I need to get back." I was working with the union. For the movies. They were stuck up in Shreveport, so I was like… People. Rita came in and chased a whole bunch of people out of there. Went back over there and started helping out for a few weeks. Took off. Figured I could make as much money over here in New Orleans. Plus I was miserable. Living in a hotel alone. And you're in Shreveport. The only thing going there is the casinos man and like— I'm not gonna— I don't even have a car with me, so— I don't know anybody. Everybody's just there to make money. Wake up at six, and you get home at five-thirty and it's getting cold. I'm miserable man. I'm used to having female companionship, and now I'm just all alone. Tired. Fuck. So, I'm like hell with this. I finally got some people. I left and came back to New Orleans. I been here ever since.

What do you think is different about New Orleans?

One time I came to a conclusion. Well, a moment of clarity. I was like, damn, I been back here two weeks, and I ain't been pissed off at nobody. I hadn't gotten pissed off at all. I'm like, God. This is the most relaxed I've ever been in this city. You know, laid back.

Do you think other people have changed? They're more accepting?

Everybody's just pretty much come into their own. Dealing with what they have and just trying to get everything done. Dealing with insurance companies. 'Cause that's what we do. Everyone's trying to get their money together. Tighten up their situation. Some people made out okay. Some people are getting screwed. I'm kind of getting tired of helping people out that I know 'cause I end up getting screwed around, so it's just what goes down from here, man. Who knows if it's gonna kick in again.

If they say there's another big one along the line of Katrina will you stay or will you leave?

I'll be here actually. 'Cause God knows, a whole bunch of other idiots are gonna stay, too.

Is there anything else you want to add or you want to tell future generations?

Run, motherfucker, run.

They Brought the *Spirit of Louisiana* and Gave it Back to Us

Stefan Schmidt
Interviewed by Kim Guise

Immediately following the storm, New Orleans fireman Stefan Schmidt worked with "the Cajun Navy" to transport people to rescue stations throughout the city.

I guess the best thing to do would be to tell you about before the hurricane just kind of what went on around here. I guess it was the day before the hurricane came in, they held us over. We were supposed to get off that day to go home. Anytime there's an emergency like a hurricane or something, they'll keep all three platoons on duty so that they have more manpower to get people out, which I don't know now if that's the best way to do it, because then you got that many more people that the city has to deal with. More firemen, police, EMS, that you got to feed and house, and they can't get to their families.

By three platoons, you mean… ?

Yeah, well, you work 24 hours for each shift, so the way we do it is we have three shifts. We have the first platoon shift that would work 24 hours, and then the second platoon comes in and they work 24 hours, and then the third. So, you work 24 hours and you're off 48 hours. Okay, so I was supposed to get off that morning and they held us over so we could all help with the hurricane efforts. We, let's see, what did we do that day? We rode around the city, around our area, and used air horns and sirens and the PA system to let the citizens know that there was a hurricane coming, which believe it or not, some people, I don't know if they don't have a TV or don't listen to the radio— there was actually people that didn't know there was a hurricane coming, believe it or not. And if you would have told me that, that there was actually people in the city that didn't know a hurricane was, a Category 5, was coming the next day, I wouldn't believe you. But I've seen it with my own eyes that people really did not know that a hurricane was even coming. And they weren't kidding. So we had to go tell people a hurricane was coming, that there was a very strong possibility that the levees, we thought, would overtop. We obviously didn't know they were going to break, but there was a good chance that some levees would overtop and that the city would have up to twenty foot of water in it. And the kind of responses we got were pretty scary. Because some people seemed like they wanted to get somewhere. You know, "What do we do?" You know, "Where do we go?" At the time we were told that there were certain locations in the city where they would pick you up if you needed to be picked up, and they'd bring you to an area of safe refuge, which was to the Superdome. With other people it seemed like you could've just told them that the Saints game was coming on at twelve o'clock, and you would've got the same response because they didn't really care. So, it was kind of scary, and it made me really scared because I knew people that— I could tell by their situation, meaning that they might be handicapped or elderly or whatever— that I knew they couldn't fend for themselves if the water did come up.

They had a woman in a wheelchair sitting on her porch in a single story house off of Orleans Avenue. And I told her, I said, "Ma'am, are you going to be able to get in your attic if the water comes up in your house." And she said, "Oh no baby, I can't swim, I can't climb." I said, "Well, are you gonna leave?" She says, "No." I said, "What you gonna do?" "I don't know." And I said, "I'm gonna tell you what's gonna happen; you're gonna drown right where you're sitting. You better make some kind of way to get out." And she said, "Well, it's in the Lord's hands." A lot of people said that, and to some extent they might be right, but the way I think is that the Lord gave you the ability to think. You know we think a lot different than other animals in that we have the ability to make decisions on the knowledge, the information that we get. And I think God would tell you, would say, "Hey, why don't you get out?" But anyway, that was a fairly common response: "Oh, I'm gonna let the Lord take care of it," which obviously, like I said, I don't agree with that way of thinking. And I don't know, some of the people that I talked to probably died; I'm sure they did. That's one of the things that I still think about: the people.

They had kids running around, just playing like they had the day off of school. And I talked to their parents, said, "Y'all are getting out?" "No, we're staying here." This is in single-story houses, so— I know that even if they did live that they were miserable sitting in their attics in 100-something degree heat, so I feel sorry for those kids. Hopefully most of the ones I saw got out. I don't know that. That's something that I do think about.

Was that on Sunday that y'all rode around? The Sunday before the hurricane came?

Yeah, I get— for some reason, and probably a lot of people that was in the city for the hurricane would tell you— the days, you get your days mixed up. I couldn't remember what day was what when that stuff happened. We were awake for so long. Like the night the hurricane was coming. Well, the night before I didn't hardly sleep because you get anxiety just thinking about it and thinking about it. It was almost a relief when the hurricane came because I was so just ready to get it over with because you keep talking about it, you keep— it's like, okay, let's just get it here and get it over with. And even myself, thought that maybe I could get a little bit more information, but not much. We've had hurricane guidelines, and it'll tell you what's gonna happen if you get twenty foot of water in the city and how long utilities are going to be out and the things that you'll see and all that. So I'm thinking about all that, and I'm still like everybody else and like, "That's not gonna happen." Every year it seems like you get the hurricane scare, and we've dodged a bullet so many times. So, I mean, still in the back of my mind I'm like, "Eh...."

When I went home to get my house ready, my wife, Amy, took all the pictures and everything, and I'm like, "What are you doing?" And she's like, "Well, you never know." I said, "Well, I guess you're right. Yeah, go ahead take them." But I was still kind of just not thinking it was really going to happen. And my house— if anyone's wondering— we didn't flood. The street got about, I'd say, 2½ to 3 foot of water on it, but the house is raised up. We were in Mid-City. My sister was in Mid-City just a few blocks away. As you went from, not to jump ahead, but after the hurricane, Delgado was like an island. For some reason it's just high there. And City Park Avenue is fairly high. They had a little water, but I drove my truck out onto City Park Avenue. So, from that point Delgado was almost like the hub, and in any direction you went, it just got deeper and deeper. And as you went down Orleans, toward the city, it got deeper and deeper. So, that was about two and a half to three foot by my house, and it got deeper as you got toward Orleans, I mean— not Orleans, Carrollton— and further into the city. And Elka was a block off of Carrollton and she just got about a foot of water in her house and I think they were raised the same height.

Let's go back to the beginning before the hurricane. I heard that at some point your crew was moved to a more central location. Is that true?

Well, what we do, we have what we call areas of safe refuge where what you want to look for is a structure that's going to withstand hurricane force winds and flooding and that normally has a few floors. And the people at the apartments, now I can't think of it....

The Esplanade?

Yeah. Park Esplanade. The people at Park Esplanade let us stay there. And they had reinforced concrete stairwells and a few floors to get out. And the building did pretty good. I think a few windows came in, but all in all, it stayed together pretty well. Yeah, we got what we could, just a few supplies and went over there. Two of the men actually stayed behind here at Engine 35. I don't know if they're just hard headed, they wanted to be here. This building did good too. It's built in 1911; it's a masonry-wall construction. It's a solid building, but anyway. So, we stayed at Park Esplanade.

How many of you went to Park Esplanade?

Just [No.] 35, just the crews from 35, which, like I said, just three platoons, so you still got, depending on how many guys are on each company, you can have a total of five men for each company, for each platoon. I don't really remember how many we ran with that day. You can only run with four, so a guy has to get detailed out every tour. But, so we had a maximum of fifteen guys; I don't think it was that many. So, we stayed over there, and we brought a few blankets, but I don't think anybody really slept too good, but we stayed there. And I remember thinking when the hurricane did hit, because you could see a little bit out the windows, I mean the rain— obviously you can't see too good in the rain— but you could see into City Park a little bit, and when I started seeing some of the oak trees falling, I said, "That's not good; because those trees have been there a long time. And when you see some of those big oak trees coming down;" I said, "They're going to have a lot of damage." And when it first started happening we didn't know about the levees. We were just worried about the wind damage really, which was bad, but obviously wasn't nothing compared to the flooding. We had the radios that were working that first day. After the hurricane, the radios weren't working anymore, but one of the guys that stayed at the Lake Marina Towers in Lakeview reported that there was a breach in the 17th Street Canal levee.

And y'all got that over the radio?

We heard him. We heard him say that. He was also seeing some fires. We couldn't respond obviously because of the hurricane, but he saw a few houses that burned, and he saw the breach in the levee, and even when I heard that, I still was kind of thinking that obviously it wasn't good. I figured there were going to be some houses that flooded, but I didn't realize how big a breach it was. I didn't think it was quite that big of a breach. I figured that— what I actually was thinking was that— water overtopped it, I didn't think that it had busted loose. So, at that point in time I wasn't all that worried about it. I didn't realize that a 200-foot section of the wall came out. Anyway, after the hurricane we came back to Engine 35 and there was no flooding around here yet. There was a bunch of branches down. Some of the people that we knew stayed behind, we checked on them.

People that you had talked to earlier?

Yeah, people that we knew that were staying.

Or friends and relatives?

Mostly neighbors. All my friends and relatives left, but I had some neighbors that we knew stayed, so we checked on them, made sure everybody was okay.

What was it like? Were people okay?

Yeah, everybody around here was doing pretty good. One of the things I was stressing to people that were staying was that even if your house makes it through the hurricane, and it doesn't flood, you're not gonna have utilities for Lord only knows how long, so why would you wanna stay in the city and not have anything? You might not even have running water. To me that was another thing. I don't know why people wanted to stay so bad. I guess a lot of people were worried about looters; I'm not sure. I guess everyone has their own reason for staying. To me, if you have a chance to leave, I don't know why you would want to stay here. But we checked on everybody, and I checked on my dog, because I had him in the kitchen, and I didn't want to bring him to the firehouse because I didn't want to have to worry about him at the same time. I figured he'd be okay at the house. He pretty much destroyed my kitchen. At the time I wasn't thinking about water coming up because it was dry. We were driving around. I figured we were good, we were fine, so I put my dog Woody out in the yard and came back because where I live at is right close to my firehouse, a few blocks away.

So, you were able to go home and come back?

Yeah, I was able to go home and come back, and a couple of the guys went out and checked on Lakeview at the same time. A few of them lived out there. And they came back, and that's when I really realized that it was bad because they got some people out. They couldn't drive too far obviously. They got a few people out and brought them to the overpass right there by Wisner where it goes over I-10.

In their vehicles? Or they went in the truck?

They went in the fire truck. A few of the guys went in the fire truck. A few other guys drove around checking on people and their houses.

So, they came back and said Lakeview's not looking— it's not good at all, and at that point, it was starting to get late. We didn't want to drive the fire truck. I think we might have went back once more, one other time. I think we got a few people out but the water was coming up, and we didn't want to sink the fire truck— which if you hear me say the pump, I'm talking about the fire truck. We call it the pump. So, we didn't have any boats or anything.

You didn't have any boats?

Well, I had my boat here, but it's big. It's a 20-foot boat, and the water, even when it come up over here, it was never high [enough] even for me to use my boat. We still couldn't have used it. It was still dry over here at that point. So we came back to Engine 35, and everybody slept here, and we tried to think about what we were going to do for the next day. So, we were trying to think about who had boats and what we were going to do— the first thing in the morning was to see if we could get boats and go into Lakeview and get people out of their houses. That morning, not knowing when we were going to eat again, we still had stuff in the refrigerator… Let me go back real quick.

We were sitting out front of Engine 35 on the apron, just the driveway, and we started seeing a little water coming up. It was coming from Bayou St. John. We said, "Well…."

So, the bayou was overflowing?

Yeah, that's what I was thinking, "Is the water coming from the bayou?"

Really, it wasn't. It wasn't coming from the bayou. It looked like it was, but it wasn't. What had happened was the water just used the bayou, the water from the lake that went through Lakeview got into the bayou, and that was the path of least resistance for it. And it just flowed from the bayou, and once it overflowed the bayou, it just overflowed like it did everywhere else. But it looked like the bayou, at first, was coming up. That night we were talking and just kind of looking at the water and said, "Gee, it sure is coming up pretty fast." And next thing you know, it's a foot up the apron; it's two foot. And it was getting pretty late, so we went to bed.

Did you have any power?

No, we never had any power. We wanted to sleep because we knew we were going to be busy. I slept upstairs, some of the guys slept downstairs. And I remember that night, the next morning, I remember laying down on the floor, and the guys downstairs started, "Aw, man…." And I could hear them walking in water downstairs. I said, "Oh, man, this ain't good." So, when I go downstairs, there's, I guess, about close to two feet of water down here.

That had come in the firehouse?

Yeah, so, we thinking about what we're gonna do. Some of the guys are trying to move their trucks.

Did you have any communication with other departments or other emergency personnel?

No, I think at that point, no. I don't think any of our radios were working. I'm trying to think the last [time] I had talked to my wife. I think the last I had talked to my family is the night the hurricane was hitting. I think the next day that was it. We never had communication. So, I wound up cooking breakfast standing in the water. Made some eggs and bacon for everybody. And Engine 26 came over on their boat. At this point you could use a pretty big boat. So, they came over….

Is Engine 26 on Jefferson Davis Parkway?

Yeah, they're on Jeff Davis. They came over and smelled the bacon and said, "What y'all doing?" I said, "Hey, it might be the last meal we get for a while." So, we ate breakfast, believe it or not, in the water. And we took the boat and went around Mid-City to see what was going on, who wanted to get out, who was staying, and if we could get any other boats to use. I think someone actually did lend us a boat. And we got together with a few of the other engine houses and wound up going to Delgado.

What about the crew in Lakeview, like Harrison Avenue? Were they with y'all?

The crew in Lakeview, we never did talk to them. I found out later on that they were doing pretty much the same thing except they had a lot more problems over there. They were getting some people out, and I remember one of the guys telling me that they got a guy out. An old man was standing on his tub, on the top of the tub, and the water was about two inches from his nose. He would have definitely drowned. I don't think he had any other way out. He was just waiting to die, pretty much. And they got him out. But we went to Delgado, and it was dry there. We were getting people together and we were trying to get some supplies together and we had some civilians staying there that didn't want to leave. They didn't want to get out. So, we were trying to find food and stuff and everything else because we didn't know how long, at that point, we were going to have to stay there.

Did people go there because it was dry? Or how did people end up there?

[In] Mid-City, by and large the people that stayed had their stuff together pretty good. They had a lot of people that planned ahead— not that they should've stayed— but a lot of them that stayed had supplies, had boats. A lot of them were just being nosy, just taking a boat, and, "What y'all doing? What's going on?" You know how New Orleans is. Ask them if they want to get out and, "No, we're going to wait and see what happens." "Okay." They had people that stayed, believe it or not— I saw a woman walking her dogs right by Delgado because there was dry land. "I'm taking my dogs for a walk." Okay.

So interesting to see, talk to people, get everyone's reaction to what happened. So, everything in Mid-City wasn't too bad. I'm sure there were some isolated incidents that I don't know about. One of the things that wasn't good was Mercy Hospital, the guys, the firemen that stayed at Mercy. They were trying to get supplies brought to them, generators and stuff. And we couldn't hardly get contact to anybody. Basically we were just civilians. We couldn't really do much. Whatever we had, we had some water, we could give out some water to people that didn't have it, some food that we wound up just getting from other people that stocked up. We had some stuff, but we didn't know how long we were staying, so we can't really give out our supplies because we might need them. Yeah, we just pretty much took everything in. We stayed at Delgado, the first, I'm trying to think, I think it was just one, that first night.

Y'all were inside or outside?

That was kind of interesting because what happened was the windows at Delgado don't open. And it was hot. And for a little while we had a generator working, I think on the roof, and they had some fans inside, but they had a lot of people so everybody couldn't get in front of the fan. And I was busy all day. I was one of the only people that had a truck, so I would drive my truck as far as I could into the water and then load up people. And everybody had gear and supplies and food. And I'd run them over to Delgado, and then I'd pick up more people. We took a boat just loaded down with stuff, supplies and water and all, and brought it to Delgado. Had to push it through the water; I don't think it was running for some reason. I was just busy all day long, so when I got to Delgado I was wore out. It was so hot inside that I had the sleeping bag, and I was looking for somewhere to sleep, and I went on the roof and I said, "Shoot, this is a lot cooler than inside." Well, that caught on. Somebody said, "What you doing?" I said, "I'm sleeping on the roof." And next thing you know we had a whole bunch of people on the roof, and some kind of way….

What building was that? I'm trying to picture—

That was the main building, Building One. And some kind of way, I think, some people got phone calls out. I think— you know, rumors get started— no one was trapped that was at Delgado; everybody was fine. But I think there was a rumor that got started that people were trapped on the roof at Delgado. Because a Coast Guard helicopter came and lowered a basket. A guy that's working here now with me jumped in and just told them what was going on because they had gotten some bad information from somebody that we were trapped, which wasn't the case. The next day, we told them we didn't need to get out that day; we were fine.

The next day was when a lot of the guys were coming in, mainly a bunch of Cajuns. We were calling it the Cajun Navy. Well, the Cajun Navy was definitely in Mid-City. A bunch of Cajuns came in with their flatboats and started getting people out. That's what I was doing that first day that I actually saw people that came in to help. I was very disappointed that after the hurricane, I was like, "Where's the trucks at? Where are these military trucks that can drive through five foot of water?" We heard helicopters and… I think we were at Delgado two nights. That's where I start getting stuff mixed up. The second night there was more helicopters around. You could just see them going around and picking up people. And, uh, when the Cajuns came in, we started getting, at that point, a lot of people that initially wanted to stay [who] wanted to get out. Okay.

Neighborhood people?

Yeah, just people; they wanted to leave. And also people that was too far for us to get to, like maybe, I don't want to say the CBD, but....

Like Broad and down that way?

Yeah, and just other areas that made their way to us some kind of way and were ready to get out. So we started putting people on boats. And what we were doing was that we had a couple of different boats going to— we were going down Canal Boulevard and the railroad track there, you couldn't go underneath it and you couldn't get over it, so you had to have another boat on the other side to transfer the people and bring them to the Interstate.

So, people would step out the boat, cross the railroad tracks, and then into another boat?

Yeah, so they had to get that kind of worked out, so these guys were coming out. To be honest with you, the first few hours I don't think we had enough boats, so I think we were picking them up actually. We'd pick up the flatboats, walk them over the railroad tracks and then we was doing that. And then later on we figured that instead of doing that we could just get the other boat ready on the other side.

These are the boats that the Cajuns brought?

Yeah, the Cajun Navy. So, we were kind of telling them where they could go.

And we were hearing rumors, too, about what was going on in the city, about how bad it was getting, so I was telling them, "Make sure you have a gun on you in case— some people they see a boat, they don't want a rescue, they want your boat." I say the term affectionately— all the "coonasses," they all had guns on them, so it was no problem.

Anyway, that went on for a while, just getting people. Some people did have injuries. We had an old man. I remember thinking how long do you have to be standing in water for your feet to get that bad. Because his— you know how you get pruned-up hands sitting in the bathtub— well he had been standing in water somewhere for so long that the skin on his feet had gotten so soft. And he was walking, I guess, in the street. He never had shoes on for some reason, I don't know why, just, man, his feet were all torn up, just bleeding, and his skin was hanging off. You see stuff like that. They had a girl that, she was walking through the water, and you can't see anything. So I think she had stepped in a hole and fell down. She tore up her leg and sprained her ankle. So, there was some injuries that we had to deal with, or just try to stabilize them as best as we could and get them out. We did that for a while and—

So, were you still together with the guys from your company here?

Yeah, we were starting to get a little spread out because different people were going on different boats in different areas. A lot of the guys, that was the last time I had seen them until like a day later. Because they'd get on a boat and were wherever, and I didn't know where they were. What wound up happening to us is that we never had very good communication with the other, with the rest of the Fire Department, and some of the guys wound up leaving and coming back. I think they just went to Baton Rouge, got some good numbers. You could use your phone in Baton Rouge, find out what's going on with the rest of the city. And what happened was, obviously, Algiers didn't flood, and most of the Fire Department wound up going to Algiers. And what they did was they took as much equipment as they could, and it wound up turning into a huge firehouse, basically. We were calling it "Camp Algiers." And that's where, later on, all the New York firemen and Chicago—the Illinoise Boys, we were calling them— were coming in [to].

The water lines were down and they had a bunch of fires. Guys were actually having to draft, suck floodwater out through the fire trucks and use that to put out the fires. And you got debris and everything floating in the water. Some of the pumps can do it, and some of them can't, so you got to figure out which one can draft and try to get it as close to the water as you can without sinking your pump. So, a lot of that going on, and then Woodland just wound up being a huge firehouse with all kind of equipment and stuff over there, and that was the jump point, the point to run out. And there was a lot of big fires after the hurricane because people can't see them, well, people's not, no one's in the neighborhoods, most everybody's gone, so by the time someone sees a fire it's already huge. Then you got to deal with, instead of having one house in flames, you might have three or four of them lit up and no water, so that was something they had to deal with. They had to get, basically like, woodland fire trucks that carry their own water. They're just used for water most of them, they just relay water to the pumps, to the fire trucks, so they can put out the fires. Because we don't have that here, this is a city. We don't have woodland fires. So, that wound up coming down, and we were using those. They had water to put out the fires. They had helicopters that came in. Anybody that watched the news saw fires they were putting out using the water tankers, us, and helicopters.

Let's go back to when you were operating with the Cajun Navy. Would you just go out and try to find people? How did you decide which ways to go?

Well, what we were doing was talking to the people that were coming in and asking them, "Where you come from? How many people are in your neighborhood? How many people are looking to get out?" They might say, "Oh, such and such is staying in his house, and there's an old lady in this house, and she wants to get out," so we'd go there and get them out. I think word was getting out that's where they picking up some people, that you know, you could go to the I-10 right there, so people were just starting to walk through it.

So, people were walking through the water to get there?

They just made their way. I mean, we're so close to Metairie right there, people know. Some people knew, some didn't know, but if you could get to the other side of the canal, there you were dry.

Were some people trying to do that? Were some people going into Metairie that way?

I guess. Like I said, we had a lot of people just come. We didn't have to go look for people, they were coming to find us, just, "Here come a bunch more or whatever," and just like I said, didn't really....

Where did you deposit them?

FEMA had pretty much set up whatever you want to call a base camp right there at the I-610, right there off of the Canal Boulevard exit. It was like a boat ramp; they were launching boats and ambulances and... I think it's Canal Boulevard, Metairie Road exit. That was a boat ramp. At the end of Veterans was another; they were launching boats there. As Veterans ends and starts into— what street is that? Around Polk, where Veterans ends, Pontchartrain Boulevard... That was being used as a boat ramp. And I had wound up leaving for a day, and because we were running out of stuff, and I didn't know— we had very bad communication— so I wound up leaving for a day and coming back in. I went to Baton Rouge, got a ride out in an ambulance. Because that's where they were running everybody to get medical treatment, was at the college. So, got a ride out to Baton Rouge and wound up leaving my dog for that day and my grandma's cat, and a bunch of other firemen had dogs.

And I came back in with another New Orleans fireman that I worked with in this engine house. For some reason our timing got messed up, and we were trying to get some supplies— we didn't get back into the city until, like, that evening, so it was getting dark. They had some boats sitting there at the end of Veterans that looked like they had some mechanical problems and all, that looked like they weren't being used.

Like abandoned boats?

Yeah, abandoned boats, a lot of them with the engine covers off and all. So, we were trying to get a boat running, and we were fooling with that for a couple of... And it was kind of aggravating because we just about finished getting one ready, and a guy comes in on a boat and says "Y'all need a boat?!" So, someone gave us his boat, me and a New Orleans fireman and two Colorado firemen.

So, they were down here already?

Colorado firemen got down here I think it was three days after the hurricane hit to help out.

Were you shocked to see them? What was it like?

"Where y'all from?" "Colorado!" It just goes to show you that if people want to help out— they're saying that they couldn't get FEMA people here. Colorado firemen drove down here in their pickup truck, so it kind of tells you something. So, yeah, they were ready to go do some stuff, so we ventured out into the night off of Veterans. At this point, I don't know if the tide was [low] or what but we were trying to get back into Mid-City, and we couldn't go over the railroad track there, you know right by Plantation Coffeehouse. We couldn't go over it, and we couldn't go under it because it had dropped just enough to where you couldn't pick up the boat unless you had something real light.

And this was like a motorboat that y'all were in?

The first one we had was like a skiff, and it was pretty heavy, so we couldn't use that. We had to turn around and went all the way to the Filmore Bridge and— well before I even did that, we were taking a ride down Canal Boulevard, and I used to live on Vicksburg Street. I said, "Let me go see my old house." And my aunt and uncle still lived across the street, so I knew what it looked like; I just wanted to see it. I knew it was flooded. I don't think I went in my aunt's house. I wanted to make sure that the second story didn't flood, but the first floor had flooded, obviously.

But [you] took the boat up into the yard?

Nah. We just went down the middle of the street, and I just looked at it. Just wanted to see it, see what my old house looked like with water in it.

Did you see any other people in the neighborhood there?

No. No one was around at all. We were the only— it was like you were in New Mexico. No one was around, pitch black. Most of the city was out of power, so you could actually see stars at nighttime. We took the boat to Filmore, and a Good Samaritan left a boat on the other side with the key in it. To me, he was doing that so people could use it. So, we transferred out of the first boat into that boat, and it was great because it was a flat boat, but it was big enough that we could put some stuff in it, but small enough that we could go in some pretty shallow water, so we went.

What did you have in it? Supplies? Water?

Yeah, we just had some stuff, some supplies. I'm trying to think what we had in it. Probably just some food and water. Went to Delgado, I think one of the guys there had his truck at Delgado, and he wanted to get it, make sure it was still running in case we needed to use it later on. But it was pretty interesting. I take it back, before we went to Delgado, we had to do something that I guess is worthy of mentioning. When we went up Marconi we got to where the pumping station is by, and there's the railroad track— before you get to Navarre— that crosses Marconi. Well, the water was high enough there that it was another one of those situations where we couldn't go under it, and we couldn't go over it, but there was a little bit of room under it, so we were trying to think what we were going to do. We had the bright idea to take the drain plug out and sink the boat about halfway and lay down on the boat on our backs so that we could fit underneath the bridge, underneath the railroad tracks, so we did that. That was pretty funny.

So, there was water in the boat?

Oh yeah, we had to lift our feet up. We had to sink it about almost the whole way. We about halfway sank the boat, so we could fit underneath the railroad track. The way I'm talking it, seems like everything is happening fast. Everything just took a while, so this is like almost probably morning, and we had been out for a while.

How long did sinking the boat take?

No, that didn't take long. Well, for one thing, when we were going down Marconi, it looked like the Atchafalaya Basin. It looked like a swamp. It's flooded, all the oak tree limbs are sticking up, and it's nighttime....

Stefan Schmidt and co-workers received a call to respond to a fire at the abandoned Carrollton Shopping Center at South Carrollton and Palmetto. Interview was continued the following day.

You were talking about when you had just come back into town after having been in Baton Rouge for a day.

Yeah, one day. Spent the night. When I went to Baton Rouge, there was only one person that I knew that lived there, so I was hoping that he'd answer the phone. And he did. And he said, "Where were you? Where are you?" I said, "I'm in front of Mike the Tiger." He said, "Well, I know where you are," so he came and got me, and we went and got a few things at Wal-Mart that night so we could come back into the city. After we had come back in we went to Delgado, took another little boat, because Delgado got dry again. It was like a little island. I just needed to get to my house. I was trying to stay out of the water this time if I could help it, so someone had a little Styrofoam cape, like. They were teasing me later on calling it the "ice chest canoe" because it looked like an ice chest, so I paddled it to my house because I still had my dog there. But I had told my neighbor before that if he didn't see me later that day to go get my dog. And when I went back there to get him, he wasn't there, so I figured that he had picked him up. And he did. He lived on Orleans and had like a two-story. He was at the top on the second floor and said that my dog Woody had had some seizures and everything; he had epilepsy. I had told him where the medicine was, but I guess there was a lot of stress involved, too. Anyway, I got the dog back, and I got my Grandma's cat back and went back to Delgado. I also went back to the firehouse here in Mid-City because they had, I think, two other dogs, two other firemen's dogs, that had lived in Lakeview. I actually didn't even know where they were at the time, I just knew they had left their dogs, so we came back and got their dogs. I was with the two Colorado firemen and another New Orleans fireman. Actually, they had stayed at Delgado doing stuff, and I went by myself and got the animals and came back.

We were trying to decide what we were going to do. I didn't really want to stay, and at that point it had kind of quieted down around here, but there were still people looking to get out. But I had to make a decision what to do. If I stayed, my dog's not doing good. I never had any food for the other dogs hardly, so we decided to try to get them out, and the other New Orleans fireman and the Colorado firemen were gonna stay here. We were trying to decide what to do because it took us three boats to get to Delgado. Well, two boats. It took three boats to get to my house, but it took two boats to get to Delgado, and we had to sink that one halfway and all. And I said, "How am I gonna do that with the dogs?" So, we started talking to this guy, one of the neighbors, and he said, "Well, I think you can get out on the railroad tracks, driving out on the railroad track to get to the Interstate. He said he was gonna show me, but he had to go do something first, but I knew about where he was talking about, so we were sitting there for a while, and I said, "Well, I'm just gonna, I'm just gonna go." And my neighbor that had helped me get my dog out, he decided he was gonna leave too; he was gonna come with me. We drove out a good ways to around where the new church is right next to the I-10, the Baptist church. And there was one spot, and I mean everything was flooded, all the cemeteries were flooded. When we were driving past the railroad track, I had to go around a coffin that was laying on the railroad track. That was the only one I'd seen. I don't know how that one came out.

Anyway, we got to one part where it was kind of steep, and the rail was real high, and my truck is four-wheel drive. I had it in four-wheel drive and got the front wheels over and hit the back rails, and then didn't get over it, so decided to try again, backed up, and hit it harder to try to jump the rails, but it didn't go over; it kind of kicked me sideways, and then I was in a really bad angle to get out, to get over it. So we started kind of going back and forth, backing up. It didn't work, we ended up sliding down the railroad track and just about flipping the truck because of the angle that we were on, and we ended up nose-diving into the water there, and that was one of the lowest points. I was like, "What are we going to do now?" Because I didn't even know if they were running boats anymore on Canal Boulevard. So, I got the animals out, got some of the stuff I had in the truck out and went to, just under a tree. And I asked my friend, my neighbor, to walk down to Canal Boulevard to see if anybody was there on a boat. That was the only way I could think of to get out. And actually, the guys we were with earlier had made it there helping out people and were running boats there. So, we got a boat, went to Veterans, where we had came in at the day before, and I took my friend's truck back to [my friend]— I stopped in Baton Rouge where my friend, his family was at, got a sandwich there, and then drove all the way to Galveston with the animals where my family was located, and had to take care of the animals there for a while until I could make arrangements to get rid of them. That was a scary point because I didn't know how I was going to get out with the animals.

So, you just left your truck there?

Yeah, I left my truck. I never did get it back. We stayed in Galveston for a little while. I contacted the fire department. They said people [fireman] were in Algiers, and they were trying to figure out who was where so they could find out when to get people back and all. They told me to stay there [in Galveston] for a few days but to keep in touch with them, which I did, and it might have been [after] four or five days I went back in, picked up another New Orleans fireman, and made it to Algiers. That's when we started. We worked for a few days. We'd be off for a little while, staying there; you couldn't really leave.

When did y'all make it back to this firehouse?

I don't remember the date. This one wasn't too bad because it was all masonry, brick walls. What we wound up doing was going to St. Pius in Lakeview as kind of like our district. The main goal was to get people, to get fire apparatus on the other side of the river in places where if you make a fire, you're not responding from the Westbank. Obviously response time is one of the main things in getting a fire out, keeping it from spreading, so they had a few locations around the city where they could put people. And that was one of the ones, that was where we stayed for a while, was St. Pius Elementary School in Lakeview. And from there we made some good fires. And we'd do a little work, come to the engine houses, we'd come to 35. And we cleaned it out as best we could and—

So, you gutted it and cleaned it out yourselves?

Well, we didn't really have much to really gut, but we got the refrigerators out, just cleaned it up, and then later on a company came in and cleaned it again, and all they did was rip anything that was good out. They probably got paid too much for it, but anyway. We had big countertops and lockers that were still good that they wound up throwing out on the curb, and when I talked to them before they said they were going to keep all that here, so I was glad. As a matter of fact, the lockers that you see downstairs, the metal lockers, we just started putting those together. We never had any lockers, and this is a year later and we're still trying to recover. And the lockers that we got were donated by someone privately because we're not getting very much from the city or anybody else. We're pretty much doing for ourselves.

But you've had a lot of help from fire departments around the country?

Yeah, it was really nice. I don't want to say fun because it's never fun to watch somebody's belongings burn, but a lot of the fires I made [fought] were houses that was pretty much worthless anyway; they were flooded; they were going to be torn down, but we had the New York guys with us, mainly New York. We had some other guys, too; we had some Chicago guys, people from all over, but mainly New York, and it was kind of fun making the fires with the New York guys, you know they had different terms and different ways of doing things, and that was pretty neat. A lot of times they would go with firemen whose houses got flooded during the daytime and help them gut out their house and do all kind of stuff. There was a lot of friendships made. Some of the guys went up to New York to visit them, so that was pretty neat. I was telling my dad, who is an ex-New Orleans fireman, who likes to talk, that he would have loved being here for that because there were so many interesting conversations going on here in the engine houses with all the New York guys. I said, "Boy, Dad you would have had a field day just talking to everybody." He's known for liking to talk. But that was a pretty neat thing.

And did they drive that fire engine down, the *Spirit of Louisiana*?

Yeah, they, a matter of fact— we had that one here for a little while, later on they brought the *Spirit of Louisiana* back and gave it back to us. That was the truck that Louisiana donated to New York after 9/11 that was just a gift, but they gave it back to us to help us out. And they also donated some other fire apparatus. I think a ladder truck and some other things.

Has the storm made your job a lot harder?

Yeah, it's harder, because even now they still have water pressure problems, and you go in these houses, and they're still contaminated and stuff; you don't know what's in them. You don't know if you're going to a fire that, even though it's an abandoned house, you don't know if there's vagrants living in it, so you could still have the possibility of a life hazard, someone being trapped. Even though you go somewhere and you say, well no one's living here, well someone could be living there, because they've still got vagrants; they've got workers coming down, and they don't have anywhere to stay, so they'll just stay in an abandoned house. A lot of them don't have gas turned on, so they'll make a little fire to stay warm, and whatever, drink tequila, and bum up the place. So, I mean it happens, believe it or not. That's something that's out there.

It's also kind of, I guess you could say disheartening, because what I did wasn't nothing to what a lot of New Orleans firemen that stayed and lost. I never lost my house. I'd feel bad when someone would say, "How you did?" I said, "Well, I did good." And you know you feel bad telling people that because you know one of my good friends that works here, he lived in Lakeview and lost everything he had. Nothing, never had anything. Lost both of his vehicles, and then you say, "Oh yeah, I did good. " You feel bad, but yeah, just the way that I think that the guys that stayed and everything, the way that the city repaid them. I don't think that they did give them credit; they're not even looking at giving guys what they've been owed all these years. I don't know if anybody watches the news, stays up with the lawsuits and all, so there's a major morale problem right now with the New Orleans Fire Department. Hopefully it'll get better.

You recently moved to the Northshore. Did the hurricane influence that decision?

To some extent. Where I was living, it was a good neighborhood and we had good neighbors, but for what I make as a fireman and what my wife makes as a social worker, we never had a big yard. We were living in half a shotgun house and we had the opportunity to go to the Northshore after the hurricane. I love Lakeview; I grew up in Lakeview, but I can't hardly afford Lakeview even after the hurricane, so if money wasn't an issue, maybe I'd stay. But to me, I could get just a better…It's a new house, it's above sea-level. That's just a decision we made. If money wasn't an issue maybe we would've talked about going somewhere else, Lakeview or Uptown or something, but I had the opportunity to make a move after the hurricane. One of the issues that we had with being a firefighter and working in New Orleans was the residency issue, which finally is gone, hopefully forever, because I don't think it was ever right. I think if you live in America, and it's a free country, you should be able to live wherever you want no matter where you work at. They changed that. It was definitely time to go.

Was that? Did that happen as a result of the storm?

That happened as a result of the storm because so many people never had anywhere to go and no one wants to buy a house somewhere thinking that, well, eventually I'm gonna have to get rid of it and move back to the city, because no one knows what the city's gonna be like or if they can afford it. Like you see it now, the prices for rent have skyrocketed. So it was a necessity really. It wasn't even an option, if you ask me, because if you can't afford to live here and your house is destroyed, what are you going to do? You gotta go somewhere.

We Have a Job We Have to Do

Rob Callahan
Interviewed by Frank Lovato

Police Captain Rob Callahan led the more than one hundred officers of the Slidell Police Department, who worked eighty-nine days straight following the storm.

What planning did the Slidell Police Department and the city do?

Well, let me give you a little history with our police department, and I can only comment on what we do at the Slidell Police Department. Each year around March, April, or May, we begin preparing for the upcoming hurricane season. We provide education to the public called a Hurricane Preparedness Forum each year, and we advise the residents of what they should or should not do in the event a storm turns and heads in our direction. We know Slidell is very low-lying; we encourage residents that in the event that there's a storm of a Category 3 or higher to please evacuate the Slidell area. We did that this year: we did on June 1st, the first day of hurricane season, not really realizing that on August 29th of last year we would actually be having the problems we did with Hurricane Katrina. So we start preparing as a police department well in advance— make sure our equipment is up in working order, our high-water vehicles or boats, we make sure that our food supplies are fully stocked, just that everything is prepared. We know June is normally not known for hurricanes, but we make sure everything is up and running for June 1st.

How about your family?

Family. Each year we encourage our employees to have a plan, and, if you've been a police officer for one minute or 21 years, such as I have been, we know that in an instance when a storm starts coming our way that we have to separate ourselves from our family, unfortunately, because we have a job we have to do. Beginning in June, our families know where they're going. Most of us have family or relatives that are north or away from this particular area, and they're prepared and ready to go. Cash is there for them, food, clothing, whatever they need. They know that within about a six-to-twelve-hour window they need to get out of town. And that's exactly what we do each year.

Where did your immediate family go?

Three daughters and three dogs and some box turtles. We sent them to my sister's house in Baton Rouge along with my parents. The whole group went to Baton Rouge.

Did you follow them or they went on their own?

No sir, I… On Sunday morning the Chief and I took a ride to the weather station here in Slidell; we wanted to get as much accurate information as possible. Ah, yeah, you can watch the weather service or the Weather Channel on TV, and you can watch the local news, but we wanted to talk to hurricane trackers at the Weather Service here in Slidell and see first hand of where the storm may or may not go. When we got to the Weather Service there was a grim look on their faces, and we knew that it was going to be a bad storm and that we were in the target zone. And to be honest with you, the guy told us, "Guys, the storm is coming right over Slidell. There's no steering currents, there's no fronts, there's nothing to push the storm in either direction. The eye will go over the city of Slidell." That was at 7:30 Sunday morning. We realized at that point that it was critical that we got people out of Slidell, number one; number two, got our families to safety so we could begin our work. And that's how the whole process started that Sunday morning when we went to the Weather Service.

I locked up the house; I really didn't think that— and I've been here for 43 years, living in the southeast of Slidell— I really didn't think that the water would stretch that far inland. I didn't raise anything up off the floor. I really didn't think that the water would stretch up that far. I did have a big fear that a tree or multiple trees would fall on the roof; I had multiple trees around my home, and I thought that was going to be the biggest damage.

So, I locked up the house and then went to the station, and for 89 days straight I worked everyday since, once the storm hit.

What is your recollection of the storm itself? Was there anything peculiar?

Well, it was similar to other storms. You have to understand that in 21 years of law enforcement here at the Slidell Police Department in Slidell, I have gone though every storm. It's required by our personnel to be available for the storm. There's no vacations, there's no fleeing to other parts of the country. You are here. And in 21 years I've been through every storm. And I knew what to expect for the most part, being a veteran on the force.

It started off like any other storm; the winds, the rains, the gloominess, I guess you could say, of an approaching storm. There was really nothing unusual at the time.

Did anybody give you any sort of hint that the lake just might dump on us?

No…

You said you didn't raise your stuff off the floor, but did you have any conception that the water would get that high?

Well, you know, and you're right… Maybe I was naive to the forces of what Mother Nature could do or what a hurricane could do. My house is about four miles from the lake, and I'm not so stupid to think it couldn't stretch that far, I just didn't think it was probable. And viewing slosh charts of the, the "perfect storm," at the perfect angle, you know there was... We were always told that for the past twenty years that there is a possibility that ten-to-twelve foot of water could be sitting at the police department, which is located in the center of Slidell. And since I'm south of that, you know, obviously there could be ten-to-twelve foot of water standing in my home. But I don't think you truly want to believe such a catastrophic thing could happen.

Did anybody tell you about the shallow bowl effect?

Well, we've been through hurricane programs put on by the United Sates, by the State, and yeah, we were totally aware of that; I don't think that we really truly believed that it could happen.

When did you first really see the effects of the storm?

It was kind of strange. The storm was huge. So, you have to understand that it took several hours for the most intense part of the storm to start reaching us. Of course you had the winds, the gales, the rains, the rain bands, coming through. But nothing out of the ordinary of a regular storm. I believe that late— I'm saying late because time seems to have fogged my mind of the storm itself— I was located at the police department there. You have to understand that we put our personnel in different locations around the city. Let me just tell you this: that in the event that we have a tornado that's spawned by the storm, we don't want a tornado hitting the main building and killing all of our personnel. You wouldn't have a police department. So we stationed people at Slidell Memorial, at Northshore Hospital, at DISA, and at the main police department.

As the storm approached, of course the winds got to unbelievable speeds; speeds that I've never seen before. I've been through Camille; I've been through Betsy, I've been through all the storms, but this was a daylight storm for us where you could be outside and see the trees cracking and the wind blowing horizontal to the ground.

Where were you? At the Police Department?

I was at the main building of the Police Department.

When the wind started coming in, we were all— we battened down the hatches— we were inside the building. I noticed something strange, and I'll bring this up, it just popped into my head. I went to the restroom on the second floor [because] we felt it was safer on the second floor. Now this building was built in 1963 or [1962], and I noticed the water in the bowl rocking back and forth. The building was rocking. You couldn't feel it, you couldn't see it, but with water you could see it rocking back and forth in the toilet. And I knew at that point we had some major problems. The force of the wind was just incredible. It was pushing on the back of the building. When the wind shifted it started pushing on the front of the building.

At that point, we have a covered balcony made of steel that we could go out on as water is going over the building, it's not affecting us. Okay? So, we were out there, the winds were horrible— the highest wind speed I'd ever seen in my life— the rain was incredible, you could hear trees cracking and falling and power lines and everything just going on at one time. As the eye got closer to us, the winds slowed down, just like you would read or hear about on TV from people, past experiences, slowed down. It got to a point where it was almost dead still. No sounds. Some light drizzle, but nothing major. And at that point we thought, "We've done pretty good. The power lines are down, the trees are down, we have no power and, and, but there's no water." Then about fifteen minutes to twenty minutes the winds turned back around, and we could watch the water in our back parking lot, and people gauge things based on what they see on a building across the way, and they could see the water rising. And it was rising at an incredible rate.

You were already on Third Street at about Cousin, and it was already up?

Yes, sir....

Three inches.

Yes sir, it was coming in. My office was located on the bottom floor. We really realized at that point this water was rising so fast, so we were going to be flooding. I ran down to my bottom floor, and I had two computers in my office. I had two CPUs on the ground — monitors on the desk. I wanted to save the hard drives, the information on my CPUs. So I unplugged one and got it undone. I stuck it on a high cabinet; I started working on the other one, I looked out at a window that goes on into the parking lot— the water was about two feet up on the outside of that window. It was like looking into a dirty aquarium.

How long did that take?

It didn't take long. I'm telling you, probably within ten to fifteen minutes it was that high. The water started pouring out of baseboards, coming into the building. It was like a fire hose. Like someone was pushing a fire hose underneath, it was just coming it; there was no way to stop it, obviously. By the time I got that second CPU up, I went back to get the keyboard thinking I was going to save my keyboard and my mouse. The water was an inch over my desk. A standard size desk.

You were thigh-high deep in water?

Thigh-high deep. Didn't realize it because the adrenaline and everything that was going on, and the fear that you're trying to save your equipment, and the flood and everything else, I didn't realize I was in thigh-deep water in my office.

Did you have any calls or times that you had to go out and rescue people?

Our policy is at around 50-55 miles per hour wind we pull our personnel in [due to] the likelihood of them getting severely injured by flying debris and that sort of thing. And we tell the community, we tell the citizens that at a certain level, we are going to pull our personnel in because it's too dangerous for them. Around fifty miles per hour we decided to pull our personnel in at that time. We did get several calls before the electricity and the phone lines went down. We had one lady that her oxygen was running extremely low; she needed oxygen, for whatever purpose. I don't even remember what her illnesses were. But she needed oxygen, and I guess she failed to plan ahead. I guess she failed to leave, so what we did at this point, as the water was gushing into the building, we were using city-owned dump trucks high enough so that we could get through to some of the neighborhoods before the large amount of water got into the area. Two of our personnel got out to the house and evacuated her. We didn't have oxygen for her, but we got her to higher ground and into one of the local hospitals.

Did you see or were you involved in any dramatic rescues?

Well, with the Governor and Mayor Nagin and our own mayor, Mayor Morris and Chief Drennan, preaching to please get out, please get out, please get out— we all know that south of I-12 is a flood, there's a possibility for a flood— we hoped that everybody listened to us and that they would leave. But we had no real idea of how many people may have stayed. We knew that the older

Slidellians, the ones that lived through Camille and Betsy and all the other storms that have gone through Slidell, and myself too, I went through Camille in Westchester over where my parents live, and it never flooded before. And my fear, and our fear, was that the elderly people would believe, "I've been through Camille. I've been through Betsy. We never got any flood water here in Westchester," or any of the other south Slidell neighborhoods. Our fear was that they would think that they would never flood, that they would stay in their homes. Next thing you know they have six, seven, eight feet of water in their homes and they would be dead.

Did you consider, or did the city consider, that that was a possibility?

There was a big— yeah, that was a big possibility. In fact the state of Louisiana sent us 2,500 body bags. And a refrigerated truck.

So the flooding was not a surprise?

Yeah, you know, Slidell flooded back in 1995. We had a rain effect over the lake, over the city, and the city flooded. I don't think that people realized what the magnitude of the storm was or what it could produce. I think the State knew. They were prepared. They had the body bags and everything else, but I don't think the citizens or even the first responders really realized what was about to take place or took place.

That morning— or that afternoon after the hurricane— what did you see as far as devastation? What was your reaction?

Well, I was located at the Slidell Police Department. We had seven feet of water in the bottom floor; we had to evacuate the police department; move our operations to higher ground. I was carted out in a boat, just like every other police officer there was carted out in a boat, and traveling....

This is a picture of the Slidell City Hall.

That's correct.

With people on top of it.

And do you know how those people got out there?

No, sir, that's what I'm asking.

The Slidell Police Department. Because what happened was all those people that decided to stay behind, that we were just talking about, they got up in their attics; they didn't realize the water was going to come up, they got on their rooftops. And when the winds got down to around forty, we were able to get our boats out, safely out, for our personnel. They started rescuing these people, okay; they were going into near— by neighborhood and plucking people off the rooftops.

Just like New Orleans.

Just like New Orleans. The first night— and the night fell— seemed to fall very quickly that night— we worked until about midnight with no lights, not knowing where power lines were that— it was obviously dangerous for us. And of course the people we were rescuing, we had no place to put these people. So we were putting them on the second floor of the City Hall for the time being, until we could figure out where to have a staging area, where to put those people. Because we didn't realize that the number of people just around the police department; just the number of people there are. And then they were evacuating themselves, if they had their own boats or they could swim out, if they could get to higher, second-floor buildings around our area.

Were there many?

The first night was about 200 people that we got out.

What did you see as far as damage?

Yes, sir. When we first got out the very next day, search and rescue was still in a big way for us, we were more concerned about the rescue of people than searching for people that were in need. The water in South Slidell did not recede very quickly. In fact, in my house— in my neighborhood— it took three days for it to leave my home.

The impression is that, at least for me, is that it went back before the end of the day.

No, sir. The Police Department itself— the water was there for about two and a half days before it receded down to a level of where you could walk or drive into the parking lot. It took an enormous amount of time for the water to recede. The damage was incredible. I can tell you right now that every street from Freemont south and every roadway was blocked by either trees, power lines, telephone poles, or water.

You were basically stuck where you were?

Yeah.

Except for the city trucks?

Yeah. I had a four-wheel drive truck, and I was able to maneuver around some tress, but some areas you couldn't get into without chainsaws, backhoes, bulldozers to open up the roadways.

Did you see any especially heroic or non-heroic actions?

Well, that's kind of hard to say. I think that every member of the Slidell Police Department was heroic that day because, you have to understand, unlike some other police agencies, we lost zero people. Nobody fled. Nobody left their posts; they were there.

From the moment that we prepared for the storm to the moment we allowed our personnel to go home after about three months— not, not to go home, but to take a day off...

Really, three months?

They stayed there, yes sir. I think that you have to understand that we all live in our community. We all know the people here. It's a small, relatively small area. We have a job to do, and you're talking about people in boats, going through hazardous areas, plucking people off of rooftops and out of their attics. It was all heroic. Communications officers, although they weren't out rescuing people, once communications was back up, they're receiving these calls.

How about regular citizens?

Well, getting back to the hero thing, there were a couple of people that got their own boats and they just went out and they started running those boats up in the neighborhoods. And they started plucking people and helping people, just like police officers were doing. They did incredible work without any kind of recognition.

You say some people helped?

There were. They pitched in, an enormous amount of people that right after the storm used their own boats to help save all the lives, to help people to higher ground. Without asking, they just took it upon themselves; they did an incredible job.

What was the general mood of the city officials on Monday?

You know, I think you hit it right on the nose. We didn't have time to be depressed. We knew what we had to do to begin getting the city safe again. You have to understand, that our first priority was search and rescue. By Thursday, we realized there was no more searching, there was no more rescuing. It was over with. We knew that we had to secure the city, number one, and start getting aid to the people. And that was the most important thing at that time. We did not have a secure city; we had a wide-open city. We had to secure the city.

But you have to understand another aspect of this. We prepare based on past history with storms. We prepare for about three days [of] food, clothing.

What is your strongest memory after the storm was gone, the wind quit blowing, and the water started receding?

I think of the incredible loss that— not Slidell and its citizens— but our own personnel [experienced]. We have about 103 people in our police department; 55 lost their homes. You have to understand from the perspective of a police officer: his job and his mission is to save lives and get the city back and up and running, for the most part. He has no time to worry about his own property; whereas other people can go back to their homes and start gutting and removing things and taking care of what they have to take care of; our police officers don't have that luxury. I didn't get a chance to go see my house until three days later. Did I think about it? Oh yeah. What did I lose? How high was the water? How bad was it? Is there any trees on my roof or in my house?

You didn't even get the chance to go look?

No. Just that feeling of not knowing what you lost personally. Another thing— our families, with no communications whatsoever, no internet, no phone, no anything— we had satellite phones that didn't work. Our families didn't know if we were okay. We didn't know if they were okay. And that weighing on a person's mind is enormous. What's my wife thinking? What's my kid thinking? Is Daddy okay? Is Mommy okay? We didn't know. And so those things coupled with working 22 to 23 hours a day, for the first two weeks was incredible stress on people. And what I really learned about the storm itself is people are very resilient in Southeast Louisiana. We worked very hard [with] little sleep, little food.

Where'd you stay? Second floor?

Well, no. Once we evacuated from the main building we stayed at the public operations building which was high and dry. It's located off of Bayou Lane by Heritage Park.

I found me a little closet that I stayed in. It was big enough for me and, and a blanket. I didn't have a mattress, but it was safe; it was dry, it was high. And that's where I stayed. I stayed there for about nearly a month.

Were you encouraged or discouraged by the way the people acted? Or both?

I was very encouraged in the beginning because you had common, normal citizens that were out rescuing people. You had common, normal citizens that stood side by side with police officers to put barricades out, to help, to do anything to help. And that encouraged, that inspired police officers. You do even more because you had all of this collectively working together during a bad time in our lives. And it was just incredible. The discouraging part, since you brought that part up, was the people that took advantage of the situation. And what I'm referring to is the looting. The breaking into houses, businesses.

It wasn't as bad as New Orleans, but you did have those people who did take advantage of the situation. Now, I was the operations commander at the time; I oversaw all the operations of everything. I told our personnel that if they found somebody coming out of a store and they had bread, they had milk, they had water, let them go. They had a true need; they were trying to survive. They're not criminals, they want to live. On the other hand, if you have a person coming out of a business that had a TV or several cartons of cigarettes under his arm, he doesn't need that to survive. Make the arrest. And that's what we did.

Did you have many?

We had probably about two dozen.

It was incredible. Well, daytime we caught a guy coming out of one of these cigarette shops and he had a white garbage bag, and it was filled to the brim— look like Santa Claus— coming out of the front window that was no longer there, and it was filled with probably fifty cartons of cigarettes. Needless to say that he went to jail for that.

We didn't have a jail. Because our police department jail is on the bottom floor and had seven foot. What we did was we made plans prior to the storm with the St. Tammany Parish jail in Covington. So we made the transports up to Covington to put them there.

If something like this would happen again, would you do anything different?

I'd move to Tennessee. No, I'm just playing. I've played this through my mind a hundred million times. I would do the same things with the family; I think that the closeness of Baton Rouge was convenient. My sister has a large enough house to house my folks, and everything worked well there. I'm very committed to this community and this city that I would still be here. As tempting as it would be to flee to the mountains of Tennessee— I mean, and people think that now. So, would I change anything? No. I think I did everything properly. I wish that I was on higher ground now than where I am because I realize that Mother Nature can stretch as far as it did. And, other than that, no I wouldn't change anything.

Was there a change in the city? Crime?

Yeah, in the past year, Slidell is no longer what Slidell used to be. And it will never be the old Slidell. Crime has risen drastically. We can contribute a lot of that to a lot of the transient workers that are in town, some of the aid workers, some of the contractors; they all took advantage of the situation. It was just incredible how they would steal from one another. We currently are experiencing— we're up about 300 percent, residential and business burglary. Three hundred percent.

How about violent crime?

Violent crimes, we've been very fortunate— knock on wood. They've occurred just outside the city limits of Slidell. The quadruple homicide that the Sheriff's office is currently investigating was about two-to-three hundred yards outside the city limits of Slidell. So, it's here, on the Northshore, it's here in St. Tammany Parish. At the end of October they had sixteen, for this year, sixteen homicides. We've had two. We normally average abut one a year. We've had two. The two that we've had were contractors from other areas that killed themselves. Not killed themselves as in suicide, but killed one another over, over disputes over money, over women, over jobs. So, crime has increased drastically; thefts are up, car thefts are up, car burglaries are up. You know, it's incredible, we would normally have two to three car burglaries in a month; I just scanned October— we had 37. We're trying to get a handle on it, but it's just been incredible.

How many folks did you lose on the Police Department?

We didn't lose any, initially. We have since lost five.

Out of a hundred and...

Hmm, a hundred and four.

That's not too bad.

No, that's not too bad, but the five who left are good, seasoned officers, well trained. And, this is why they left: they didn't want to leave, but they had to. Their wives made better money in their jobs; they were transferred out of New Orleans to other areas throughout the United States. A good friend of mine, Reggie Ralph, a detective twelve years, lot of experience, a very good guy... His wife was transferred to Arizona. He had two options: get a divorce or move with her. And he took the move; which is the right thing to do, obviously. But, yeah, we've lost five so far.

How about the newcomers [to Slidell]? Has there been a positive or a negative change?

I think both. I think that a lot of the newcomers, on a negative side of it, may bring their "garbage," bring their "trash" with them, from wherever they came from. And it shows. And we've made numerous, numerous arrests from people that were living in other areas before Hurricane Katrina and that are now residents of this area.

We've had a lot of people that came down to help, to help get Slidell, this area, back and up and running and decided, "You know, it's a great place, it's great people," and they just decided to stay. So, yeah, we've met a lot of people that way.

There's a large contingent of people who consider themselves Slidellians. Has that changed?

I think so. I've lived here all my life. Knew just about everybody. But a lot of the "Old Slidellians" have decided to move, and that's a shame. A lot of my parents' friends, people that I grew up with, their children have moved away from this area. I think that in the next several years there's going to be big changes to Slidell; I think there are a lot of positive things that are going to come about the storm— I know it sounds bizarre to hear that after going though what we went through— but I think that people here realize the value of life now, of property, and I can see people being more caring. Now, you can't say that about the drivers: drivers, now that's something totally different. But there's just a different mindset I see, particularly in my neighborhood amongst the people. I think there's a good, positive change coming to the city. There's a lot of businesses, believe it or not, that are coming in.

There's a picture, supposedly, of you, with your dog, and that's down South Slidell? You went and got your dog?

I had the dog with me at the police department. I had her in my office. My wife couldn't take— you can see how large the dog is— couldn't take the dog. Although I didn't need that burden, I knew that my wife couldn't take the dog in the small car that we had at the time, so I kept the dog with me. Had her in the office. As the water came in, I brought her up to the second floor and put her in a closet. And she stayed with me; she was my friend there for three days straight at the police department. But at some point we had to evacuate, and I loaded her up in a boat— didn't know what I was going to do with her— because at this point, though I love my animals, or my dog, I didn't know what to do with her. I had a job to be a policeman, not caretaker of this dog, who was deathly scared, obviously, of what was going on as well. But, yeah, I got off the police boat, I carried her up to dry land, and there was a photographer there that snapped my picture, and though I heard that it was in the newspaper somewhere, I didn't really realize where, when, or what it looked like.

The Mud Took Our Shoes

Douglas Hitt
In Her Own Words

A thirty-foot wall of water rearranged all the furniture in Hitt's home. She found a shelter where she slept in her car and used the branches of a fallen tree for a bathroom. From Texarkana, Arkansas, she traveled to Canton, Mississippi. (Note: Douglas Hitt is the mother of Louvin Skinner and grandmother of Stephanie and Caroline Skinner, whose stories follow this one.)

I was born July 8, 1921, in a little house in Independence, Louisiana. My mother was a farm girl. My father was what I call a town boy. He lived in town. My grandmother had fourteen children, eleven of whom survived to adulthood.

I planned to stay in my house through the storm because a year before we were supposed to have a hurricane come through and it didn't. It just didn't. So I was just going to stick it out and stay in my little house. I think my granddaughter, Stephanie, called me and got very upset because we weren't leaving. She must've called her mother, my daughter, Louvin, because she called and said, "Mother, this is going to be a very bad storm. You must leave. This is a dangerous storm." I said, "Okay." We left immediately. Before my neighbors did. They were still packing their car. My husband and I threw one change of clothes in a suitcase and went to Poplarville, Mississippi. The first shelter was full and turned us away. We wound up at the First Baptist Church where we stayed for two days. The ladies in the church were just wonderful. They fed us well and took good care of us. The day after the storm we went home. We had no trouble. Trees had already been cut off of the highway. At one point an underpass was flooded, it was the only time I was afraid on the way back, but we managed to get through the water without stalling. So, we got to Bay St. Louis and when we saw our house was still standing we thought, "Oh good. It made it." But then we had to park outside because of all the tree branches and mud blocking the driveway. We had to walk through slippery mud to get to the front door. But we couldn't get the door open. So then we went back around the driveway. There was all kinds of debris: tree branches and things that had floated there and stayed. Mud sucked the shoes off our feet. We finally got to the back door and pushed it open. That was the shock. Water had been in the house almost six feet deep. Furniture had floated everywhere. It was all turned over on its back. There was no passage for us. In our muddy feet we climbed across our bed and tried to pick our way to the front of the house. It was utter chaos. I had a 100-year-old upright Chickering piano. It was turned over on its back. The refrigerator was on its back. It was such a shock. And it was morning. It was such a beautiful day. People were already picking wet carpets out of their houses and wet clothes from the trees. All we could do was turn around and walk out. We couldn't get our door locked, so we left it standing open. I wanted air to circulate. The floor was covered in ankle-deep mud. Our clothes are still shut up in those closets. Four months later they're still there. I hate to think what they look like now.

That night we stayed with a neighbor. What happened was a thirty-foot wall of water inundated Bay St. Louis. That's what destroyed us. But our neighbor across the street didn't get as much water. On our second night, my husband foolishly thought we were going to go home to sleep on our wet beds. I don't know what he was thinking. He slipped and fell and hit his head on a piece of furniture. I couldn't get any traction to get him up. He was wallowing around in the mud. I gave him a flashlight and went to find a police station. I did my best in the dark. There were no streetlights. I pulled into what looked like a station and found a lady sitting in a chair. I told her that my husband had fallen in my house and couldn't get up. A fire truck followed me back to the house. He was covered in mud. I was covered in mud. We didn't have any shoes. The fireman said we couldn't stay there, that we had to go to a shelter. The first one we tried was full. The second one was just half a block from our house. So we went there. People were outside of the building. I leaned my head out of the car window and yelled, "Is this the shelter?" They said yes, so we pulled into the parking lot.

Our car is such that we could push down the back seat so that it was like a double bed. We had two pillows and two blankets. There were no bathroom facilities. People were going behind the school, and that's what we had to do. But a big tree had fallen across the parking lot and offered lots of privacy. So I went up in the branches of that tree and that became my bathroom. And I am a tenderfoot. I can't walk barefoot anywhere. Whenever I had to walk on the pavement to go to the bathroom, and I have to get up a few times every night, it was so painful. The second day we were, there the tree cutters came and cut that tree up all nice and neat, and I lost my private bathroom.

The second night we were there, some nurses got flown in. One looked at my husband with his big knot on his head and brush burns on his arms and face. The pupils of his eyes were pinpoints. This was in the morning. She said that the next morning, if his pupils weren't dilated he needed medical attention. She was very worried. The next morning I rolled over and pulled my husband's eyelids back and his pupils hadn't dilated. He said he felt badly and wanted to go to the hospital. He acted like there wasn't even a storm. He wanted me to find his regular doctor. So we went to the hospital, which was closed. But medical tents were set up. And, I don't think a doctor saw my husband because they wouldn't let me in the tent. I believe it was a nurse. They gave him a tetanus shot and bandaged his head up. They put us back in the car and sent us back to the school shelter. So, we tried to get some sleep.

That's where we were when a young man stuck his head in our car and said, "Are you Mrs. Hitt?" I said, "Yes." He said, "We've been looking for you for two days." And I told him I was glad he found us. He was a friend of my granddaughter. Our neighbor had seen him and his brother at our house and shouted to them that we were at this shelter. That's how they found us. We were so muddy. They took us to northern Mississippi where they lived. Their mother was a nurse. She had just come back from thirty hours at a hospital but she took care of us. She washed our feet off of all the mud, gave us clothes and heavy socks. We were there with them for a few hours but the young men called one of my granddaughters in Lafayette.

In the middle of the night my granddaughter drove to Saucier, Mississippi, and picked us up at about two in the morning. We spent a night there, just outside of Lafayette, but I just can't remember it. My memory is vague. Then they called my daughter and her husband who had evacuated to Texarkana, Arkansas, with some of my other granddaughters. They came and picked us up and brought us up to Texarkana where we spent two and a half months. There was a big apartment complex up there where they rented several apartments to house their family. It was very pleasant. The people of Texarkana were wonderful to us. The Walgreens Drugstore filled our prescriptions and wouldn't even charge us for them. Everyone was so good. I needed a haircut. I was about to start cutting my own hair. I found a beauty shop, and when they found out that I was an evacuee they wouldn't let me pay. Everyone was so kind to us. I love Texarkana.

After a while, we went to Canton, Mississippi, because we thought it would be better to be closer to home, to Bay St. Louis. We stayed there a month and a half. My daughter and her husband found an apartment in New Orleans that was furnished. They lost most of their furniture. Two or three weeks after we were in Canton she visited and said that the apartment beneath her was vacant and asked if we wanted it. It only had a bed in it. But we took it because we just wanted to be with family. In Canton we were all alone. That's when it hit me. The delayed reaction. I couldn't do anything but cry. I couldn't talk to my family on the phone because all I could do was cry. I had to write my brother a letter 'cause I knew I couldn't talk to him without crying.

It's unbelievable and unreal. Like being in a nightmare. We're all devastated. I haven't been back to Bay St. Louis in two months. We're going to go back in January and I know it's going to be a shock to me again, but it's what we have to do. We were so happy there. It's where we were going to live for the rest of our lives. I'm back in New Orleans now on a temporary basis. We just have to decide what we want to do with our Bay St. Louis property.

We Lost Five Households

Louvin Skinner
In Her Own Words

Louvin Skinner worried for days about the whereabouts of her parents and other displaced family members. Before Katrina, her family all lived within New Orleans but are now scattered throughout the United States. (Note: Louvin Skinner is the daughter of Douglas Hitt, whose story precedes this one, and she is the mother of Stephanie and Caroline Skinner, whose stories follow this one.)

I've lived in New Orleans almost fifty years; my husband's lived here his entire life. We have never, ever evacuated, but that Saturday night we were watching the television and watching the pictures of Katrina in the Gulf, and it was so overwhelming, and the weatherman, maybe Bob Breck, was just talking about what a powerful and strong storm this was. My husband and I looked at each other and just said, "We're outta here." This was the first time, and we just started calling our children to make sure they were leaving. So, we packed up a gym bag with about three days worth of stuff. We figured we'd be back in three. At my children's insistence we took along our 19-year-old cat. Usually we'd leave her for about three days at a time with no problem. But we packed her up in the back of the car and left at about six Sunday morning with a caravan of our children, miscellaneous spouses, friends, and boyfriends. We had two pick-up trucks, three cars, four black labs, six cats, and eight adults including a student who had arrived the night before from Colombia and probably had no clue what we were doing with her, but we scooped her up and took her with us to Texarkana, of all places, because my girls found a place there that would take pets.

We did ride Betsy out on Chartres Street in the French Quarter. I don't even know if we lost power. So, we had never left before. With

Katrina, we were concerned because it was so big and so strong, and I guess the storm winds. In New Orleans the storm surge had never been a problem for us. Obviously, we knew it was a problem in the Lower Ninth Ward and lower lying areas, but we had never had issues with flooding in our neighborhood. Really, it was the wind that scared us.

The trip between New Orleans and Texarkana took twelve hours. Normally it would take six or seven hours. We headed out on the Westbank because we didn't want to get caught in traffic going to Baton Rouge. Everyone decided they just had to take I-10 to Baton Rouge. It took us about four hours to get to Lafayette on Highway 90. And from then it started to ease up and, it was pretty smooth going from there. However, negotiating our way through Shreveport to get to Texarkana took an extra hour. Of course, we arrived and went to the wrong motel. Other than little glitches it was okay. The old cat was a very good traveler. The children arrived with all of their relationships intact, if not strained, after hours in cars with animals climbing all over them, but we got settled down in the hotel around six p.m.

By Monday evening we were very concerned about the Gulf Coast. Mainly because my parents lived in Bay St. Louis. They are 84 and 89 and very stubborn. We were not sure if we had persuaded them to evacuate. That first day, that Monday, there wasn't a lot of news because the storm was still going on. We knew that it was bad, that there was a lot of destruction. But, it wasn't until Tuesday that the word began to get out that the levees had breached. The first levee we heard about was the 17th Street Canal. And, by that time, of course, there was 24-hour coverage of the storm. The 17th Street Canal was extremely serious and concerned us a great deal, but, our houses did not seem to be— except one daughter had an apartment in Lakeview, and my son-in-law-to-be owned a house in

Lakeview— our houses seemed to be, more or less, out of danger. Later in the day, we learned that the London Avenue Canal had two breaches, and that was very bad news for us.

I went down into the lobby of this motel, which was full of people with their pets, sitting around tables glued to the television set and being very, very quiet. We stood in the back and just watched the city go under. Nobody would say anything. It was so quiet. You'd run into people in the hallway later, and so many of the people were from St. Bernard, and they already knew it had been obliterated. And, it was really, really bizarre. Not bizarre, otherworldly, like it's not happening to you; it's happening on television to somebody else. And you know that's your house going under, but you're not there. It's kind of like an out-of-body experience, just watching this happen and not being able to do anything about it.

My parents were missing for three days. We had another elderly couple we were worried about who were missing for seven days. Ultimately we collected everybody and got them to Texarkana, but those first few days were just really, really strange. And we just packed for three days. I carried everything I owned in a duffle bag. Everything I had fit in a gym bag. We knew we weren't going home soon.

My husband had the presence of mind to ask the lady at the front desk if there were any apartments around. She pointed behind the motel to an apartment complex called The Links, and they had furnished corporate apartments. We walked right over there and put deposits down on four apartments because we knew nobody was going back anytime soon. The next day we moved out of the hotel with animals in tow and into these apartments. We were really very, very lucky.

We were still hopeful that our house hadn't gone under. In the past, it hadn't even gotten water on the lawn. It's on a terraced lot and it's raised and we were very hopeful. My youngest daughter, who was just starting out, bought a house around the corner from us, and she was hopeful too. But one of my other daughters, who is very good at the computer and evacuated with her laptop, started getting on the internet and pulling up the aerial photographs of the city, and you could literally pinpoint your house and see the depth of the water. By Thursday we realized that we had a serious, serious problem. Beyond loss of electricity. My youngest daughter had six to seven feet in her house. We had three feet in our house. The houses down on slabs were really hard hit. And, of course, the water sat there for three weeks. We had, in the downstairs hallway on a closet door, for years and years, one of the charts that you measure the growth of all your children and friends and whoever passed through our home. And, that chart was still stuck up on that wall. When we got back we could see that the water peaked briefly at three feet and dropped to about two feet where it stayed for some time. That chart is now upstairs and will be laminated the way it is.

It was very disturbing to watch the coverage. Sometimes we just had to turn it off. To see the people being plucked off the roofs. And all we heard about the Gulf Coast was that it was just gone. And they were right. When we got back we saw that it was gone. But to see these people on the roofs, and to realize that the dire predictions that everybody had ignored, the computer projections of the city of New Orleans underwater that we never thought we would see in our lifetime, actually happened, is so mind-boggling. You couldn't get your brain around what really happened. It was bad enough to see the people at the Superdome and at the Convention Center, but the ones stuck up on the interstate interchanges with nothing, not even any shelter, but to see the crowds of people, and no one could even bother to drop them food or water for six days? It was mind-boggling. You'd just have to stop. You couldn't watch it all the time. It was too much. You just couldn't comprehend what was really happening. It was like watching a Hollywood movie with stunts but these weren't stunts. It was really happening and these were real people.

Having lived in New Orleans for as long as I have, those of us that lived there understood the demographics of the city. We understood that those left behind had no cars, no transportation. These were the people that for the most part rented and did not necessarily own their own homes. These were the people who had no way out. Largely, these were the elderly. And all over the city, the elderly refused to evacuate, which is why we wound up taking care of so many elderly. Although my parents did evacuate for a short time, the other elderly couple just plain ol' didn't want to leave. It was too much trouble. My family and friends, well, it is pure luck that they got out.

The national media, in a way, has misstated what happened because most people died in Gentilly and in Lakeview, and the majority of them were elderly. They would not leave, and some could not leave. Of course there are exceptions. We would sit around and think what could we have done differently? And it's hard to think of what you could have done differently. Bringing the buses in— the buses needed fuel, they needed drivers. There was no fuel to be had, no drivers. Half of the buses were under water. No one predicted, well, they predicted it, but nobody believed the levees would breach the way that they did. And had the levees not breached, the transportation wouldn't have been underwater. You would've been able to get these people, but there wouldn't have been that great of a need to get them out. Everything conspired, so I can't really fault, certainly not the local officials— I really believe that almost everyone that wanted to evacuate were able to do it. And the ones that were left did not want to evacuate until they realized they were in big trouble. They were in big trouble because of the breached levees, not because of the hurricane. Then it was too late to get them out the normal way. The only way to get them out was to pluck them out with the helicopters. That was really a horror to watch. It's true that the faces that you saw were majority black, but they were not all black. That's largely because they were the ones who chose to stay. I understand that buses were sent down before the water came up and people still wouldn't leave. I think it is very unfair to call this a racial issue. Katrina and the levee breaches, well, that is everybody's problem. And some people were in a more difficult position just for a lot of reasons, but it wasn't because nobody tried to help them. Sometimes the disaster is so large and so difficult that all the planning in the world can't keep all these horrible things from happening. But this got the whole city. It did not get just the Lower Ninth Ward. It did not get just the poor and the black. This got everybody.

I have friends who lived in the French Quarter and Uptown who weren't so affected by the hurricane. That's the original city, which was settled along the crescent. And now we know why, well, we always knew why it was settled the way it was. Our dear friends in the French Quarter— when my husband and I needed to come down and look at our property and take the next step, we had no place to go— they generously offered to have us stay with them for three nights. The woman and I were talking, sipping wine on a balcony in the French Quarter on a delightful evening, and she's a very smart, articulate, perceptive and compassionate woman, and she said to me, "You know, I've driven around and seen some of the devastation, and I hope, I like to think that we understand what people are going through." And I looked at her and said, "You don't; you can't possibly understand." It happened to her city, but not to her. They had some wind damage and some insurance claims, but they still had a house. They had a place to live. This is not a woman who is unsympathetic or uncaring. It's just that, I've decided, you really can't understand until it happens to you, until you walk into a house that is still standing, and to have nothing left. My daughter's house took five or six feet of water. She couldn't salvage one thing. She lost her car and her job.

Our house was a real disconnect. It's a two-story house. It took probably no more than maybe 36 inches of water. It was enough to float every piece of furniture, including a grand piano, around, topple everything, cover everything with mud and silt, have mold growing up the walls reaching the ceiling, not even being able to walk through your house. We had furniture from the living room float into the dining room and our china cabinets were on the side, the refrigerator on its side, I mean, you can't explain it. Pictures can't explain it. You have to see it to understand what it is. I just walked in, and we were warned by my daughters who had been there before, but still, you walk in, and it takes your breath away. But upstairs looked like my husband and I just went to work and didn't come back. It was pristine. Smelled a little musty. It was like the city: the damaged parts right up next to the undamaged parts. You hear eighty percent of the city got flooded. Well, that doesn't mean anything until you drive for miles and miles and see nothing but destruction. When I brought my parents down for the first time four months after the storm my mother looked around and said, "I didn't realize this part of the city flooded. I didn't realize there was this much damage." As much as you explain to people, and as many photographs as they see, it just doesn't do it til you're here. And you can smell it, and you start to sneeze, and your eyes start to water on any particular day. Weeks after we got back here every one of us had a bad cold.

One thing I've always loved and hated about New Orleans is that the air, humid and hot, hits you in the face. Now it hits you in the face with all kinds of junk in it and it doesn't smell good. It's just indescribable. And something that nobody can understand. Nobody in Washington, nobody in New York. To just, in a few days, to have nothing left, to have nothing that you hoped for.

We lost five households. That's a lot. Most of us had insurance. We were very lucky; we all got out. We didn't have to go through the trauma of being rescued. But to think of what you've lost, you can't think about it. You have to think about what's next. We came down and looked at our house and it was a disaster. My youngest daughter was the one who was perhaps most upset, but then, she lost the most. She and her husband were just starting out and thought they had a pretty good handle on it. All I could tell my children, and this is when we were still in Texarkana, my husband and I, not that we don't have a future, but we're winding down and retiring and enjoying the rest of our lives. All of our children are young and just starting careers and households, and they all had a future planned out. All I could tell them was that you still have a future, it just isn't the one you thought you would have. That's been the way I've approached it. It's been an interesting four months, very difficult for some of them, in many ways for all of them. They're all landing on their feet and settling into a new future. The way it's going to be, not the way we planned it, the way it's going to be. It's not necessarily going to better or worse. It's just going to be different.

For my husband and me, we were planning to retire to Bay St. Louis, to our house on the Gulf Coast. Amazingly, our little house on the Gulf Coast, a tree clipped the back of it and it's still standing and being rented out to people who desperately need it. What we do now is figure out how we handle our retirement. What my children do is figure out how they're going to handle their futures.

Ransacked Memories

Stephanie Skinner
In Her Own Words

Stephanie Skinner returned to a city where everything was dead; all that was living seemed to be people in military uniforms packed into RTA buses, standing at checkpoints, and rolling around in Humvees. (Note: Stephanie Skinner is the grandaughter of Douglas Hitt and daugther of Louvin Skinner, whose stories precede this one, and she is the sister of Caroline Skinner, whose story follows this one.)

I was 28 when Katrina hit. I had just gotten married in April, just gotten back from our honeymoon in August. The night before the hurricane we were at a party. We weren't going to evacuate. I was asleep on Saturday night, and for some reason I woke up at four a.m. We had the weather channel on, 'cause I'd gone to bed with it on. The mayor issued the mandatory evacuation. They were saying the storm had strengthened to a Category 5, and everybody was panicked. I woke up Dave, my husband, and said we had to evacuate. Not immediately, but soon. The next day we left and went to Texarkana with the rest of my family. We stayed at a La Quinta for a week before Dave went back, about a week after the hurricane hit. He was going stir-crazy. I stayed, and we all moved into an apartment complex called The Links. I was there for about a week before Dave came back. He'd stayed in Kenner with his parents for just about four days. About a week after he came back, we left together, went back to New Orleans and lived with his parents in Kenner for several months.

The first night he and I were back, Dave decided he was going to try to get into Gentilly to check on our house and on my parents' house. He just wanted to see what had happened, 'cause he wasn't able to see it the first trip back. I thought from watching TV that I was prepared for what I would see, but looking back, I had no idea. No idea that it was going to be like it was. When we were driving through Metairie, I thought that was pretty bad. I mean, there was storm destruction in Metairie, and I figured, "Well, Metairie didn't really flood, and so Orleans Parish must look a hell of a lot worse than this." I thought that prepared me, but no, it didn't.

That next morning, Dave woke up at about four a.m. He went with a friend into Gentilly. I asked him to check on my parents' house too, which is right around the block from ours. Dave is a contractor, and he has a big truck. His dad also had some sort of pass to get through the National Guard checkpoints, 'cause civilians weren't supposed to be back in Orleans Parish yet. I didn't think he'd get in. But he called me at about 7:30 a.m. and said, "We're here. Try and come meet us. Take my dad's pass."

You see, I had this jewelry box, and I don't know why I did this, but before we evacuated something made me lock my jewelry box and put it in a top drawer in my bedroom. And that drawer was above my waist. The only reason I put it in a drawer was, well, because I remember thinking it wouldn't float away. I didn't do that with anything else. It's weird that I actually had a thought that it would float away when, really, we had no idea that everything would float away.

I got in our other truck and decided not to take the interstate. The day before the traffic was a nightmare. So, I thought I would take back roads through Old Metairie and down Metairie Road. When I got to the underpass they had blockades, and they wanted to know why I wanted to go into Orleans Parish. I explained to them that my husband was waiting for me, and I wanted to see my house and my parents' house. I even told them that I had to go find my jewelry box. Dave kept calling me, and he couldn't figure out which drawer the jewelry box was in.

Dave tried to prepare me. He said it was all fucked up, that it was crazy, but I don't think you can explain it second-hand. So, I keep begging the National Guard at the Orleans Parish line to let me through, and finally, when I explained that I lived five minutes away from where we were and that my husband was waiting for me, they let me go. I went up Metairie Road, which turns into City Park Avenue. I made a left on Wisner, and I was going to make a right on Mirabeau.

As soon as you got into New Orleans proper, everything was gray. Everything was dead. There were no bugs, birds; nothing was alive. And it was just me; there wasn't anybody else around. I kept going down Wisner and took a right on Mirabeau. It was wild. It was like an atomic bomb had gone off. It wasn't even gray; there was no color at all. It was just… wet mud and dry mud. Everything was dead and desolate. Then I saw a big RTA bus, the kind that you've seen every day from the time you were a kid, [usually] filled with old ladies, and it had been taken over by the military. They were just cruising up and down St. Bernard Avenue. I thought that was strange, but I kept going. Then I started seeing more of the military Humvees. People were in them with guns. There were no civilians. It was a military zone.

I get to the London Avenue Canal, and I see this truck stopped at the top of the bridge. And I think, "What is he doing?" There were trees down everywhere and electrical wires. It was scary, 'cause I knew that if anything happened to me, it'd be a real problem. But I kept going. When I got to the top of the bridge, I saw that there was still water on the other side. Clearly, I couldn't go that way. So, I turned around and started to find another way.

I was in awe. It was unbelievable. It was unbelievable. It was hard to get your mind around it. This was the place where I grew up, and it was unrecognizable. I kept looking around me, and it was like someone just waved a wand, and everything that was green and alive, where people used to live and garden, someone had just waved this wand over everything. It was unreal. There were not even birds. No insects. Nothing was alive. At all. And this guy was just standing outside of his truck at the top of the bridge, just staring straight ahead over the levee to the other side.

I turned around, started going back to find another way in, and there was still a few inches of wet mud caked on the street. A huge tree was down. I slowed down, and my tires locked up. I started fishtailing, careening towards this big tree that was tangled with electrical wires. I kept thinking, "I know this truck has four-wheel drive. I guess if I get stuck or run into the tree, I could go find the military people." I wasn't worried that no one would find me, but I was nervous. There was nobody living in the vicinity, obviously there was no activity, human or otherwise. So, I stopped the car, and I just sat there for a second and thought, "Holy shit."

I went back to the interstate and drove east, and then Dave called me. The phone service was spotty. It had been at least an hour since I told him I was leaving. He'd been trying to call me but couldn't get through. I know he was worried. At this point I was on the interstate, passing City Park. I explained where I was. I remember, as I was talking to him, looking around me. And there's Lakeview on one side of the interstate, the LSU Dental School on the other side, and Mid-City, the Fair Grounds, and [I'm] thinking, "Everything is ruined. It's totally and completely ruined." I got to Elysian Fields, and there was another RTA bus filled with military. There was barbed wire blocking the Elysian Fields exit. I had lost Dave at St. Bernard. The phone went dead. And I had to explain to them 'cause they didn't want to let me through; I said, "My husband's going to think I'm dead, 'cause I just got off the phone with him." It was wild. There was nothing there. And they were so nice. I wasn't crying like I am now. But I was firm about wanting to go see my husband. These guys were young, in their early twenties, and one of them told me that he was from the Midwest, and there were lots of tornadoes in his town, but that he'd never seen anything like this. I had been through parts of Lakeview and Gentilly, so I sort of knew what it would be like. Then I saw Dave pull up. He talked to them and explained that we just wanted to get this jewelry box and check on my parents' house because they were still in Texarkana wondering if they even had a house. They took the keys to my truck and let us go. They said to be as fast as we could. I walked down the ramp with Dave. Everything was demolished.

We went to our house first. It was crazy. There was no house that had escaped. Every house had been flooded. There was just nothing. We had no house. Really, it was gone. The water line in my house was about seven feet high. It was surreal. Everything was in a different place. The sofas had floated. It was disgusting. It smelled awful. It smelled like Katrina. There's no other way to describe it. It was musty, moldy, and I had closed the door to our bedroom in case the windows blew out. I didn't want rainwater to get in the rest of the house. Dave had to kick the bedroom door open 'cause it was swollen shut. And he had to kick it hard. But my bedroom smelled like I had a refrigerator in it. I almost threw up. The smell was overpowering. I ran in, got my jewelry box, and ran out.

I wasn't that upset when I saw my house. But then we went to Mom and Dad's house. That was upsetting. Because what are you going to tell them? How are you going to tell them? And all this time, we were holding on to some hope 'cause we lived on the ridge in Gentilly. I went into their house, and it was like someone had just ransacked memories. A lifetime of memories for my parents. My house, that was different. We hadn't created that many memories there. But Mom and Dad's house, well, that was our home. That was home base for everyone. Seeing their house was more difficult by far than seeing our house. And my dad, he just kept asking me to see about his piano, he just wanted to know if the piano made it. And all I could think was, "I don't think anything is going to make it out of this." Dave put me back in his car and went back to the interstate. He walked me back up the on-ramp. I didn't cry then. I'm surprised I'm crying now. I guess I was just in shock then. After that, I didn't go back into New Orleans for at least a week.

Now, living back in Gentilly, I have to look at pictures to remember the place that it was that first day I went in. You can't undo twenty years of what your neighborhood was like in nine months. It's kind of sad because even being surrounded by the chaos and abandoned houses, I still remember it the way it was when I was a kid: alive, green, so many trees.

About two months ago I was driving down Elysian Fields, and I passed Filmore. I started looking at the roofs because that's one way you can figure out if people are doing anything to their houses. I started noticing all the holes in the roofs. It took me months to realize that every hole in a roof is a person who was living there, who stayed for the storm, and who tried to escape water.

It's sad for the people who left, but it's a whole lot sadder for the people who didn't leave. And it doesn't matter if they should've left or why they didn't. These were good people, and they were my neighbors. And you just see that, and it's heartbreaking. But the more I see activity, I do feel like I'm home. Maybe more than I did before because everyone around you has been through so much, you share a common bond. I'm close to so many of my neighbors now, and I didn't really talk to them before the storm. The one's who have come back are really my neighbors.

If I Had Known

Caroline Skinner
In Her Own Words

After Katrina, Caroline Skinner rented a home in Texarkana. Upon returning to New Orleans, she discovered that nothing was the same in the place where she grew up. (Note: Caroline Skinner is the sister of Stephanie Skinner, the daughter of Louvin Skinner, and the granddaughter of Douglas Hitt, all of whose stories precede this one.)

Friday, August 26th, 7:30 a.m.

One of my four sisters calls to tell me that Katrina has veered offtrack and is heading in our direction. What? Should we make reservations at that La Quinta in Texarkana? Don't they accept animals? I'm groggy. My new roommate is flying in from Colombia today. I have cleaning to do. We count the people and the animals: my new roommate and I, Mom and Dad, another sister and her husband, our godparents, four black labs and six cats. I decide we should get six rooms. Last time we cancelled anyway.

8:00 a.m.

My mother calls. Do you have a full tank of gas? Uhhh, shit...I don't. Go to Roger's on Franklin and Robert E. Lee. Your father said there isn't a line yet. I roll out of bed. I neither brush my teeth nor put on a bra. By the time I get to Roger's twenty minutes later there is an hour-long wait. It seems everyone in Gentilly Terrace is there, leaning on their cars in the bright sun, waiting for the click of the gas nozzle. One guy with a van has been at a pump for twenty minutes. He's smoking a cigarette. "Christ," I think.

9:30 a.m.

Hmm... maybe I should refill my prescriptions. That wouldn't be good if I ran out of Klonopin and Zoloft while evacuating. Bad news from the pharmacist; I have no more refills of my Klonopin. I buy five gallons of water, a jar of peanuts, packs of granola bars, and a few cans of Bush Beans. At my apartment, I count how many Klonopin I have left. Enough for two weeks. "Cool," I think, "I'm good."

10:30 a.m.

I go back to sleep. When I wake up, "that hurricane" will be heading back toward Florida. They always go to Florida.

12 p.m.

Katrina isn't going to Florida. Mayor Nagin looks frightened. I'm supposed to pick my new roommate up from the airport at 3:30. The traffic is bumper to bumper on I-10 West. I'll never get there in time. She doesn't speak English. I decide to stay put, to page her when the plane lands and have a cab bring her home. The coverage of the storm is non-stop. It's red, all red, and the eye is tight as a pinhole. I chew on my thumb and look out of the window. Will we really have to leave this time?

I call my mother, forever the optimist. She and my father rode Betsy out in the French Quarter. They've lived in Gentilly for over thirty years. It never floods. Not even street flooding in heavy rains.

"Our neighborhood is built on a natural ridge," she says. My mother has a Masters in Urban Planning. She knows these things. "If we leave it's because the electricity will go out for God knows how long. It could be off for more than a week."

"But it's not like we're going to die if we stay?"

"No, honey, we aren't going to die. We'll just be uncomfortable for a while. But we'll see. Your father and I think we might actually leave for this one. It's nasty."

"But, this isn't a matter of life and death?" I want reassurance.

"No," she reassures me, "It's a matter of eating out of cans for a week and being without air-conditioning. But grandmother and granddaddy, they should leave." My grandparents live in Bay St. Louis. Their little house could be lifted and dropped somewhere else in Mississippi.

"Are they leaving?" I ask.

"They say no. I can't make them."

I'm pulling my hair in frustration. "What do you mean you can't make them? They could fucking die! They're your parents and they're 84 and 89! You can too make them leave!"

"Tell me what to do," she yells. "You tell me how to force them to go to a shelter."

I hang up on her. My two cats are on the front porch watching green parrots line up on the power line. They live in a large palm tree across the street. I walk out and stare at the tree. Sometimes the parrots look like ripe limes clustered at the base of the palm fronds. I call my mother back.

"If we leave you're taking Wink, right?" Wink is the family cat. She's twenty years old. I picked her out when I was thirteen.

"Yes," she says, "If we leave we are taking Wink."

I could walk around Gentilly Terrace blindfolded. At the age of ten, I fell off my bike on the corner of Painters and Selma. My friend Susan's brother, Kenny, on whom I had an enormous crush, carried me four blocks home in his arms. Susan's parents still live on Painters. My best friend from elementary school lives around the corner from my apartment. I'd just moved back from New York about a year ago, full-circle to the old hood. Chilly Gentilly. Krewe of Dreux. The Bacchus Lounge. A week earlier I shot pool alone at the Golden Cue. For the first time in a year, it was starting to feel like home again.

9:00 p.m.

I've tried to explain to Catalina, my new roommate, that she must pack a small bag.

"For how many days?" she wants to know. I shrug.

"About four, I guess."

I drive her around what we both think will be her new neighborhood. I bring her to the University of New Orleans. "This is the building where you will be taking your classes. I'll be in the building right across the grass."

"*Sí*," she says.

I drive by the local Catholic Church. "You can walk to this church from our apartment," I tell her. I used to go to that church. "This," I say, "is the bus stop that will take you to campus."

"It's so much," she says. "And how come we are leaving tomorrow?"

"Hurricane," I say. "Do you know what a hurricane is?" She nods. "Hurricane is coming here." I point around us with my finger. "Not safe," I say.

"No safe?" she asks. "No safe," I repeat. She stutters, trying to get the right words out. "We leave, we will be safe?" I nod. "You are coming with *mi familia*." Ah. She understands. Away from the storm. The wind and water. Yes, yes. She understands.

11:00 p.m.

My friends from New York start calling. "Jesus," they say, "What are you going to do?"

"We're leaving. Going to Texarkana." I accentuate the "Tex" in "Texarkana."

"Why Texarkana?" Everyone wants to know.

"'Cause they take pets."

"Hotels and shelters don't waive pet policies?"

"Nope," I say, "which is why a lot of people don't leave. I wouldn't leave my cats."

"No way." It's unanimous. Nobody I know would leave without their pets.

"What are you packing?" my best friend Nancy asks.

"Dunno. All of my underwear, running shoes in case there's a gym at the hotel, a bathing suit, some T-shirts. Just light stuff. It's boiling in Arkansas. My computer, of course."

"Call me when you get up there," Nancy says. My cell phone still has a New York area code. It didn't occur to me what an advantage that and my computer would give my family.

Sunday, August 28th, 5:00 a.m.

My mother calls to wake me up. I bang on Catalina's door. She doesn't answer. "Shit," I think. This is not comfortable. We don't know each other.

"Cata," I yell, "you have to wake up!" I do this three times before she groans.

"I'm sorry, but we're leaving very soon. Very soon." She's bleary-eyed. I don't think she knows where she is, that she isn't in Colombia.

"Cata, do you remember? We're going away from the storm this morning."

"Ahh." She scratches her head. "I take a shower." She has long hair. My stomach is in knots. My parents will be outside in ten minutes.

"You need to move fast. Fast."

"Okay. Okay."

My parents and I wait twenty minutes for her to get ready. She's disoriented when she stumbles down the stairs with a backpack, her wet hair stuck to her back. I'm hungry. There is movement up and down the street. My cats are moaning in their carry-cases, which I strap in carefully like baby seats. We haven't even left and I'm already apologizing to them.

Tuesday, November 23rd, 12:00 a.m.

Is it a coincidence that when I prepare to write this narrative I get tired? That all I want to do is sleep? "If I get into bed," I think, "and lay in the dark, I can organize my thoughts." I am in bed now with my computer. This is the fifth bed I've slept in since August 26th. A furnished corporate apartment in Texarkana. From my window I see the golf course, an IHOP sign and the American flag. I live with four cats. Two are my own. One is my sister's, an inbred barnyard tuxedo cat. The other is the cat I picked out when I was thirteen at the SPCA on Japonica Street. She's twenty years old, deaf as a doorknob, and sleeps through the cat fights. Every morning at five a.m. she meows, or rather, she screams like an old lady who's lived on Lucky Strikes and whiskey. I love her. She lets me sleep with my head on her stomach. This is the cat I saved and the cat I left when

I moved to New York. It is the right thing, having her close to me. When I took her from my parents before they moved back to New Orleans (their new apartment is "no pets"), my father cried.

The cats are confused. Two of them are having a pissing contest on top of the refrigerator. When they urinate it drips into the freezer, which I have to wipe out every day. They also pee on the washing machine, in the bathtub, on the bathroom floor. My black cat, Ruby, sleeps on the pillow next to me. Annie, a one-eyed scrappy calico, sleeps at the foot of the bed. They're survivors, both doomed to die by veterinarians at a Brooklyn rescue. My catastrophe cats.

I only have two friends outside of New Orleans that haven't bailed on me. Talking to me isn't fun. Why do I have to explain to an outsider that Clorox will not clean my fucking refrigerator? And that I wasn't a complacent person before the storm and didn't need to have my life shaken up?

This is my life:

"Well, this used to be where my mother hung the spare tire for us to swing from." Dead magnolia.

"Out there, where you don't see anything, that's where I won a transistor radio at the July 4th Fishing Rodeo in Bay St. Louis when I was ten."

"What are these bruises on my arms and knees? Oh, just fell over the fridge trying to salvage the Elsie soup cup my grandmother served hot chocolate in when we were kids. Landed in six inches of sludge and decided to just sit there for a few minutes."

I'm a real downer. Incapable of small talk. The cycle of my brain: school, my godmother is losing it, school, I'm self-medicating with pancakes at IHOP, school, I'm a bad granddaughter, school, school,

I've gained weight even though I have access to a gym, why can't I exercise, I'm lazy, school, I should've spent more time with my grandparents, sleep more, sleep even more, sleep until you wake up and realize you have 48 hours to write a story, food, eat a spoonful of peanut butter, the skin under my eyes is loose, I have belly fat for the first time in my life, and how am I going to write my Katrina Narrative? I want to piss on top of the fridge to show how stressed and sad I am.

My 83-year-old godmother asks me each time I see her, "Are you going to leave me? Please don't go. You don't need to go back to school now. It isn't going anywhere. Will you drive me to Walgreens? I tee-tee on myself and need some Poise Pads. What if Leonard (her 88-year-old husband) dies? I can't be by myself. Don't leave me."

Am I skipping too far ahead? Is this narrative not coherent?

I know about incontinence, the best over-the-counter laxative (medicine for my godfather's overactive bladder "tightens him up"). My godmother will only take two showers a week. She's lost thirty pounds. I've learned to press her tibia with my thumb to test for edema. If my thumb leaves an imprint, there's too much fluid in her ankles. It makes her urinate all day. The doctor gave her Zoloft. It gives her blurry vision. So now she's taking Lexapro. What she really needs is a Xanax, but she keeps popping narcotic painkillers left over from a back injury. She needs sleep and six hours of peace. The doctor won't give her Xanax. Osteoporosis. What if she's dizzy and breaks a hip? How about he refer us to a shrink who knows what he's talking about?

What does she see every night? Does she replay the five days in the house with no food and electricity? A neighbor waded through the water every day to bring them canned food. A boat finally picked them up and dropped them off at the Liberal Arts Building [at

UNO]. They can't remember how many people were there, but they remember that they were the only white people. A product of their time. I know they defecated along with everyone else outside. They chased a Coast Guard helicopter in order to get to it before it took off without them. They dropped my godmother and she fractured her tailbone.

I'm tired. I don't know if I should go backwards or stay in the present. Just writing for an hour makes me want to sleep for five.

Sunday, August 28th, 12 p.m., somewhere between Texarkana and New Orleans

My calico cat, Annabelle, is hyperventilating. It's my fault. We stopped to eat lunch at a BBQ place and left the two cats in the back of the car. I covered them with a reflective sunshade. I left the windows cracked. But now my mother and I are cradling her in my arms. My mother is using a straw to suck water out of a cup. We are trying to get the other end of the straw in Annabelle's mouth, to wet her tongue. Ruby, my other cat, is breathing funny. They're going to die, I think. I was stupid, stupid, stupid for leaving them in the heat, but we've been driving for six hours and needed to eat. I'm paralyzed with terror. I don't want to leave the parking lot. My mother forces Annabelle back into the carry case and grabs me by the shoulders. "The only thing that will help is to get her into the hotel room. We have to leave. NOW!"

So we do. I drive and cry. My new roommate checks every few minutes to see that my cats are breathing. I just want to get to the hotel. It isn't safe for me to be driving. This I know. I can barely keep my eyes open.

We don't know if my grandparents in Bay St. Louis have evacuated. My mother finally got scared and called the sheriff to find out where the nearest shelter is. They've closed all shelters near the water. They'll have to drive to Kiln. They don't want to go, but my mother screams and cries at them on the phone and tells them they'll die if they don't. They aren't answering their phone anymore.

This drive is never going to end. I will never be able to lie in a dark hotel room with my cats. I will never be able to sleep. That's what I want more than anything: to sleep through the night and to wake up and turn on CNN. To see that the storm has passed.

Tuesday, November 29th

I am sorry that I signed up for this course, that I promised to write my own narrative and collect narratives from my family and strangers. My chest hurts every time I try to put this on paper. I can't get my arms around it. Three months later I'm living alone in Texarkana. I've stayed in order to care for my godparents. Did I write this already? I'm afraid I'm repeating myself.

There are three boxes of photographs on my apartment floor. One hundred years of photographs, the plastic slips that contain them still filled with water. Hurricane water. The storm surge is in my apartment. I'm afraid to go through them. I know that nothing is left.

I still have bruises on my legs from falling down over an upside-down sofa (and refrigerator) in my Grandparents' house in Bay St. Louis. Everyday I visit my godparents in a retirement home in Texarkana. They tell me their story in bits and pieces. I will record them, but they aren't ready yet. I know this. I will record my grandmother but she isn't ready yet. Or I am not ready yet. My godmother mentioned that they had crabs on the floor of their house before they were rescued. They were down to half a carton of cranberry juice and one can of Coke. She's in shock. I'm trying to make her bathe more than twice a week. I took her to buy new shoes yesterday and told her that she smelled bad. On Thanksgiving, she gave me her gold wedding band to wear around my neck. "This," she said, "is the hardest ring to get."

My narrative will be shorter than everyone else's. I want to do everything but remember the week after the storm. The five days we didn't know if our grandparents were dead or alive. The seven days we thought our elderly godparents died in Gentilly.

If I had known, I would've looked harder at the palm tree across the street from my apartment, the one that was home to so many wild parrots. It's gone. I would've stared at the magnolia tree in my parents' backyard. It's dead. And I can't stop thinking about the fireplace my mother designed herself. What exactly did it look like? No matter. It's gone. The yellow growth chart my mother used to track our height for thirty years. It's gone. Gone. Gone. Gone. My little sister's, Susannah's, first house. Her wedding pictures. The necklace I brought her from Paris. My granny's kitchen table. The wood-carved screen my grandmother brought back from Mexico. Gone. My great-great grandfather's barrister bookshelves. Disintegrated. My other sister, Johanna, was able to salvage two things from her apartment in Lakeview: a diamond ring that belonged to our granny (her boyfriend kicked over the TV and saw it in the muck) and a ceramic table that belonged to my grandmother. It was too heavy for the flood waters to move, but they dropped it trying to carry it back to the truck and it broke in half.

I thought I had an apartment to return to. My landlord evicted me. As I write this, my mother is moving stuff into a new apartment. She's packing my personal items. Things that must make her wonder how well she knows her daughter. My sister tried to go to my apartment to grab my vibrator before my mother found it. "What the fuck," I finally said. What don't we know about each other now? I saw my mother puke in the lobby bathroom of a Hampton Inn in Canton, Mississippi. She was hung over. My mother doesn't get drunk very often. Seeing house slabs wiped clean and sheets and curtains flapping in wind-stripped trees will drive you to drink.

My knees were still weak from walking through our gutted family home when I tore the eviction notice from my apartment door. I ran around to my landlord's entrance and banged on her door until one of my knuckles started to bleed. The man who lives across the street in an old stone bungalow that was once flanked by two beautiful trees that reminded me of Christmas, was walking his poodle, Rooly, and drinking a glass of scotch while he hosed down the sidewalk. Not much water coming from the spout. I used to wave at him from my front porch. He knew my sister lived here before me. He looked at me as though I were a stranger. My mother stood in the street asking him if he knew where my landlord was. He kept shrugging. She waved the eviction notice in the air for everyone on the block to see.

"Rachel is evicting my daughter!" She screamed. "This woman is evicting my daughter!" What she really wanted to say was this, "We have lived in this neighborhood for over thirty years. I walked each of my children to school at St. James Elementary on Gentilly Boulevard. I took them to church there every Sunday. I put four pumpkins, bought from the French Market and personally carved by my daughters, on our doorstep every Halloween and gave your children candy. I lit up my azalea bush with white lights on Christmas and put our decorated tree in the window for everyone to enjoy. I did all of this, and now my daughter is being evicted from her past." But maybe, just maybe, that's what I wanted to say. In any case, my landlord will not answer her door.

I've always felt blessed to have three homes: New Orleans, Bay St. Louis, and New York City. Of the three, one remains as I left it a little more than a year ago. I can return there to touch my memories. This is the bar where I kissed Cosmo, my ex-boyfriend. This bench in Prospect Park, this is where I'd stop to stretch my calves after a run. Oh, and my friend Keith and I would sit here to drink cider in the fall when the leaves changed. Here is the table where my best friend, Nancy, and I had brunch every Sunday.

I'm afraid of how quickly memories dissolve without touchstones. This is why my legs are black and blue from diving over a wet sofa to pick up a decorated heart encrusted in the mud of my grandmother's floor. It's why I won't open any of the swollen photo albums on the floor of my temporary corporate apartment. I know they can no longer remind me of what my grandmother's uncles looked like or how beautiful her Aunt Prue was. Everyday I remember a picture of my great-grandmother. We called her Mimi. She lived until I was a teenager. In the photo, she is eighteen, looking over her shoulder at the photographer. Her black hair is piled on top of her head except for a few loose strands. It's the eyes I don't want to forget. They are enormous and brown. I always thought them incredibly sad. I close my eyes at night and imagine that photo and her sadness. It's as though she's looking at me, saying, "I know."

I'm getting on my knees now to pick through an album. I believe it's the one that contained this photo. Annabelle and Ruby are sniffing around the box. I sneeze; pieces of Katrina on the floor in front of me.

Can I touch it?

Can You Tell Me How We Get Saved?

Toni
Interviewed by Jamie Mathews

The day before Katrina, Toni began to evacuate but turned around when a friend invited her to party in an abandoned dairy in Mid-City.

Let's begin by talking about the evacuation. You initially tried to leave?

Well, the night before, I was bartending at my job at Finn McCool's in Mid-City, and I was working 10:00 p.m. to 2:00 a.m. My grandma had called me the day before, and said, "We're leaving, we're leaving, we're leaving. So you gotta come," and I didn't get the message until the next day, and nobody really thought that it was going to be a big thing, the hurricane. So, I worked, and by the time I got off and went home, it was pretty much around 3:30, 4:00 a.m., and I went to sleep the next morning, and [then I] got a phone call from my dad, freaking out, telling me I had to leave. If I hadn't worked that night I probably would have left earlier, but I was kind of forced to leave that morning with everybody else.

Where did you go? Where were you intending to go?

Well, first of all, I was supposed to go to my friend Ashleigh's house with another friend of mine, and we were going to stay at her house, and just ride out the storm. But then when the storm got so big and everybody started leaving, then they called and said, "We're leaving, we're leaving." I called my grandmother, the one who called me before, and I said, "All right, I'm coming to where you guys are," and she said, "Oh, we already left. We called you last night to see if you wanted to come, and you didn't answer, so we left." [They were] at my aunt's house [in Alabama], and I'm bad with directions, so I didn't know how to get there or whatever. I called my other aunt, and she said I couldn't bring my cats. And so, I was like, forget that; I'm not going to leave my cats behind. I have three cats. Then I called my dad in Texas, and I said, "Okay, well, I'm coming to you." And he said, "Okay, okay." I said, "Well, I just wanna tell you I'm bringing my cats." And he was like, "Well, Toni, how many cats do you have?" And I said, "Three." And he said, "Oh come on, three cats?" So, I freaked out and cursed him out and told him, "I don't know what's wrong with this family. Everybody I've called is like 'No cats.' And maybe I'll just stay here and die with my cats." And he said, "Well, no, no, no, no, no. Just bring your cats and come on."

I only had one cat carrier. I wasn't really prepared. I had like two gallons of water. I had all the cat food, and the litter box and stuff, and some of my things, my personal things, my laptop, and some clothes. I loaded it all up in my car, and I was going. It was pretty much smooth sailing, and my one cat had an accident, and he had diarrhea all over my car. And so, I was like, "I cannot drive to Texas," and usually it takes about six hours to drive to Texas, but with all of the traffic, it would probably be like thirteen hours and what not. I was like, "I cannot drive to Texas in traffic, with diarrhea all over my car." So, I pulled over; I got off the interstate because it was pretty much smooth at that point. I hadn't hit bumper-to-bumper traffic yet.

How long had you been on the road by now?

Probably about— I don't know— fifteen minutes.

I got off on the first exit, which led me to Lakeside Mall, and it had rained the night before, so there were puddles everywhere. I took my cat, and I pretty much dunked him in a couple of puddles to get— you know— to clean him. And then I took a blanket I had in the car and started wiping it all up, but it still smelled pretty bad. I left that in a puddle. And so I get back on the interstate, and I hit the traffic. It was bumper-to-bumper traffic, and it's like middle of August, I mean, late August, so it's sweltering. I don't have air-conditioning in my car. I was sitting there sweating, and my cats started freaking out, and they were jumping all over my car. They were drooling this foamy drool, and they're all panting and crying, and it was freaking me out. Not to mention, I'm really claustrophobic, and everywhere I looked, from left to right, there were cars. In front of me, behind me, to the side of me. Every time I'd blink, I'd see splotches, black and white splotches. I was drinking right out of the gallon of water, and I kept telling myself, "Don't pass out, don't pass out." If someone would've been in the car with me, it would have been a little bit easier. If I had somebody to talk to, or somebody to help me with the cats, but I was by myself.

My friend, Maria, calls me on my cell, and says, "What are you doing?" I said, "I'm on my way to Texas." I was only in Kenner by then. I'd been in the car for about an hour and a half by now, and I was in Kenner [about ten miles from New Orleans].

And so Maria calls me, and she says, "Well. I have a hotel room downtown. And me and Chris," another mutual friend, "we're going there. We're going to stay at the hotel. It should be fine, and we'll be high up, and it should be okay." I said, "Are you sure?" And she was like, "Yes. Come back. Just come back."

So, I turned the car around.

This guy we know, Tim, owned a lot of property in Mid-City, and along with most of his property, he has an old dairy from the 1950s. It's pretty much made out of concrete. It's a huge building that takes up a whole block, and it's about five stories high with two roofs. [Maria] said, "Well, he's having a barbecue, and a bunch of us are going there to have a rooftop barbecue before the storm." I was like,

"Well, let's meet there." So, I drop my cats back off at my house to let them calm down for a little bit, and I go to Tim's house— the dairy.

We get to the party, and a bunch of people started showing up; a bunch of people that I play kickball with and that are on my kickball team started showing up. Tim, who is my first baseman, says, "Well, I just don't understand why you three are going to go to the hotel. This place is concrete. Nothing's going to blow it down. We should all stay together."

I pretty much trusted him. He's older; he's wiser. Okay, well, I talked Chris and Maria into staying, and we all decided to stay there. Little by little, more people started showing up over the rest of the afternoon and night. By the end of the night, we had sixteen people, counting myself.

This was Sunday night?

Sunday night. Six cats.

But your cats were still at your apartment, right?

By the time we decided to stay, Tim said, "Well, go back to your house, go get your cats, and come back." So I went back to my house, got my cats, and came back.

Tell me about the party, about the actual night before it happened. What kind of hurricane supplies did you have?

There were sixteen people counting me. Six cats, and let me think… I think… seven dogs. And when we first got there, everybody, right before it started raining, decided, we were like, "Okay, we have to figure out how much food we have here and how much more we need," because the grocery stores were already closed down. And we already were filling up bathtubs and stuff like that with water, and anything we could find empty— buckets at Tim's house and stuff like that— we were filling them up with water.

Everybody started saying, "I have stuff at my house, and we'll go get it." My friend, Chris, his mom had left, and he has the keys to his mom's house. So, he was like, "Let's raid her fridge and her pantry." We went to my house and got all the rest of my food that I had. We went to Chris's house and got his stuff. We had, like, big boxes; a big box of frozen hot dogs, a big box of frozen hamburger patties. We got beer. We went back to Chris's mom's house and took all of her stuff out of the fridge.

We brought all the stuff back to Tim's, and, likewise, other people were doing the same thing. They were going to their apartments and getting stuff. After the first night of cooking dinner for everybody, nobody was frugal. It was like, "Hey, let's just eat!" Everybody was just eating everything, wasting drinks. After the first night we were low on food. The hurricane happened, and we sat there the whole night. And Tim has this whole entertainment center, and he has all these movies. Everybody was sitting together, watching movies like *Sin City*.

You had electricity?

Yeah. We watched *Office Space*. We just sat back and watched. My friends were texting me, "Are you still there?" And I was like, "Yeah, we're watching *Office Space*, ha ha. You're still stuck in traffic." Then the electricity goes off. And the wind was crazy. On top of his roof, one of his roofs, he had this big metal thing, almost like a metal chimney thing with this mushroom-looking thing on top of it. But it's old, rusty, nasty… Just been there for years, and the wind came so hard that it just ripped the thing off. You could hear it rolling along on the roof. You could hear ching-cha-ching-cha-ching. The windows were going back and forth. They had taken all the windows out before the storm, and put these plastic sheeting things that you make patios out of, the roofs you use for your patios. They had put that on there so the windows wouldn't break through. Before the hurricane started, all the guys were going around taking all of the glass out of the windows so that nothing would explode, putting wood on the inside, and drilling that in so no glass would get in.

Chris and one of his friends decided they wanted to go up on the roof during the storm. They climbed up on the roof, and the wind's blowing, and I'm screaming at them like, "Chris, I really don't appreciate that you're doing that!" And he was like, "Well, you don't appreciate it, do you?" I was like, "Shut up. Just come down."

The wind keeps picking up and picking up. I climbed up there on the roof right when it first started, when it was probably about sixty mile-an-hour winds, and I just had my back up against the wall. But it was really strong… It felt like it could take you away.

How were you afterwards? After the hurricane, what were you thinking?

Well, it was scary at first because the wind was blowing so hard. And then when the electricity went out, it was kind of creepy because all you could hear was just the wind. We went into this little, this hallway where they had taken all the windows out, and they had put the plastic sheeting on. You could see through it a little bit… The trees blowing, it was just gray and creepy.

After the hurricane, did you go outside at all? Did you think you were in the clear?

Well, I remember the first time I went outside because I pretty much fell asleep. I went into the first little bedroom and lay on the floor with my cats. I tried to get all three of them to come lay with me because I knew they were probably freaking out, but two of them wouldn't come. But the one that slept on the pillow most of the time, Tater, he came and lay next to me. We fell asleep on the floor, but when the door opens to that room, it opens in, and I was kind of behind the door but didn't realize it. My friend Chris was looking for me, and he couldn't find me. They were opening doors, looking all through the dairy, and they couldn't find me. They thought that I had gotten blown away. When they finally found me, I was sleeping.

How long between the hurricane and the water rising?

Right away it started happening, and you could see it coming in. Tim said, "Okay, well, we need to go get my stuff…Will everybody come help me?" And we were walking up and down the stairs, three flights of stairs, bringing stuff up and down, up and down, up and down. We pretty much managed to clean out all of his files and made sure everything was okay.

Well, when the water started rising. How fast did it rise?

It didn't rise that fast. But over the next three days, I guess it rose pretty fast because it was just like, before you knew it. We had parked in this gated area where it was like a driveway thing and really big, and he said, "Everybody park their cars in here because the further it gets, the higher it goes. So your car won't get flooded as much." Little by little, you could see the first car flooding and the lights would come on because the water would hit the batteries, and this is in the middle of the night. The lights would come on, and then all of a sudden, the alarm, if the car had an alarm, you could hear, "Bing bing bing bing" until it was like, "Brrraaa", and then it would die. The lights would stay on until the battery died completely. Then you hear the next car's alarm going off, ("Beep beep beep") and then the next one, and the next one, and the next one.

What were you thinking? Did you go out on the roof and look?

Oh, yeah. The next day we started. When we first got to the party, my friend Craig said that his across-the-street neighbor left town, and he said, "Whatever you need, you have the key to my apartment. Take my canoe. Take my guns. Take my food out of the fridge. Anything you need, just take it." So, when Trent showed up to Tim's house, he had a canoe and some guns. He went back and got the food when we all went on our grocery runs... Like, get as much food as you can. In the beginning somebody else brought a canoe, too, so we had two canoes, and Tim had a generator.

How many guns?

I think Trent had some guns. Tim had some guns. I think that's about it. I don't know how many guns. I never really asked. I don't really care to know about guns. We were pretty good. Tim had these big jugs of Kentwood [water], the ones that you put into the water coolers. We had big jugs of those, and the ones that he emptied, we filled. We were doing alright. Um, the next day...

Which is Tuesday?

No, it was on... Monday?

The hurricane was on Monday...

Yeah, yeah, right. We decided, me and Chris and Maria, to take one of the canoes and go canoeing around the city, around Mid-City. We checked out things. We realized the water was rising more and more. And there was a person— there were two people— wading through the water. If you were standing in it, it was a little bit above your hips, at your chest, pretty much. That's how high it was on this guy, and he had two bags. He was holding two bags filled with clothes or whatever. There was a girl, also. I was like, "Where are you guys coming from? We would give you a ride in the canoe, but there are three of us in it right now. There's no room for anybody to get in." They were like, "No, can we put our bags in there? Can you bring our bags to our place?" I was like, "Yeah. Tell us your address, and we'll go drop it off." They were like, "Okay, we live on Palmyra." I used to live on Palmyra. So, we put their bags in the canoe, and we canoed their bags to their porch and set it there. And we waited for them to come back because we didn't want to leave. They finally waded their way back, and they were like, "Thank you so much. We were at a hotel downtown, and it just started getting really bad. Once the electricity went out, all the people that worked at the hotel left. The managers left. There was just nothing but people going crazy. They were smashing things, looting things. It got really scary. So, I wanted to get out of there, and she was like, I wanted to get out of there, too. So we decided to come back home. We thought it would be better. We just needed to get our stuff."

We canoed down the street a little bit more, and we passed by the bar where I work. The water was pretty high then. Down the street from the bar was one of the bar patrons, this guy Rick. He has this really high staircase up to his house. It's probably the fourth floor. There are little apartments under his house, and they were screwed. They were flooded. But the staircase went all the way up, and his little apartment was fine. I was like, "Rick! Rick! What's up?" He calls down like, "Hey Toni! What's going on? Y'all want a beer?" So, we hooked up our canoe, and we climbed up the stairs. We sat on the stairs drinking beer because we had pretty much run out of beer at Tim's. We didn't have anything. After all the storm and the water, we just wanted a beer. So we sat there and drank, and it was ice cold because it was in ice. We sat there and talked for a little bit. Then we realized we had to get back because the sun was going down. And that's when it started getting scary because, as we were going back, there were a lot of people just sitting on porches. They were like,

"Hey! Hey! We want the canoe, we want the canoe!" Chris was like, "Yeah, right, whatever." And it started getting darker.

There was this little Spanish couple, and they were walking. They were old, and they really didn't speak English. They spoke a little bit of English, and Maria knew a little bit of Spanish. So she tried to figure out what they were saying, and she pretty much figured out that they wanted to get to this church. Maria jumped out of the canoe so the old lady could get in. I'm short. Maria's much taller than me. She's like, "You can't get out, because it'll come up to your chin." I was like, "Yeah, you're right." She walked with the old man and let the old lady sit in the boat, and we brought them to the church. Then we were going back to Tim's, and we just heard people screaming at us some more, "We want the boat! We want the boat!" And then all of a sudden it was getting darker, and you couldn't really see too well. All of a sudden you hear this, "Splash, splash, splash." It was people jumping into the water, like coming towards us. So we were like, "We have to get out of here." We started paddling really fast. We got back to Tim's, and I was like, "I'm not going out there again."

That night we realized we weren't going to have enough supplies because we noticed the water kept rising. We were like, "We're going to be here for a while, so what are we going to do?" When we were paddling back to Tim's house, we noticed that a lot of people were coming back from the grocery stores. There were three grocery stores in one block, pretty much. You have Robert's, and around the corner from Robert's, about a block down was Sav-A-Center, and right next door to the Sav-A-Center is Winn Dixie. We were like, "Okay, well, the next morning, we're going to have to go get supplies." So, the next morning we decided— I don't know if the time is perfect— I'm not sure which day is which because it kind of just squished into one.

So, the next day, a bunch of people decided to go to the grocery store. They were like, "You want to come?" I was like, "No, I don't want to go out in the canoe again." "I'm just going to sit here and watch the news." We didn't have electricity, but we had a generator, and the generator was working. And after the storm had happened, Tim had DirecTV, and we hooked up the satellite, and it worked. It was amazing, I mean, in the middle of New Orleans, there's flooding, and all this stuff. They're like, "Can you watch the news and keep us up to date on what's going on?" So I sat there and watched the news and gave news reports. They all went out. It was this guy Dan, this guy Serge, and this crazy guy Sonny, who plays center field on my kickball team. He's got crazy curly hair, and he's loud and obnoxious, just insane. Anyway, Sonny, and then Chris, they all went to get food or whatnot. Well, they canoed, and they passed this one bar, and they were like, "Look, the window's open. Let's go in there." They go into the bar, and they're like, "All right, what can we get from here? We need to get some food." It's a bar that had a grill, but they realized that the water had come up too high.

Do you know what bar it was?

It was, um, (snaps fingers), it's on…It had the chicken fingers, and it was open real late at night…

Beachcorner?

No, it's um…

Oh, oh, Tyler's.

Yes, yes, yes. Okay, they went to Tyler's, and they went in through the window. When they got there, the water had risen pretty high, so the food was kind of ruined. But all the liquor was still on the counters and behind them on the shelves. So, they just started loading up liquor into a box or whatnot, and put it into the boat. Before they put it into the boat, they sat at the bar. They were sitting there on the barstools, with water up to their chest. They were like, "I wonder if the keg is working." So one guy, Serge, pulled the keg, and it worked, and it was still kind of cold. So, they sat at the bar, and drank a pint of beer with water up to there. They were like "Oh, this great! Woo, yeah woo, we're drinking beer." They get to the boat, and they're all happy about the score they made, all the liquor that they got, and they saw a bunch of people leaving the Sav-a-Center. They were like, "Fuck it, we're going to go to Sav-A-Center." So they go to the Sav-a-Center, and they kept one guy outside with the boats, two canoes. They go in, and Dan said that he walked in, and there were just people everywhere taking stuff, loading it up. And all he heard was a guy kicking a shelf, ("boom, boom, boom"), kicking the shelf with his foot. And like over to the left and right of him were ice chests falling everywhere. So, Dan, Sonny, and Serge went and grabbed ice chests.

They walked over to the counter where the cigarettes were, and there was a guy standing back there with his elbows on the counter, like he was ready to take an order. Dan walks up to the counter, and the guy goes, "What you need?" It's pitch black in the Sav-a-Center, and Dan was like, "All right, I need a bottle of Jaeger, I need this, I need that...." And Serge was like, "Yeah, we need those cigarettes." They filled up an entire ice chest with nothing but cigarettes, and another ice chest with nothing but liquor.

So, we have one ice chest of liquor, a whole ice chest of cigarettes of every flavor you could imagine, and then just one ice chest with like, pasta, pasta sauce, peanuts, whatever the hell they decided. They come back like, "We scored!" They came in through where all the cars were parked. There was a fence, and then there's like a little, narrow staircase that went down. We called it "The Dock." They got off right there in the boats, and they just started passing stuff up. We were like, "Woo, three ice chests!" We open one, and it's cigarettes, phew! I was smoking then, and if I would've quit smoking I'm sure I would've gotten really sick because your immune system pretty much quits if you quit smoking, or I don't know, something like that. Anyway, I was like, "All right, cigarettes." We open the next one, liquor. And then a box of liquor. We open the next one, and we were like, "Oh, okay, you got some food." Well, one of the girls that was with us, Sarah, she was pissed. She was like, "What the hell? We send you out to get stuff, and you come back…" When they went out to go get the stuff, we were sending them to our apartments. You know, I gave Sonny my key and was like, "Get whatever you need, blankets, pillows, anything like that. Any food left behind." And that's when they went to Tyler's, and they saw the grocery store and all that stuff. We didn't expect them to go to the grocery store. We didn't expect it at all. So she was like, "You come back, when you have this whole entire grocery store," and she's pissed, "And you come back with nothing but liquor? How are we going to survive with this?" And so Sonny gets upset, and he's like, "All right! All right fine. Make a grocery list, and I'll go back tomorrow."

While they were out getting groceries and stuff, Tim said he was up on the roof and some guy was screaming at him. He was like, "Hey, I want to come up there." And Tim was like, "No, man. We're doing things here. We can't let you up." And he was like, "Well, if you don't let me up, I'm just going to force my way up." Tim was like, "Oh yeah? Well, let me go get my gun." And the guy was like, "All right, we'll see what happens. We'll see what happens." So, that night, Tim decides— this was the whole third night— Tim decides that we have to start keeping watch from the roof because there are people getting desperate. The water's rising, and he was afraid people were going to start trying to come up in our place and violently come up. So, Chris [kept watch] the first night with Sonny. And I did it the second night with Chris. He had to stay up all the time and watch because he wanted to do it. Chris was really upset because when we got the boat, he wanted to be able to help people. Go around and save people. And Tim said, "No, we need this boat for us. There are sixteen of us. What happens if we need it? What happens if the boat gets taken? What happens if it breaks? We need to save ourselves." And that's the only reason that Chris stayed, because he thought he could help people. It really broke his heart that he couldn't go around and help people.

Tim really wanted to help people. I mean, we had meetings every night to discuss what we needed to do and what was best for our group. It was like a little commune. We talked about not wasting food, water, and drinks when we went to go on top of the roof to guard, to keep a look out of everything. We discussed a lot of things. And everybody had a role. Tim really wanted to help, but he didn't want Chris to go out and pick up people and everything. He had all this wood that didn't get ruined from the Habitat [for Humanity] people. So, him and Trent and a whole bunch of other guys sat on the roof and made rafts and paddles. And they threw them off the roof into the water. People that would come by, if they were wading in the water, he was like, "Take that! Get to the interstate. Get someplace where it's safe." He helped a bunch of people by making rafts out of wood, so they could go.

The night that I was on the roof keeping guard with Chris, it was really creepy because it was dark. You could see the stars. It was always beautiful. It was the only time in New Orleans that you could look up in the sky, and you could see the stars. They were really bright, and it kind of made you forget where you were. It was dark, and you couldn't see the water surrounding you. All you saw were stars. We sat up on the roof, and we just watched the stars. And all you could hear were dogs crying and howling. I was like, "Chris, this is really disturbing." I was like, "They're dying out there." He was like, "I don't know what's more disturbing. Last night, all I could hear was people screaming for help from every direction. And then tonight, all I hear are dogs crying." It was really depressing. It kind of gets to you after a while. The next morning was the last time they decided to go out because cops started coming out, and cops started driving boats looking for looters.

And we were watching— we had DirecTV the whole time. We knew everything that was going on. We knew what was going on at the Superdome. We knew what was going on at the Convention Center. We knew it was a really bad place to be. We knew that Coast Guard boats were dropping people off at the interstate, and they would wait there for days for busses to come. We didn't want to be a part of that. Every day we were on the rooftop, helicopters and Black Hawks would pass over us. The last day [the guys] went, they tried to make a long haul. They brought all three boats, all of the ice chests, and they filled up boats with [jugs of] water. All the boats were filled up with [jugs]; all the ice chests were filled up with food. And they stopped at Harry's Ace Hardware and picked up a trillion gas cans. From there, they were like, "We need to get gas." They noticed there was a used car lot on Carrollton. So they went to Bohn Ford and they tapped into one of the tankers and filled up every single one of those gas cans.

One of the girls had gone on the last day to the Sav-a-Center. Everybody only had a couple outfits with us, like clothes, shirts and stuff, and just being in those clothes was disgusting. You're wading in water downstairs trying to collect Tim's stuff. Your shoes are disgusting; everything's just disgusting because you can't shower. You know, it was just gross. So, she comes back with shirts for the guys out of Sav-a-Center, the shirts that were hanging up that are like "Louisiana Cougars" and little-boy shirts for girls. She cut the sleeves off, and she cut the necks off to make them tank tops because it was really hot. So, I still have my "Louisiana Cougars" cut-off tank top, and I'm really excited about— I'm probably going to frame it. Anyway, so I wore that shirt with this nasty skirt that I had worn for days. It was like gray, and it's like, got muck on it. I wore that for the rest of the time I was there. That's all I wore because it was so hot. We had these big industrial fans, and he put it facing backwards out of the door to suck the heat out. So we didn't really get much air blowing on us; it was just sucking the hot air out. It was calm. I mean, it wasn't cool, but it wasn't sweltering.

And anytime anybody had to use the bathroom, since the toilets don't flush anymore, we set up a bucket system. There was a big garbage bag inside of a bucket. And then we had these little grocery bags. You put the grocery bag over the bucket, do your business, then you tie up the little grocery bag, and you drop it into the big garbage bag. Then once that garbage bag was full, we tied it up, and threw it into the water because we didn't know what else to do with it. I mean, we're not going to keep human feces around or anything. The last time they went to the store, we told them to go into the pharmacy and get any antibiotics that we needed for any infections or anything because of stagnant water, mosquitoes. I think that we were afraid that somebody was going to get deathly ill, and we needed something to help us just in case that happened. And one guy we knew did get pretty ill, but he was all right. We had vitamins, and we gave him some antibiotics. So, we prepared for that, and we just got all the food we could: vegetables, fruit, anything that hadn't gone bad yet, and all the gas. We were set; we were good.

Meanwhile, everybody's trying to use their phone, and all the networks are down, and you can't get through. One time, somebody would be like, "I got through!" And so everybody would use that one person's phone to call their family. My dad never used text [messaging] before. I'd text everyone, and tell them, "I'm okay." I was getting texts the whole time. So anytime anybody wanted to talk to me, they could text me. I was getting texts all the time by people. My dad's like, "I'm sending a helicopter!" And then the next day, "Can you get to the Causeway because I'm sending a boat?" And I was like, "Shit, how am I supposed to get there?" So, the next day, Tim was all frustrated, and there were these skylights that were all on his roof. They [the guys] go down to where all the cars were parked, and they were just taking the shingles that have blown off the roof onto the top of the roof, and he was taking them and throwing them, throwing the shingles on top of the glass watching the glass shatter and break everywhere down below. He was like, "Toni, do it with me, it's a lot of fun. It relieves so much stress." So, we were smashing things, smashing the glass, watching it break on top of the cars that were already flooded. That was a release. And then I found these perfect little horseshoe-shaped metal pieces on the roof, and there were these little poles that were sticking up, so we started playing horseshoes on the roof. And then we were throwing stuff in the water, and seeing how far we could throw. We were making games up just to pass the time because we didn't know what else to do. People were doing crafts and making necklaces. We had some fishing wire, so we'd make fishing wire necklaces with a big K on it, and then I made little eye of the hurricane jewels. I made them out of tape and put them on fishing-net wire. Everybody had either a little K or a little eye of the hurricane.

Instead of staying in one tight-knit group, everybody's kind of walking away from each other. You go up on the roof, and you see one person in that corner of the roof and one person in that corner. You know, everybody's just sort of separating and getting tired of each other pretty quickly. We're starting to make "Survivor" references, like, "The first person I'd vote off of the island is...." A couple people kind of got on my nerves, too. I'm not going to say anything, but it's just the way they treated other people. At times I didn't talk anymore. Towards the end of the time, I was quiet. I kind of kept to myself, and the only person I really hung out with was Chris. Maria swore it was affecting me in a weird way, and I wasn't myself, and I was freaking out. But I never— I just wanted to stay out of everybody's way. I don't want to be a part of that. And I could tell Tim was getting aggravated, so the first chance I could get to leave, I was going to. But I had my cats. So, Chris went out one more time in the motorboat with Sonny and Dan. And they were looking to go help some people because they could hear people crying for help and stuff.

They went out, and before Chris knew it, his boat was filled with people, and there was one more couple sitting on a porch. There' s just enough room for two more people, but Sonny and Dan had to get out of the boat. So, they're like, "Well, get out, just come back for us." It's pitch black. Chris is like, "All right, I'll be right back. I'm going to drop them off at the interstate, and I'll be right back. So Dan and Sonny are just wading in the water, and they start waiting for Chris. They keep looking for a place to hold on to, and they kind of float. They float away from where Chris had left them, and they ended up on a street where they knew a cemetery was. All of a sudden they felt like they were bumping into things. And things were kind of floating next to them, and they didn't know if it was bodies, or what it was, what was happening. So they started freaking out and trying to get away as soon as they could, and they're trying to get to houses, but there's nothing to hold on to. And Dan pretty much, in his head, he told me that he had pretty much given up. He was just going to let go. And Sonny freaked out; he was like, "You're not going to die on me!" He just ran up to a house and started ripping siding off, pulling off wood, and giving it to Dan. And Dan was floating on it, and so was Sonny, and they were screaming for Chris. They were like, "Chris! Chris!" And Chris didn't know where they were. You know, there's no light on the boat. They had a couple of flashlights, but the one flashlight Sonny and Dan had had gone out. And that's what kind of freaked them out in the first place was that their flashlight went out. They're in complete dark. And they're looking for Chris. Chris wasn't coming. Finally, Chris turned and went down a street, and he heard his name. He pulled them out of the water, and they came back.

Chris called his brother, Charlie. His brother worked for Entergy and was delivering food. He was delivering food to Entergy, and he said, "Chris, if you can get down here to Jefferson Highway, I can get you out. They're only letting a couple people into the city, and they're only work people. So bring whoever you want, not too many people, you know. I can get you out."

We didn't know what was ahead of us. We didn't know if— we were just going to walk. We were just going to swim and walk to Jefferson Highway because they were saying, "We don't want you to take the boat." Tim said, "If it's just you two, y'all can't take the boat because we're going to need it. But if you get more than one person, if it's three of you, four of you, go ahead and take the boat." So, Trent wanted to come and Maria wanted to come. But after the meeting, Maria said she didn't want to go. She was like, "I'm going to stay with the group." And then there were some rumors going around that me and Chris decided that we were going to leave that night and steal the canoe without anybody knowing. I'm like, "That is bullshit."

The next morning we woke up, and Tim had made us these little care packages with some antibiotics in it, three bottles of water, some ointment for our skin in case we got cut or anything, some tuna, some peanuts, stuff like that. I had my cats, and I only had one cat carrier. I have three cats. Tim helped me drill holes into this ice chest that had wheels. I put one of my cats in there, and they were just crying and crying and crying. Remember, it's August; it's hot. It's just hot, and you put the cat in the ice chest? Come on, that's cruelty. I couldn't do it. And I didn't know what to do; I didn't want to leave my cats, but I didn't want to take them with me because they might have a heat stroke in an ice chest. I didn't know how long we'd be walking. I didn't know how— I didn't know what was going to happen. If it was just me, I would have gone. If it was just me and Chris— no animals— I would have done it. I would have waded in the water. I would have swam if I had to. I don't care, I mean, I just didn't want to put my cats through that. I told Chris, I was just like, "Go." He was like, "Toni, this is ridiculous, you need to come." And I was like, "No, just go." When he left, I completely lost it. I mean, I couldn't stop crying. He was my link. I mean, we were together the whole time. We did everything together, and we discussed everything. We had each other's backs. And when he left, it was just like, what am I going to do now?

Do you know what day he left?

It was a Friday morning. I had my bag packed. I was gone, but my cats freaked out. It was like, "I'm leaving. I'm going." Then something happens, and you're stuck again. That is the worst feeling ever. Sara was making little care packages for everybody just in case the Coast Guard or the helicopters came and said, "Now you have to leave. We've passed you a couple of times, you know. Now you have to leave. We're forcing you to." So, we're getting ready. We're getting ready just in case they're telling us that we have to leave.

Later on that afternoon we heard somebody screaming up at us like, "Hey! Hey! Y'all in there?" And we looked out of the window, and it's three Coast Guard boats. And they were like, "Y'all want to come?" And we asked them a million questions. We were like, "Where are we going? Are we going to get on a bus? Are we going to have to wait on the interstate? Can we bring our animals? What's going on?" And they answered them all correct in our minds. They were like, "Yes, we'll pick you up, bring you to the interstate, and you'll take a bus out tonight and you can bring your animals, so come on."

So, me and Sara were really excited. We were like, "Okay." One of the guys had brought one of these big cat carriers, and he told me I could use it because he was going to take my little cat carrier. Because he had one cat but this really big cat carrier. We're all excited, and the cats just look at us. They run in opposite directions like, "Oh my God, you scared the shit out of me." Same thing happened to her [Sarah],; all of her cats [vanished]. And so, the only cat that I saw was Tater. He didn't run away fast enough. I grabbed him, and I swept him up, and I threw him in the little cat carrier because I'm not going to bring the big one. I was going to come back for Buster and Peety, my other two cats.

I climbed down the steps onto the dock where the Coast Guard guy was, and he helped me onto the boat with Sara, and Petri, the girl who busted her head open, Cassia, and my friend Trent. We all went with the Coast Guard. And they dropped us off onto the interstate. Well, first we drove around Mid-City in the boats, then we get into a truck in the back of a pickup, and in the pickup, a guy took a picture of us, a photographer. And we drive in the back of the truck all the way to the top of the interstate, and they dropped us off. We were like, "Okay, so when's the bus going to come?" They were like, "We don't know."

We knew we didn't want to go to the Superdome. We knew we didn't want to go to the Convention Center, because there were rapes and shootouts and people killing each other, and we're like, "God." So we were like, "Why don't we just walk across the bridge? Let's walk across the bridge, get to Metairie, and we'll figure out where to go from there." Since Chris left that morning, we knew he was going to be sticking around in Jefferson Parish. If there was a way that we could get to Jefferson Parish, we could catch up with Chris and his brother, and his brother could get us out of the city. We climbed to the top of the bridge, and there was a bunch of news cameras up there. Everybody's shooting news, everybody's interviewing people, and this German news lady comes up to us, and she's like, "Hey what are y'all doing? Where are y'all going?" And she's filming us. She's like, "Can we film you?" We're like, "Yeah, yeah, that's fine." And she's like, "Where you going?" And we're like, "We were just thinking about walking to the bridge and see if we can cross, so we can get away. You know, I mean, we're young, we have energy, we'll be fine. And we'd rather save a seat on the bus for some elderly person or a child that needs it. We can save ourselves. We can walk." She's like. "Okay, that's really good." We got almost to the top, and a guy was at the very top of the bridge with a gun pointed at us.

What bridge? Going to the Westbank [the Crescent City Connection Bridge]?

Yes. We're like, "Can't we just cross?" And he was like, "Go back! Go back!" So we're pretty much heartbroken. We're like, "Shit. What are we going to do now, right?" We were going back down the bridge to where we were, and the news lady comes up to us, and she's like, "What happened?" We were like, "Well, they won't let us cross." And Petri was pissed; he was just like, "Well, I don't understand. They won't even let us save ourselves. All we want to do is cross." [Mayor] Nagin was telling people, "Walk! Walk across the bridge. Get to freedom. Get to where you need to go." And then guards are telling people to go back, and that's ridiculous.

So, we go back to the bridge. We're sitting there, and we see bus after bus after bus after bus pass us and go to the Superdome. We were like, "All right, well are we ever going to get on a bus?" Then the ration guy comes in the truck, the army truck. And they drop off boxes and boxes of MREs [Meals Ready to Eat], and rations, and all of this stuff. So, the lady walks up to us, the one that Sara let use the phone, and she opens the box. And she had a huge family. I mean, she had three little kids, two teenagers, a grandma, her, and another lady. There are all of these people in her family. And she opens it, and gives us three MREs to thank us for letting her use the phone. It was like a bartering system. It was creepy, and Sara was like, "No. We don't need it. We have some stuff." And she was like, "Take it. You let me use your phone. That was really helpful." So, we had three MREs, but we were afraid to eat. We were like, "Okay. We don't want to eat because we don't want to have to use the bathroom on the interstate." We were just basically drinking water, and I never peed when I was on the interstate because the more water I'd drink, the more I'd sweat out. I was just constantly drinking water. I ate a couple of handfuls of peanuts for protein, but other than that, nobody ate. Nobody. We went two days without eating because we were afraid.

You walk up to the interstate, and it's like a shanty town. People had built semi-shelters out of blankets and old crates. I was like, "God. How long have these people been up here?" The lady that gave us the MREs had been up there for four days. And there's no shade. There's no shelter. We sat up there for one day, and I was brown. I had gotten so much sun that it was ridiculous. And I don't know if it was sun, or dirt, or what. I was disgusting. I was like, "I'm not going to be like this. We're not going to be here that long." We had to sleep on the interstate that night. The whole night, sleeping on concrete, and getting eaten by ants. And you're afraid to sleep because you're afraid somebody's going to steal your bag or your phone. I had money; I had cash on me because I had bartended the whole weekend. So I had like $500 on me. And I was like, "Where am I going to put this money? Should I put it on me? Should I put it in my bag?" Well, I ended up putting it in the cat carrier with Tater. Because I thought nobody's going to look in a cat carrier for money. Tater guarded my money and my phone. The next morning I woke up, and Tater was crying. It was like a little alarm clock; [at] 6:00 a.m., I wake up. I get no sleep at all. And I was like, "Shhh, be quiet." There were people all over the place. I didn't want to wake them up. Once he heard my voice, he got louder. I tried to give him food but he wouldn't eat. I tried to give him water; he wouldn't eat. I was like, "Maybe he just wants to get out and stretch his legs." So I took my shoelaces off my shoes and tied them into a leash, like a choke chain kind of leash, and locked it around his neck. I walked him on the interstate with a pair of shoelaces. And he was okay. He didn't use the bathroom. I put him back in his cage, and he stopped crying. I think he just wanted to walk.

Then the sun started coming out. It started getting bright again, and I was like, "Okay, we're going to need some shelter." I look around, and we're just tired of sitting on the concrete. I see these crates that hold Kentwood waters, the little bottles. So I grabbed four or five crates. I just walked up and down the interstate grabbing crates. And then I grabbed cardboard boxes and anything that could block us from the sun. I found a pillow, and I was like. "Woo! A pillow! Where'd this come from?" So I grabbed the pillow, and I put it on the crate, and just sat on it. We were waiting for buses and waiting for buses, and I was like, "Okay, we're going to have to get supplies. We're going to need supplies. We're going to have to do this, and we need this to live." So, we get to the Convention Center, and we see this guy in scrubs, and we're like, "Excuse me. Can you tell me how we get in, to get saved?" And he's like, "Just go around that way. You'll see a line for buses, and you'll see a line for helicopters." And we're all looking at each other like, "What do y'all want to do, bus or helicopter?" And we're like, "Black Hawk, all the way!" So we get in line. And honestly, we wait in line for an hour. Geraldo's there. He's filming. The National Guard has come in, took control of the Convention Center, and it's in order. People are waiting in line. There's no pushing, no shoving. People are getting on the helicopters and getting out.

We're waiting in line for an hour, and we get there, and I'm like, "Is my cat going to be okay on here?" And he's like, "Yeah, yeah, yeah, you're cat's okay." It was so loud, and I could feel Tater running around in the cat carrier. He's flopping around. All I could see is his mouth moving "meow, meow." I can't even hear him. And there's a photographer there, and he makes a sad face at me, and he takes a picture of Tater, and it's digital, and he shows me, and he looks so sad. We get on the helicopter, and we get in, and it flies us to the airport. We get to the airport, and there's ice water, these big canisters of ice water. And I hadn't had an iced drink in so long. Because even at Tim's house we didn't refrigerate everything, so we were drinking hot water. Even the Cokes weren't cold. The first time I had an ice cold Coke was when that German lady was like, "Do you guys want anything? Do you want anything at all?" And we were like, "No." And she's like, "What about a Coke? Do you want a Coke?" I was like, "Oh my god." I hadn't had an ice cold can of Coke in five days, and it was dripping. It was sweating. Ice was falling off of it. I drank it, and it was the best Coke I'd ever had.

We get to the airport, and we're drinking the water, and it's so good. There's one door to get into the airport. One door, and there were four lines forming to get into the one door. And at the door, there was this huge squish. And I'm really claustrophobic. My body's being squished against thirty people. I'm talking to Trent like, "I don't know if I can do this. I don't know if I can do this. I'm going to pass out. There's like, so many people, and I can't be in the middle of it. I cannot stand crowds. I don't go to concerts for that reason." And he's like, "Look behind you." And the line is wrapped around to where you can't even see the end of it anymore. He was like, "Do you want to go to the end of the line? Do you want to wait a couple days before? You have to do this now."

We get through, and when we get to the first line, the guards are there, and they're like, "Okay, we need you to— if you have any lighters, razor blades, anything, guns or anything, we're not looking. Throw it out right now. Once you get up to the metal detectors, we will put you in custody if you have any of these things that we just mentioned. We are looking the other way right now if you want to put anything on the floor." We saw a bunch of things wrapped in shirts on the side, you know. People were throwing their guns down. This one guy had a bag of lighters. I don't know where that came from, or why he had a bag of lighters, but he did. Anyway, so we get past that, and we get to another line. People were passing out turkey sandwiches, and they were passing out water and chips and cookies. We get through that line, and we're waiting in another line. And the guy at the top of the line was like, "Okay, we have a plane that's going to either San Antonio or Austin. Where do you guys want to go?" He gave us a choice. We were like, "We want to go to San Antonio." Because we had some friends over there. My dad lives in Texas anyway, so he was going to come get me no matter where I was in Texas. He was like, "Okay, this plane goes to San Antonio." We [got] to Austin.

How do you feel about the whole thing today; how's it still affecting you?

Well, I would say that if I had to do it all over again, I would probably do it again just to have the experience of it all. You never know what kind of person you are until you have to go through something like that. You realize how strong you are, or how much it takes to break you. I mean, I guess I'm pretty sad that I went back later to go find my cats, and they were gone. The SPCA had come. I have been searching for them for a while. I've checked shelters; I've gone online. I've looked for them. And if I had to do it over again knowing that I'd lose my cats, knowing that my car would be flooded that badly, that my laptop would be looted... Everything that I'd ever done, written, or anything on my computer was lost, all of my songs, all of my writings; everything was gone. I probably wouldn't because maybe, then... I don't know. My cats might have a good home.

The SPCA thought that they were doing something good when they were going in, but they didn't. It wasn't very organized, and you can't find your animals. But for the most part, I still... I still have breakdowns now and then. Just from the stress involved in it. I still think about things and all the stuff that I had lost. I lived in Mid-City, so my place was completely flooded, and I lost everything. And I had to start all over again. Everything that was sentimental to me was lost except for my photographs. For some reason, I grabbed all of my photo albums when I left. I went back to my apartment, and I tried to save everything I could, but most of it was ruined. Being in a place now, and looking around, and not seeing anything that's mine, still really bothers me. It's going to take a while for me to just get over that fact.

It Looked Like Mogadishu

Michael Ward Prevost
Interviewed by Anita Louise Hedgepeth

Michael W. Prevost remained in his home as the massive breach of the London Avenue Canal levee inundated his neighborhood with approximately nine feet of water.

You are a true New Orleanian, born in the Ninth Ward and raised in and around the New Orleans area all of your life. Can you tell me a little bit about what your life was like pre-Katrina?

Pre-Katrina? Sure. I had bought a house out on Paris Avenue near Robert E. Lee [Boulevard] about three years before Katrina came. Before that I had been living in Venetian Isles, right on the water, which was a wonderful house. But my daughter, at the time, felt like she was too far away from the city. So we sold that house, and we moved out by the lakefront on Paris, and it was a little bit of a commute into Newman [Isidore Newman School], but when I would drive home, I sort of liked living out there. I liked being that far away from school. I liked being near the lakefront. I would go out to the old beach, old Pontchartrain Beach quite a bit. Sometimes I'd bring a fishing pole, sometimes I'd just go walk around out there. And I was swimming in the lake. In the last few years it's been clear for swimming. I love the water— I love all aspects of water except when it comes in floods. Life was good; life was really good. I'd been working at Newman for twelve years, very comfortable here. I take a lot of summer vacations. My daughter spent a lot of time with me out there at that house. Her mom lived in Lakeview, which was only about a mile and a half from my house, so we all lived in the same vicinity, and that's about it. Life was good— is still good.

So you still have hope, and you're keeping your head straight about things?

I am, I am. A couple of years before Katrina came, I joined a Buddhist Dharma group and started learning a lot about Buddhism and practicing a little bit, or practicing a lot, in fact, and reading a lot. In just the few months before Katrina came, I had a Tibetan Lama stay with me for two weeks. He was visiting New Orleans. He's a rinpoche, a reincarnated Lama. One of the central tenants of Buddhism is this whole notion of impenitence, that, particularly, our things and what we accumulate, and even to a certain extent, our personalities and the self… I don't want to get into all of that. But I think some of those notions, which I really sort of believe in my bones and blood, was a good preparation for accepting, on some level, the losses that occurred with these things, this house, and so on and so forth. So, it was timely, in some ways.

You mentioned that your home is on Paris Avenue. Can tell us what the proximity is to the London Avenue Canal and the 17th Street Canal?

I absolutely can. It is approximately five blocks and then maybe, say a half a block up from the breach on the western side breach [of the London Avenue Canal]. That was the breach that flooded my neighborhood, without any doubts. I paddled over to that— I think it would have been Tuesday morning— to see the breach. That house was very close to London. I jogged a lot. I still do run a lot, and that was my jogging path. I'd jog up to London, jog along the levee of the London Avenue Canal up to the lakefront. I'm really close. That breach, that's where I would take, when I would pick up people, and I don't know if we want to go into that now, but when I would pick up people in the neighborhood and take them to UNO [University of New Orleans], I actually didn't take them to UNO. I took them to the London Robert E. Lee levee and somebody had a truck there, and he would take the truck down the levee, or up the levee, to the lakefront, and believe it or not, Lakeshore Boulevard was high and dry. And he would drive them in to UNO that way. That's sort of how it was worked out. I spent a lot of time on the London Avenue Canal levee. Even after all the people in my neighborhood were picked up and rescued, there were a few of us, a few people— I called them "the survivalists"— they would hang out there. Everybody would sort of come out of their little hiding places, if you will, and meet on the levee in the light of day and exchange stories and opinions and who was leaving and what have you heard? A lot of these folks were armed to the teeth. They were very nice and very kind to me, not threatening at all, but we were hearing, as you know, the rumors that were rampant about everything. A couple of the guys assured me they had nothing to worry about. They had big dogs and rifles and guns, pistols. I would paddle out to the London Avenue Canal sometimes just to have company and meet folks over there.

Let's talk about the rescues. What was the water level in your neighborhood at the highest point?

Katrina was coming, and I know this doesn't answer your question, but I sort of think of it chronologically; that's how I sort of have it stored in my head. Katrina was coming, but my sister's birthday was August 27th, and she was having a big birthday party. It was going to be a really good party, and I wasn't going to miss it. I'm really close to her, and she's having a bunch of people over that I know, so we all went to that— we were all having a good time at the party. It wasn't a "hurricane party," as the part of the lore of Camille and what have you, but a lot of the conversation was about who was going to evacuate the next day, which would have been Sunday. And I remember jokingly telling some of the people who didn't know what they were going to do, "Hey, you can come to my house. I have a canoe, and, you know, I can paddle you around." It was a big joke, never thinking that that would ever happen.

Sunday I got a call from my sister and a few friends, and they were like, "We're leaving, we're packing, we're leaving now." They got up the next morning and looked back at the news. At that point I started turning on the television, and Katrina looked huge. It took up most of the Gulf of Mexico, or it appeared to, and it was a [Category] 5 heading to New Orleans, and there was a mandatory evacuation. I had never evacuated before, but I was thinking, "This looks grim." But in the end I didn't evacuate because, I think probably the primary reason is, I'm lazy. The idea of getting stuck in traffic for ten, twelve, fourteen hours is anathema to me. Maybe I don't have the patience for it. Then I have some perverse sense of adventure— let's see what this thing's going to do. And I did know I had a boat and, I mean, I did say, "You know if the water comes in I can get in this boat and float around, and if anybody needs help, I can help." But I think the primary reason was not altruism but really laziness or fear of gridlock or whatever it is. So I didn't leave. I got a few more phone calls during the course of the night or course of the evening. Into Sunday evening, I got my last phone call from a friend in Folsom [Louisiana], "Mike, come on, pack up your dog. Let's go." And I thought about it long and hard and just chose not to do it. I went to bed early that night because I was still tired from the party, actually, and not getting much sleep. I was still putting up lawn furniture that evening, Sunday evening, and moved my motorcycle into the house, brought the boat into the house, some life jackets in the boat and paddles— still really not thinking that I would need them. I wasn't a boy scout, but I was sure acting like one, in that I did have a sense of preparedness. I went to bed.

By about 2:00 a.m. my electricity was out. I remember that because the air conditioner went out. I woke up the next morning really early and ate some breakfast. It must have been 6:00 or 7:00 am. I had these big sliding glass doors in the back leading to my patio, and the trees, the pine trees in my yard and the yard behind, were just bending at sixty-to-eighty-degree angles, a couple snapping off. I just lay on the sofa and watched the show, so to speak. This is a powerful hurricane— that's what was going through my mind. That, and there's no electricity. And then I talked to a friend of mine, Bonnie, who stayed Uptown. I called her, and we talked, "This is something, huh?" and she's like, "Yeah," and then we lost phone contact. Then at about, I want to say 9:00 a.m., water started to gather in the street in front of my house and in my front yard. I bought this house because it had never flooded. It didn't flood for [Hurricane] Betsy, any of the May floods, and I'm like, "Okay, I'll take it." It's a slab, brick fortress of a house, single story, common to the area. I'm thinking, "Water? It's not raining that much." I didn't give it thought after that, like where's the water coming from. By about 10:00 a.m. the water is up to my doorsill. Not long after that, water literally starts to bubble up, gurgle up, through the foundation of the house and starts pooling under the carpet. I'm thinking, "Okay, I'm going to flood." So I started raising things up to tables. Then the water continued, I'd say it rose about a foot an hour from that point on. There I was, frantically moving things up from table to counter, from counter to top of closets, sort of thinking, "The water will surely stop soon." And that was being sort of the optimist that I am; "Eventually it's going to stop." And it kept getting higher and higher. My mattresses were floating, so I started putting clothes on mattresses.

I put my dog, by the way, Chelsea, a mixed-breed, great dog, was floating around on my sofa in the living room looking at me with this quizzical look like what is going on, and what have you gotten me into this time? The water got so high that the refrigerator floated up, and then it slammed into one of the doorjambs, and it made an incredible sound. It scared me, and I had to wade back into the den to see what had happened, and there was the refrigerator floating out from the kitchen towards the den. I took that as a bad sign. At that point, I took the canoe. The water was over my motorcycle. The canoe was floating, and I pulled it into the den, put Chelsea into the canoe, and began to fill the canoe up with things like a rain parka, food, cell phone, flashlight, radio, some extra clothes, a bed quilt. I had also, earlier, pulled down my attic stairs and loaded up the attic with bed clothes, axe, saw, food, and some books and candles. I would only go into the attic if I knew the water had stopped rising. There was no way I was going into the attic since I had a boat, even though I had the saw in the attic, so I could cut my way out. I remembered the Betsy stuff about people trapped in their attics. Most New Orleanians know that now. I got the boat in the house.

Now, the water was four or five feet high, and it was up against the plate glass doors and the picture windows. It was kind of funny— you didn't know if you were looking out into an aquarium or you were in the aquarium. I remember thinking, "How come these doors aren't shattering with the pressure of the water?" but, of course, there was water in and out so it was equalized. I don't know much about Physics. So, I'm waiting for the plate glass windows to shatter, but that never happened. At about 1:30 or 2:00 p.m. I opened the sliding glass door, and water doesn't pour in because there's as much water in as there is out, so it's all equalized. I push the canoe out into my patio, which is protected on three sides by brick walls. I climb into the canoe there and decide to wait it out. So, Chelsea and I wait it out in the canoe, and the water is getting higher and higher to the point where, by that evening, which is now 4:30 or 5:00 p.m. I'm having to lay down in the canoe because it's pushing itself up against the ceiling of the patio. Now, I'm not afraid because I know that I can paddle my way out of here if I have to, that I'm not going to be smashed. But the wind was still gusting at fifty to sixty miles an hour, gusting higher at about 4:00, 4:30 p.m. I did try to go out once, and it pushed me all around, and I couldn't control my canoe even though it was a lake canoe with a nice small keel on the bottom. I had to go back into the patio and just wait it out. It was wild. It's hard to describe. The ants were training up by the thousands up higher and higher. You could see them on the glass. Those little reptiles, lizard-type reptiles, "skinks," we called them as kids— I don't know what they're called— were suctioned up to the top of the glass and freaked out like everything else. This was all on the patio with me. I just sort of lay down in there and waited and waited.

At about 5:30 p.m. I paddled out, and the wind did not push me around. I paddled out to the front of my house for the first time, and the water was, I'd say eight and a half feet deep, nine feet deep. Eight feet deep, whatever. Deep, let's say. All you could see were the crowns of the oak trees or the magnolia trees on the boulevard and only the rooftops. You couldn't see the foundation of the house.

It was eerie, surreally beautiful, that was my description, and it really does fit. It was like things you normally see but in a context you would normally never see them in. It was beyond real, like a dream. I felt like I was in some national water park or something. I paddled, and you could see, from the Rite Aid drugstore, a dumpster had floated by and an ice machine, I mean the big ice machine that they store all the bags of ice in, had floated by. There were cars. I'd be paddling, and I could see cars underneath me, and they looked like sort of watery corpses, if you will, and they would be three or four feet underneath my canoe. And all the cars' trunks had been sprung open, and at first, I thought, "Did everybody leave in such a hurry they left their trunks open?" And then I realized that it must be something about the water pressure that springs the trunks. As soon as I got no more than a house or so away from my house, paddling on Paris up towards Robert E. Lee, which is a half a block away, people started calling out, "Help, help, hey you, help!" Two or three voices. One guy was a guy that I knew from my neighborhood, and I picked him up, and another guy was a young man that was living in one of the apartment buildings on the left-hand side, and I took those two guys immediately to a flat-roofed house in my neighborhood because if you were going to stay on a roof, you wanted a comfortable roof. So, I took them to a flat-roofed house, which was still a foot or two above water level.

Then, there's a huge apartment complex on the comer of Robert E. Lee and Paris— a lot of UNO students, a lot of people in general— it's huge. I would guess there are 150 apartments in it, so it's really big. A couple of people called to me from those apartments from out of their windows, but they were on second-floor apartments. I would paddle over there, and they were like, "Help us, help us!" And I'm like, "I can only take you to a place that's as high as you are now, so I'm happy to take you or you can just stay there." I think they were afraid the water was just going to keep getting higher and higher. Two of these guys were Chinese UNO students, and one of them was like, "We have just come over from China two weeks ago. We have never seen so much water." And I'm like, "Neither have I. This is new to all of us." There were a number of people up on the roof of that apartment building, and by that time helicopters were already starting to pass over, but these were helicopters that were just surveying the damage. We're talking about 6:30 p.m. in the evening, Monday. So, I left. The folks on the roof, they were higher than anyplace I could take them. We didn't know anything at that point. We didn't know where the water came from. We didn't know if there were evacuation sites. There were no rescue boats. There was nothing going on. I took the two guys from my neighborhood and put them on the roof there, left all the other folks where they were, and then spent the first night with those guys on the roof on Paris Avenue. It was one of the most beautiful nights I've ever slept outside under the stars. The juxtaposition of these experiences was phenomenal. It was kind of weirdly interesting and beautiful. But the hurricane had cleared out all the crap in the atmosphere, and it was clear; it was cool, really cool. In fact, I slept under the quilt that I had put in the boat that night.

There were no lights, of course. You could see every star in the sky; you could see the Milky Way, which is that white blur of lights where there are so many stars, where it's just a blur of light. You could see that in the New Orleans, Louisiana, sky. It was like sleeping on the top of the Rocky Mountains. It was incredible. The next morning I got up early; I started paddling around. At that point the Chinese guys were still there, and I said, "Let me paddle around and figure out what's going on." Still no rescue boats. I paddled to the London Avenue levee, and at that point there were a few people on the levee— the guy with the truck, he was staying in a house closer to the lake, so his house didn't have any water, or it was his in-laws' house, I can't remember. But his truck, he parked it up on the levee. And he said, "They're going to be using UNO, the new business building," is what he told me, "as the Evacuation center." I said, "Great— because I have people in my neighborhood." On my way back, I paddled past that apartment building where the Chinese guys were staying, and in one of the apartments, overlooking Robert E. Lee, the window on the second floor was wide open. I paddled right up to the window, being curious, and knowing that I'm not going to an evacuation center— I can get into the reasons for that later— but I paddled up to the window and said, "Hey! Anybody there?" Nobody was there, so I tied my boat up, and I jumped into this apartment. I started looking around knowing that I was going to need a place to stay, and this guy had three gallons of drinking water. I know it was a guy because I got to know him through his apartment. A loaf of really good, almost like homemade, whole-wheat bread, peanut butter, honey, Mars bars, which are like good chocolate bars, a pack of those little mini-bars, and two Red Bulls, which I had never had a Red Bull before. But they work if you don't have coffee, you know. I'll never look down my nose at a Red Bull again. I jumped into this apartment, and I'm like, "Wow, this guy should have… he could have stayed."

I had some beef jerky, a box of cereal, a jug or so of water, a gallon, so I was okay. But this, this was like… I could live here for a week, easy. So, I paddled back to the roof to find the two guys that I had left, and I said, "Look, here's the deal." These were African-American guys, and the only reason it matters is because I think of what decisions they made. I said, "I found an apartment, and it's really nice, and it's got food, and you guys are welcome to stay with me. And I found out that UNO is being used as an evacuation [center]." They both wanted to go to the evacuation center; there was no doubt about it. And later on, I think that because they were African-American, they may have been questioned about being in that apartment. Not that African-Americans didn't live there, but while I was there for five days, when the rescue boats and all of these authorities would come up and see me in it, not one of them asked me if it was my apartment. I'm wondering now in retrospect, had those guys been there with me, would that have been the same, given particularly all of the stories we were hearing out of Central City, inner city, Superdome, blah, blah, blah. Anyway, they wanted to go to UNO. I brought them, and the guy in the truck took them to UNO. I went back, got the Chinese guys; they were ready to go. I took them to UNO that day. At this point, we're talking now around 1:00 p.m.,

I'd say by 2:00 or 3:00 p.m. rescue boats started showing up in my neighborhood. A lot of these guys looked like Wildlife & Fisheries guys that were coming from elsewhere.

The folks that were up on the roof of the apartment building that I had seen the first evening were gone. I don't know where they went, but I assume they were rescued somehow. They were not there.

I sort of made my home, I commandeered, which is now a common word in the New Orleans parlance, that apartment and went back and took a nap. And then I got out that evening and started paddling around, and the rescue boats would ask me... They were getting calls from specific addresses, but they didn't live there, so they didn't know "Where's Warrington, where's..." you know, they knew Robert E. Lee, but they didn't know the side streets. I would help them as best as I could to tell them where things were, take a ride with them. Then, that would have been, yeah, that was Tuesday. By that point, helicopters night and day, 24-7, and I think they were taking people from UNO to Causeway [Boulevard)/l-10]. I don't know where they were taking them. I just kept flashing on all of those Vietnam movies. I was in high school for Vietnam, so I didn't go, I wasn't drafted, but it surely was a part of my upbringing, and I'd seen enough of those movies. And the helicopter sound was constant. It kind of reminded me of that era. Wednesday, there were four elderly people left in the apartment building, the same apartment complex I was staying in, just the next building over. I had been paddling back and forth, and I didn't know they were there. They had been really quiet. It was Wednesday— I knew they were there Tuesday night because I was paddling in for the night, and they raised the window. I'm talking people, four of the them, in their seventies, late seventies. They were elderly, and a couple of them weren't doing real well. One was a little confused, and he wanted to walk back home to his house. I stopped at the window and stayed in my boat and talked to one of them who was very bright and lucid, and she made total sense. She was a character; she was funny, and she had a sense of humor despite all of the stuff that was going on. I said, "Well, it's late now, and how about first thing in the morning I'll paddle over here, and I'll take you guys two at a time over to UNO?" And they said, "Great."

That Wednesday morning I went back over and got the elderly folks, and that was tough; getting them out of the window into my canoe was really difficult. I really thought we were going to tip over. By the way, the water had gone up. It was about eight feet on Monday evening, but it went up a foot. Tuesday, it was nine feet. But after Tuesday evening, it started to drop a little bit and started to go down,not much, but it was not going back up. I had to get them out of the second-floor window into about a 4 ½-foot drop into my canoe, and they weren't, you know, adept at climbing down too well. The first one hit the canoe, and I thought, this is it, we're going to go over. We managed somehow, and two at a time I brought them over to UNO. Those were really the last folks that I paddled over. There were no people that I could tell. I would paddle through neighborhoods. The beauty of having the canoe was that it didn't have a motor, so it didn't make noise. I could hear really well. Plus, if I needed to portage it, I could pull it over levees or whatever. I almost commandeered a little sixteen-foot flatboat with a 40-Yamaha [motor] on it. I loosened it from the trailer— I almost took it. And I thought, "I don't need it; the canoe's good." So I left it there. But [the owner] left the key in it, so I thought that was an invitation to me. But anyway, I didn't need it. So, those were the last folks. I concentrated on dogs after that. A lot of dogs were left, and there was one heartbreaking story. Some were on the tops of roofs, and I would pick them up and give them to the rescue boats. One was in the top of a tree, and he was barking and barking, like, "Help me," barking, "Help me, help me." I would paddle up to him, and when I would get close, because he was so scared, he would snap at me. I could not take the chance of being bitten with no first aid, and I had to paddle away from him, and then he would bark this forlorn bark. It was one of the two times I literally broke down into tears because I had to just leave him in the top of the tree. It was really sad. I spent the next day or day and a half looking for dogs, throwing them in the canoe, and bringing them to the rescue boats. That was fun... I mean, not fun, but it was real rewarding to me.

This is Wednesday and Thursday?

Yeah, mostly Wednesday and Thursday morning. I paddled over to my friends' house who left their two dogs, and he called and said, "Could you go check on the dogs?" I paddled over there in ten feet, nine feet of water. I banged on the house with my paddle and called the dogs, and I heard no sound back, so I assumed they had drowned. But those dogs were safe; they survived. They were floating together on the sofa. My guess is they were so scared that they didn't even bark to let me know that they were alive— that they were traumatized. When the water went down— what was it, three, four weeks later— they sent in animal rescue people, and those dogs were alive, rehabilitated— they're back with the owners. But I paddled away thinking they had drowned, and again, it was one of the low, low times of the experience.

You sound like a pet fan and a pet lover. Did that affect your decision not to evacuate or go to the evacuation shelters?

It didn't. I didn't know what was going on. In retrospect it would, given the story I end up having to tell about what happened to Chelsea. I didn't hear they were not letting dogs. Here was the deal... I had a radio, so I could hear them pleading for federal help, and I heard [Aaron] Broussard and [Ray] Nagin, and it was comical, although sad. But I knew things were crazy in the city, and that if I did leave I wasn't going towards the city, that I was going to go towards the suburbs. What I knew is that once I paddle into civilization, although you would be hard-pressed to call that civilization, that I would be giving up my autonomy. I've got this boat. I've got this food. I can move around as I please, and I can take care of myself. Once I give that up, I'm at the mercy of some authority figure telling me what I have to do. I don't like that notion. Never have, probably since adolescence. So, it was more about that than it was about the whole pet situation, although, in the end, I paddled out on that Friday morning and paddled all the way across Lakeview, stopped and put some food out for a friend's cat that was up on the third floor. Actually, it was my ex-wife's house— my old house— that had three stories. They left the cat, but the cat was on the third floor and high and dry. I had extra water, and the food was left, so I left enough water and food to last the cat a month, and I knocked the window out in case Felix wanted to get out on the roof and catch a squirrel or something and have some exercise. I paddled all the way and beached my canoe on the I-10/610 split.

I ran into lots of rescue boats along the way. Once they were certain I didn't need rescuing, they told me where to go. I beached the canoe there. It was hard to give up the canoe. It was a great craft. It really was, and I should have written my name and address all over it, so maybe it would have been returned to me. I would love to have it. But I didn't find it when I came back to New Orleans. Chelsea and I got out— there were a couple of ambulances there, some state troopers on the high-rise part of it. It was closer to Lakeview, the I-10/610 split. The ambulance guys didn't know what to make of us at first. I had a backpack on the front, the back, my dog, a gallon of water in my hand. I hadn't bathed. It was really hot after that very beautiful, cool night. I slept with a wet rag around my neck, and you'd wake up all during the night, sponge-bathe yourself just to stay cool. So, you can imagine what you look like after a week of that. They were looking at me, and they were like, "Are you okay?" And I'm like, "Yeah, we're fine." And they're like, "Well, do you need a ride?" And I'm like, "Yeah, a ride would be great!" At first they told me they were going to take me to the airport, and I was like, "Great!" Of course, I didn't know the airport was a mess, but I'm thinking, "I can get right on a plane and go to friends' houses!" I had a wallet and a charge card. Then he finds out from his superior that he's got to take me to the Causeway/I-10. Well, that's where they take me, and I get out there and, as soon as I got out there, I realize why I did not want to give up my independence. It looked like a scene out of Mogadishu or some starving village in Africa. That's what it seemed like to me. Mostly African-American people, and I guess that's why I have sort of this African sort of image in my head. There were white folks there, too. Litter everywhere, hot, no shade, no order, chaos everywhere. "Buses are supposed to be coming," they say. I get out of the ambulance, and the state trooper's waiting, and he said, "The only way out is there are going to be buses coming, and you can't take your dog." He says there is an SPCA truck from Houston; you can give your dog up to the Houston people and then get him later— be reunited. The ambulance driver offers to do that for me and, this is the one… I was thinking clearly the whole— I think I was thinking pretty clearly, maybe not— the whole time I was back there.

But once I got into this sort of chaos, the stimulation there was beyond what I had been used to. Imagine paddling around five days mostly by yourself. So I said, "Sure, go ahead and do that." She had a collar, a rabies medal on her. But, in retrospect, I should have done a lot of things differently. Then, he says, "I'll take her for you, and you can go get in line." So I give up Chelsea… say goodbye. He takes Chelsea. I asked this other state trooper where's the line for the buses. By the way, there are no buses there. He says, "You see that crowd of people over there up at the front near the highway? That's the line." Well, I walk up there, and it's not a line; it's people just pushing against each other. There is no order. It's just like some sort of Darwinist experiment. It's like who's going to push the hardest to get to the front? I stand sort of back from that a few steps, and I think, after about forty minutes, no buses— I think, I can't do this... This is crazy. This is making me nuts, just standing here. So I decide to walk out of the I-10/Causeway place. I walk back towards where the SPCA trucks are . They're gone. The SPCA trucks are gone. I'm thinking, "No big deal, she's gone to Houston." I decide to walk out. The state trooper stops me, and he says, "You can't walk out of here! There are roving gangs of looters everywhere, and you won't be safe." I assure him of what I've been doing, and that I'll walk out, and I know this neighborhood, I grew up around here, blah, blah, blah, I went to Rummel. He eventually lets me, so I put my money in my front pocket, and I start walking down the highway.

I start flagging down every car that passes very animatedly. And sure enough, this guy in a Ford, a white SUV, he pulls up and stops, and the electric window goes down, and I can feel the air conditioning pouring out. He goes, "Yep, can I help you?" And I'm like, "Yeah, can you give me a ride to Airline Highway?" I had heard that the Sam's (Wholesale Club) on Airline Highway was also kind of a makeshift place where you could get food. Salvation Army was there. I thought if I can get to Sam's, I can walk to my mom's house. That's my neighborhood, you know, I can really make my way somehow. He was very reluctant to let me in his car. He thought I was a "bad guy." He eventually let me in. At that point I find out he's a commercial roofer who's come in from Houston. He's the supervisor, and he's putting a roof on Ochsner Hospital. At that point I start telling him, "Ah, I used to work at Ochsner. I was a social worker there." I'm trying to ingratiate myself to this guy to let him know I'm okay. He's pulling his crew out of New Orleans, by the way, because they've been hassled so much by gangs of people on Jefferson Highway. And he says, "Well, I'm pulling my crew out, we're all going back to Houston. We'll come back in a few more days and try it again." Meanwhile, I must have said enough to him that he figured I was okay, and he said, "I tell you what, come with me to Houston, and I'll drive you all the way to Baton Rouge, which is where my hotel room is," and I'm like, "Great, because my sister's in Baton Rouge with her friends. I've got an address."

Later, after Ochsner's stop, we're heading up to Baton Rouge, and he pulls over and pulls out his laptop. He's got Mapquest, and we plug in the address, and he literally drives me up to the doorstep of where my sister's staying with her friends. So, that morning I went from paddling— I got up at dawn, by the way, and left. Part of the reason is I did see two looters the night before, and I'm thinking, okay, looters are starting to come around, I don't want to be here, there's nothing else to do here, and I'm just staying because I don't want to leave. But I went from paddling out at dawn that morning to by, 3:30-4:00 p.m., I've had a hot shower, and I'm sitting in a Greek restaurant, an air-conditioned Greek restaurant eating a Greek meal. To me, that was a miraculous day, that Friday.

The Chelsea story is really unhappy; it's sad, very sad. I ended up never finding Chelsea. I found out that none of the dogs were taken directly to Houston. They were all taken to a central center. When I told them about the collar and so on and so forth, they said— by the way, I had people spend hours, days, and weeks looking for my dog. These people, the commitment people have was beyond my commitment. I'm like, "I feel guilty, you guys are looking more than me," and they were like, "No, we know you don't have a computer, blah, blah, blah." They would reduce me to tears, these people were so dedicated. Pet detectives, you know? They found out that the collars were taken and lots of dogs didn't have collars. Collars were taken off of dogs to walk the other dogs that didn't have collars. Having a collar didn't mean that your dog would have a collar once it got somewhere. I never found Chelsea, and it's obviously the biggest regret I have. The other regret, second-biggest regret, was with my daughter. I have a fifteen-year-old daughter; she was fourteen at the time. She called me Sunday morning, and she goes, "Dad, Mom and I are leaving for Houston. What are you doing?" And I lied. I said, "I'm going across the lake." We chastise our kids for lying to us, but there I was lying to her. I didn't want her to worry.

Needless to say, nobody could get in contact with me for days. But I did have a cell phone, and I would only turn it on for a half an hour each evening so I could save the battery. I would try like heck to get hold of people.

Wednesday afternoon I start getting text messages. Wednesday evening my phone rings, and it's my daughter. She goes, "Daddy, where are you?" I said, "I'm in New Orleans, Honey." She starts crying, and she says, "Why are you there?" And then I realized that the decisions we make, the consequences they have for people around us... That my decision in some ways was kind of a selfish decision, and I didn't really think through the kinds of consequences that it might have on people, particularly my daughter, who means a lot to me and is dependent upon me. That was a good lesson. And I said, "I'm fine, Honey, and I'm trying to help out. There's no danger here."

And I never was in any acute danger or never felt that my life was at risk at any point along the way. But losing Chelsea and then having Maddie [Prevost, his daughter] so worried, sick, sad, and, in some ways disappointed, were really solemn, sad occasions.

Can you tell me more about the "survivalist mindset?" I know you said they would gather at the London Avenue Canal. What was the idea, the frame of mind, going on at that time?

I think it's hard to know what those folks' motivations were. I think, in some respects, they were trying to protect their houses or something that they had of value. Nobody's going to take that from them, and there was just this sense of protection and defense of private property. We would talk about looters because we were hearing lots of stories, and they were like, "Let them come to my neighborhood!" It was almost like they were inviting it. I didn't have that particular mindset. For me, I grew up hunting and fishing— I'm comfortable in the water, and I like a little sense of adventure, and that was about it for me. It's hard for me to know. This is an aside: they kept offering me beer and cigarettes, "Aw, man, you want some beer, you want some beer? You want some cigarettes?" And I'd be like, "No." And they had a duffle bag of cigarettes and cigars, I'm talking this high [motions to denote approximately three feet]. So, somebody was around when one of the corner drugstores was, you know, "commandeered" because that's the only way it could be explained. They had cartons and cartons of cigarettes and those cigars you buy at drugstores, cheap cigars. They had ice chests of beer and things. I did not want any beer. I felt like this whole experience was an altered state of consciousness, so I wanted to keep what few wits I had about me. I wasn't interested, but they had that. Some of them were drinking beer and smoking and armed, just out to protect their property. They were very nice to me, very kind, offered me whatever I wanted, and real sweet. But I wouldn't have wanted to cross them, I can tell you that.

You did not see much looting in the area?

No. I saw two guys who were definitely looting trying to get across Robert E. Lee. They were on the lakeside of Robert E. Lee, which hadn't flooded very much. They had walked through— which is a very affluent area too— Lake Terrace, maybe? They were trying to cross Robert E. Lee, and they had packs on the front, the back, and were carrying stuff. Well, Robert E. Lee was seven and a half, eight feet deep when they were trying to cross it. They were screaming at each other, "I told you not to take so much… There's no way you're going to be able to get across!" Literally, if they would have tried to cross Robert E. Lee, which they did, you know the metaphor, they would have drowned in their greed. They turned around and walked back the way they came. I was hiding out in my apartment. I was in an apartment across from them.

Also, one night, a boat came through. It was evening, and it was a brand new Bay Stealth bay boat. I know those particular boats, beautiful boats. That fishing boat was brand new, looked like it was just off the showroom. There were about seven guys on it, and they passed through the neighborhood. They saw my canoe, and I heard one of them— because I had it tied up outside— I heard one of them say, "Hey, there's a canoe!" I jumped out. I was sleeping in the window, and I immediately put my hand up like this to them [motions with hand up, palm front], and they were like, "Oh, that's your canoe, okay." They were definitely going to take it. The point being, my sense was they were not up to anything good. They didn't ask me if I needed any help, if there was anything I needed. Most people that would come through would ask, "Are you alright? Do you need anything? Do you want to come out with us? We'll take you out." These guys had no offers of help. My sense was they were boating around the neighborhood looking for stuff they could take. I didn't see them take anything, so I'm not sure. But those were the only two incidents.

You work with the students closely on a daily basis, and when Newman reopened in January of 2006, did you notice any signs of post-traumatic stress or anything the students were going through or having difficulty with?

Yeah, it was hard to tell. One thing that was easy to tell was how happy the kids were to be back at school, back in New Orleans, back with their friends, more than anything. So, even if some of the kids were suffering, as they were because they lost their houses and everything that was in them, they were so happy to be back with their friends that it would mask it. It would be hard to tell who was having a problem to the point that it was interrupting their daily or emotional functioning. They were also so happy to be back in a normal routine in the school and with their friends. The kids who lost houses, they definitely were grieving and were emotional periodically and wanted to talk about it. The kids who didn't lose as much, they were, rightfully so, less affected, the kids who lived Uptown and what have you. But you know, even those kids, who had summerhouses in Bay St. Louis and whatever, lost those, which was difficult. Some of those kids' parents also lost jobs or their businesses were now threatened, and everything was uncertain. Even kids without, the ones who didn't lose their houses, were still a bit anxious about it. But there are two things: adolescence, you know about. There is a sort of natural narcissism to adolescence, and if it's not affecting them right now or not affecting their friends right now, they can put it on the back burner and enjoy their lives. A lot of it was about just trying to have fun. Michelle [Beloney], the other social worker, and I decided to go into the classrooms and have Katrina conversations. We can't not have a conversation. Some of the kids didn't really want to talk about it; they felt like they had been "Katrina-ed" out. But once you'd start the conversation and sort of get it rolling, most everybody would pay attention if not, in fact, participate. We had these Katrina conversations, and basically it was just two hours— it was two days, two class periods, one day right after the other. We'd talk about the city, the uncertainty, what went on, if anybody wanted to talk about their neighborhoods. I'd ask, "Where have you been? Have you taken a tour?" I had a bunch of questions that I could throw out as conversation starters. We looked at jobs and businesses so that I could get them to think about all the things.

But the bottom line— this has been much harder on adults, I think, in general. I'm generalizing here. Go ask the kids in Chalmette or the Ninth Ward, and you might get a different response, and rightfully so. Maybe it's harder on the kids who came from a community that's completely devastated. Then I'd say it's equally hard on adults and kids. But in our community, I found it to be much harder on adults. They were the ones having to deal with Katrina, FEMA, SBA, do we move our businesses, is my law firm going to have a practice here, contractors, rebuilding the house. That was all adult stuff. Now, adult stress percolates down to kids, but I found that it was the adults, by far and away, in our community, that were more stressed out than the kids, in general.

Did working with the children help you to work through your own issues, like losing your home?

Yeah, well, it really helped. Yes, it did. What it felt like was we were all in this together. We were all peers. I was maybe the adult facilitating the conversation, but I was right in there with them. I talked about my stuff, not too much, because as an adult you can tend to dominate things, but I let them know a little bit about where I lived and what happened. But not too much. But, yeah, I joined in and shared. Not just for me, although I'm sure for me, but also to let them know we're all in this together, we're all going through the same experience, more or less, all this uncertainty, which is really a hard thing to deal with. We like the world to be certain and predictable, and it surely wasn't then and probably still isn't now. Or maybe that's an illusion to begin with.

You recently went to California and spoke to a group of students there. What was their perspective, or how was it speaking to a group that was unaffected by the storm?

It was a wonderful experience. It was a private school, a high school, a group of kids, maybe 450 kids, and 100 faculty members. I have this incredible *Times Picayune* slide presentation that a friend of mine loaned me that was part of the presentation that I did. But I also told my story a little bit in the middle. Well, if that slide presentation doesn't get your attention, nothing will. The kids— you could have heard a pin drop— they were just moved and asked really relevant questions. When I told my story, they laughed when it was funny— it was really a healthy thing for me to do. It was maybe the healthiest thing I've done because when I'm talking to a group in California, I'm a lot more myself— I share a lot more personal stuff. This is an aside, but I think it's a great part of the story. In October, I'm at a birthday party for my mother, and a friend of mine brings three nurses who have volunteered to come down here and help from different states: two from Alaska and one from New Jersey. They're FEMA nurses, but they're really just nurses down here helping, working at Touro [Infirmary]. I end up falling in love with one of the nurses from Alaska, albeit who knows if that will ever work out, but I could say that. I had a picture of the nurses in my slide presentation, and I said that they're representative of all the people who came down here to help, and people just felt so compelled to help that they would leave their jobs, some people would move down here permanently, and I'm so— it's unbelievable— I feel privileged to be a part of the human race. I said, "In fact, I fell in love with one of them!" You could just hear everyone "oohhing" and "aahhing," and it was just a wonderful fun kind of thing for me to do. It was just good. I could say, "Yeah, it's like a line from the Dylan song, right, 'They say the darkest hour is right before the dawn.'" Even in dark times, if you keep your eyes open, sometimes there are shafts of light that come down, and if you're aware, there are opportunities. And through the presentation, I could feel the openness, the energy, and the compassion in the room, and it allowed me, I think, to just be swept up into the flow of it. In some ways, I think it may have been more healing for me. They were very moved, and I felt good keeping it in the minds of people elsewhere that we've got a long way to go. "Come down and visit! It's still a nice city!" I did my little New Orleans spiel.

If another storm comes like Katrina, would you stay or would you go?

I would stay. My first— I don't know that I could; I don't know that my daughter would let me. But I would stay. I'd need to have a boat, which I don't have right now. It's the first time in my life I've ever been boatless. But I would stay.

The Cajun Navy

Manning Billeaud
Interviewed by Shannon Billeaud

Manning Billeaud joined the nearly 500 good samaritans called "The Cajun Navy," who used their boats to help New Orleans residents left stranded by the storm.

You've lived here in Lafayette, Louisiana, your entire life, and it's two hours away from New Orleans. What relationship have you had with New Orleans before the storm?

Well, I had three daughters living in New Orleans. And that was one of my reasons for wanting to go down there.

What did you think when you first heard that the levees broke? What was the first thing in your mind?

Worst-case scenario. I had just finished reading *Bayou Farewell* and a number of other books that pretty much predicted what would happen. You know, it was kinda ironic in that at first they said— I think it was CNN or one of them— said everything was fine, New Orleans was spared. Then the levees broke. And then you watched it on TV and the lack of response— seemed like the only thing was good was the video the news reporting, the rest of it was awful... to sit here and watch it and not be able to do anything.

How exactly did you get involved with the "Cajun Navy," and why did you get involved?

Well, by Tuesday morning everybody was glued to the TV watching it, and there was nothing anybody was doing. The state had done a great job evacuating people who wanted to leave. I think that's kind of a— a lot of people don't believe that but I believe that to be a fact, 'cause we were there [in New Orleans, days before Katrina hit.] We saw everybody get out of town who could get out. And then Tuesday morning the situation was pretty helpless. You know— then the governor put out a plea for help and asked any private citizen in boats to try to come in and try to help. So, there's a friend of mine— an old acquaintance by the name of Nick Gautreaux who's a senator or representative— I guess he's a representative, from Vermillion Parish. He got on the news and organized an effort for everybody to meet at the Acadiana Mall at 4:30 the next morning [Wednesday]. So, at that point, my fishing buddy Mike Pears called me, and we said, "Well, alright we'll go." That was late in the afternoon, early evening. We had to go get the boat, the little boat, gas it up, bring extra fuel for his pick-up truck, and buy water and everything that we thought that we would have needed because we knew there was gonna be nothing down there [in New Orleans]. We got there about 4:45 a.m., which I'm glad we were late 'cause there was about 500 vehicles with boats in the Acadiana Mall parking lot. Everybody was just amazed at the turnout. Way up in the front towards the building itself was kinda an organizational effort. We couldn't really hear or anything, so my buddy [Pears] and I decided since we had pulled up late and we were out on the outer perimeter of all the vehicles, that as soon as they said go, we took off.

And we basically go to New Orleans at about 80 or 90 [mph] with virtually no traffic on the roads. There was about twnety cars and trucks or twenty trucks and boats that left together because we had already fueled up vehicles and trucks. A lot of people, I don't think, had gotten ahead of it enough to be able to do that. They had to fuel up in Lafayette or, at the very minimum, Breaux Bridge because after that— I don't think there was power at that point forward anywhere else east of us. So, we took off. And it was almost a race on the highway. When we got to La Place we picked up a police escort.

And at that point we were running third in line because we didn't wanna be first.

My buddy's [Pears] pretty competitive, so we picked up a police escort in La Place and basically drove 80 mph across the [Bonnet Carré] Spillway into New Orleans. And just— was just amazed at the stillness. It was twilight when we got into the city and exited off of Vets [Veterans Boulevard] somewheres. And the smell was fuel. A lot of stuff was knocked down, but it wasn't like blown away knocked down. It was heavily damaged. Then, when we got to the area of Vets, you could start really seeing the water 'cause before that we really couldn't see the water. It was dark, and we came to a complete stop. At that point there was about fifty or sixty trucks and boats that came to a complete stop. There was a Marine guy in a wetsuit with a jet ski on a trailer. And he would— it was completely disorganized. Nobody's fault, but there was just like, no game plan. So, I noticed this guy [from] the Acadiana Mall parking lot who kinda seemed like he was on key. Then I saw him again, and he was one of the first ones there. I saw him talking to the police— to this Marine. I asked him who he was. He said his name was Duff. He lived in New Orleans. We decided we'd go follow him, and we took off. We went down to Vets and got photographs of it. Nobody wanted to launch there. It was just power lines and looked really eery. Then he said, "I got a better idea." We took off, and we went through Old Metairie. The water was really deep in some spots, so we'd have to jump off the road into parking lots, hop curbs, get back on the road, and do all that. We were in a three-quarter-ton truck, so we had a lot of free board.

Finally we got to where the 17th Street Canal bridge crosses Old Metairie Road. And that's where the water really started in, where it was solid water into that graveyard area. We turned the boats, turned the trailers around, and we had to physically push the boats off of there and then push them through debris and power lines that were turned off. And then that's when we took off and headed towards the interstate.

Did you bring your gun?

No. Didn't bring a gun. My buddy brought a pair of waders, and I should've put them on, but I didn't. We just had shorts and some Tevas.

I remember running into some guys from Henderson in these crawfish boats with these pro-drive outboards and they told us to watch out for the underwater fire hydrants, which we hadn't thought of. We took off, and we went by the graveyard, and then we eventually ended up at the intersection of I-10 and Old Metairie Rd., which turns into City Park Avenue. By coincidence we were there the Saturday before the storm, leaving, getting some of my daughters'— you being one of them— stuff moved around. Unfortunately, yours in the basement, and fortunately for your sister, hers on the fourth floor.

Most of the city was under water. How did y'all decide which part of the city to go into?

Well, first off, we met a pair of kids— one of them— I can't remember their names; it will come to me. They were Tulane medical students, who had gone to their first day of school and then the hurricane hit and [they] lost their vehicles, most of their vehicles and all of their possessions. One of them borrowed a boat and a pickup truck; they had been working all night. [They] had evacuated the people that were in the pumping stations somewheres out on Lakefront, and then they had made it back to the train up on I-10. They were ferrying people— this was early morning, I'm talking about like 6:30, 6:45 a.m. They were transporting people from I-10 where it went back underwater at City Park [Ave.] over to the train trestle. And there was a group of boats, from— a lot of them from Lafayette and the St. James Parish Sheriffs department— who would stage them. We would bring them to the train trestle, and we would have to haul them up there because it was kind of a steep embankment. Then they would load them up on a boat on the other side of the train trestle. I think they were bringing them— I think they told me to the [I-]610, which was where the dry ground started. And I remember seeing the people coming down the interstates in pairs and fours and sixes and families and a lot of them had shopping carts; some of them had valet carts from hotels. Everybody [had] a garbage bag with whatever they could carry with them.

And the first... Three kids we picked up were from Slidell, and they had stayed the hurricane in their grandmother's home in Slidell. [They] had to go up in the attic, had to break out of the side vent, had to crawl up on the roof, [and] spent the night there. [They] saw the rescue helicopters passing overhead, which I suspect were going into St. Bernard or the Lower Nine or whatever. And at the end of the day, they decided they had to get out, so they swam, walked, and finally got to I-10. They circled and they had walked all the way around the city, swam and crossed and walked. On Wednesday morning about— I don't know— 7:30, 8:00 a.m., they came walking up. We asked them if they wanted to go to Baton Rouge, and they were like, "You kidding?" We said, "No." We gave them some water and asked them what water they had been drinking, and they said, "You don't want to know." [We] asked them if they had food, and they said they had run into an Army vehicle, which was probably one of those big National Guard deuce-and-a-quarters that had medical and food supplies on it. When it stopped for them, some thug ran up with a gun, stuck it in the guy's face, so he had no alternative but to take off. We gave them some sandwiches that we had— we didn't think to bring too much more food than that— [and] some water. We transported them— and I remember one of them's name was Tig. That was his nickname, like Tiger.

How many people do you think y'all got?

Well, what happened was Mike and I and Duff— Duff lives somewhere off of City Park [Ave.]— went in that area on two boats. We had a hard time because the water would get shallow; then it would get deeper. The power lines were across the road, with the oak trees and the oak tree limbs. And we had to drag— we had trouble getting across that train trestle that crosses City Park [Ave.] We got as far as Delgado. And there was— the water was about knee-deep to waist-deep down there. But we were told that at that point it was getting much deeper as you went towards the park and toward Bayou St. John. We were approached by four policemen or security guys from Delgado Community College that asked what we were doing there, and we said, you know, governor put out a plea for help and all that, and that's what we're doing. They were dragging a twelve-foot flat-bottom boat with a rope, and they each had like one or two guns. You could tell they had been doing this for days, and they asked if we had guns. Mike and I said no. Duff said he had a twelve-gauge Ithaca Deer-Slayer, which is basically a cop gun. It's a riot gun. And they told us to take it out, pull the plug, which increases the shell capacity, and be prepared to use it because the night before two punks had tried to take that little bitty flat-bottom away from four armed policemen.

Mike wanted to poke around and take pictures and talk to the people. There was a lot of people in the neighborhood. There were people on balconies— actually, when we were going in there was a guy standing in waist-deep water talking on a pay phone. It was kinda weird. So, I went up there [to Delgado], and one of them wanted me to meet the chief— his name was Ron Doucet. I got to know him through the course of the day. I met Ron Doucet, [and] he said he had 200 people there, but they were running out of provisions. I forget— I think he had 125 firefighters who stayed behind to help. They had parked there trucks up in the medians, so they were high and dry.

Is this at Delgado?

At Delgado Community College. And then they had a mixture of faculty, some folks from the neighborhood, faculty children, some old folks who were sick and infirm, and he [Doucet] said he'd like to get them out of there. And I told him, I said, "Well, the worst case is— it's getting hot— would be to move everybody to the interstate and not have any water." 'Cause he had about, I think he said 500 gallons left. They started out with like two or three thousand gallons. And they were running out of food and water. So I told them I would go back to the interstate, which takes about 45 minutes to go through all that crud again, 'cause you can't— you gotta go in a boat; you can't just walk the whole thing. So, we did that, went back. I went over to the trestle, and I talked to the St. James [Parish] Sheriff deputy that we spoke with earlier. He said, "Two hundred people?" And I said, "Yeah, but we can walk most of them out."

So, meanwhile, we went, and we saw these guys, the two young guys from Tulane— they had found or absconded what they— not only their outboard motor and little flat-bottom boat, but they had an eighteen-foot, like eight-foot-wide flat-bottom with no motor that they had borrowed. They said they "found" it.

They were loading it up, I have pictures with them with probably fourteen people in it. Damn near sinking it. They'd tow it behind the other one. Well, what was his name? Anyway, I agreed to get one of them to walk back into the neighborhood with me. At that point we started— we made, I guess three trips back there. Ron Doucet sent some of the students in front. They had to cut through the chain link fence that keeps people, normal pedestrians, from crossing between the grave yards on the interstate or just crossing the interstate. They keep a big fence. He sent them in there with wire cutters, and they cut holes so that the people who could walk out [could] walk to the fence, crawl through the hole, and then walk the train trestle all the way down to where it crossed. And there they had to get a boat. Everybody else, all the young kids and old people, we had to put them in a flat-bottom, this big flat-bottom and drag them out of the neighborhood. And we made two trips with that. Most everybody else was walking out at that point. Ron Doucet wasn't gonna leave anybody back. And the firefighters I think finally went on their own. I don't know where they went.

It was bad because as the water went down there were red ants everywhere. The water had peaked that day around noon is what I was told. 'Cause we looked at the photographs a couple days later— at the fly overs— and you could actually see our truck with the boat trailer at the 17th Street Canal bridge. I remember hitting something underwater and going back and seeing and it was a car. You could see the car from the aerial photograph, too. But as the water got low, we'd have to get them out. They had these two little twin girls; their daddy must have been a faculty member at Delgado. When they were walking on the median, when I first picked them up, they were full of red ants. We had to dunk them under water. And there was red ants in the boat. Anything that wasn't wet had red ants on it. We got them back there [to the trestle]. The water really started falling, so you had to be careful if you went back into those neighborhoods 'cause— actually, you could get stuck back there.

And the crawfish guys, the ones from Henderson and from Loreauville, were great. They could go back in there at forty miles per hour in a foot of water, running in the curb— you know the roads are turtle back, so the water funnels on the side, and they would just run thirty miles per hour, be back fifteen minutes later with five old people, turn around, go right back in, come bring out a bunch of kids. They were going back and forth. Then the airboats were trying to run back and forth, but they had problems going underneath parts of the interstate 'cause of the— what they call the fan— the prop on it. While I was in the neighborhood, Mike [Pears] kept the little boat. And I went back [with one of the Tulane students], and the kid's name was Francois. When I went back with Francois, Mike went back with the little boat, and he continually ferried people from where I-10 went under over to the train trestle. He did that for like half of the day.

Midday, when we got hot and tired, we parked under the interstate in about ten feet of water, eight feet of water, where it was safe in the shade and ate lunch. And then went back and moved people. Then, at about 4:00 p.m., we saw— we never saw [before that]— we saw helicopters, but we kept thinking, "Man, there's gotta be more help than this." At about 4:30 I told Mike, I said, "Mike, we gotta get out of here. We don't wanna be here after dark. I think we've done what we could," because the amount of the people coming down the interstate had dwindled. And we actually saw Air Force One fly over twice. We saw the helicopters, but again, not a lot of them, so we went back up and showed Francois and them… A lot of people had to drag their boats over the trestle, which is huge. My brother Moose had to do it. So, we showed him, and he followed us in his boat up Old Metairie Road 'til it got shallow enough 'til you had to walk it through the trees and power lines. And then, when we got to the bridge, we had to turn the truck around, back the boat in. And there was a— somebody brought a Zodiac, and they had a Down Syndrome child that was about ten years old— I remember this, and the grandparents were with him. They must have lived right around there in Metairie somewheres. And the child was in a bad way— I don't know if the child was going into shock. You could tell something [wasn't] right. So Mike ran up the road— well waded and rode up the road— 'til he found an EMS and brought them back down there. They were tending to the child.

So, we loaded up, and we were getting out of there, and I remember these huge military dump trucks coming in with sand. We thought, "Why on earth would they have sand?" And didn't know this was— they were staging to fill those super sandbags to drop on the breaches in the, I guess, Orleans Street or 17th Street Canal levees. But we didn't know where it was. The water had gone down a little bit. We talked to some people, gave a couple of them a ride up the road, gave them some water. When we got back onto Vets, went to Causeway, and when we got to Causeway crossing I-10, [it] was amazing.

We stopped for an hour, and I can't believe they let us do it. We were in the middle of that super huge triage. They were landing helicopters… There was a guy with a red glove, and he was military or something. There were probably five, six, seven thousand people down below us. There was a huge outdoor triage set up in the shade. There was this guy with the red glove, [and he] would walk out into one of the big grass/clover leaf areas on the intersection of I-10 and Causeway, and he'd go and lower his hands, and they would drop four or five Black Hawk helicopters, and then the other ones, the gray ones— the Navy versions called them Sea Hawks, same aircraft. And they would drop them down all at once. They'd land. And the prop wash would be throwing junk in the air, and plastic cups and stuff. And people just tumbled out of there; children with no shoes, no shirts, families. Sad. Didn't look like a lot of daddies, just mamas and grandmamas and aunts and kids. Saw one of them fall down, gave him CPR, and then in front of us, down the interstate they would roll land the Sikorskys, which are those huge helicopters. They kind of land them like an airplane— where they roll them down. And then behind us they were landing the Coast Guard Jumpers, the colorful ones, and those are these French helicopters. And we'd see them, and they'd land, and they'd take families out. What we were thinking was— and they were kinda flying a route that the Sikorskys and the Black Hawks were doing— some of those were going into the 'Dome and Convention Center at some point and picking up people. But the Coast Guard Jumpers were going into the— into St. Bernard and Plaquemines Parish, we think. We're not sure. But probably St. Bernard.

And I remember, they have that cage, that rescue cage that if they can't strap to you and pick you up, they just put you in this cage. One of them had this old guy in there, and they— he couldn't even get him out of the basket or cage, so they just had to pick him up and take him out. And you watched all of Acadian Ambulance, the National Guard, the State Police, the Wildlife and Fisheries. And there were no public buses— at all. We were there for well over an hour, and we never saw one public bus. It was all private.

At the Triage?

At the triage, picking people up. It was all private— looks like small rural church buses or metropolitan church buses from St. Francisville, from Baker, up in Tangipahoa— everywhere… Whoever could. But there was thousands and thousands and thousands of people sitting down there. And it was hot. I mean, there wasn't enough provisions, and that was on Wednesday. My friends went back on Friday and said there was like twelve thousand people, said it was awful. We took pictures, but, I mean, some of the pictures were pretty graphic— down into the triage. I told Mike, you know, I don't really wanna be too intrusive with the pictures, but, I mean, it's probably good that you took them. Somebody needed to know what happened. We stayed up there for well over an hour until some deputy pulled up and said, "What in the hell are y'all doing here? Get out of here! Y'all are in the way." When we were leaving there was a barrage of rescue craft coming in those Zodiacs. I don't remember where they were from. And I remember at one point there was like a dozen of them. These are like $250,000 rubber boats with radar and everything. We saw Missouri rescue people. You name it, they were there. And then that's when we took off and went back [home]. I wasn't gonna go back the next day. I just— I think it was getting too dangerous 'cause we heard about all the gun shots.

How many people do you think were in the "Cajun Navy?"

Oh, I don't know. I mean there was 500 of them— estimated 500 boats at the Acadiana Mall. I was told they turned about 400 of them back. But a lot of people just found other ways to get in the city. I would tell you that there was probably— and I'm just gonna guess at it— I don't know. And especially if you look at the coverage, most of what you see is all private boats that the people that didn't live in metropolitan New Orleans that came in there— baby, there was probably a thousand of them. In addition to that, they had the Texas Wildlife and Fisheries. I think the biggest heroes were the Louisiana/Texas Wildlife and Fisheries and Coast Guard Jumpers. Those guys were not only— they were dropping in between power lines and buildings and getting shot at.

Yeah. I read that the Wildlife and Fisheries had organized the Navy.

No. No. What I remember of it was that Kathleen Blanco was frustrated with the lack of federal response and put out a plea for help to the private sector. That's when Nick Gautreaux, down here, organized the effort to meet at the Acadiana Mall. It's really a shame that they—and it wasn't anybody's fault—they got there, and nobody really knew where to go. We were really lucky we ran into somebody from New Orleans. I mean, I saw people pulling boats over this huge train trestle, and we were able to drive around it. I mean, there were parts of the city that you didn't need to go in. I had a friend who stayed there who was Director of Emergency Preparedness at Charity Hospital. They had to go in there with armed guards to get infants out.

Did you mostly get people out of Delgado or from neighborhoods as well?

Out of the neighborhoods. When they saw us moving a bunch of people from Delgado, a lot of people we had seen or had seen us started coming out of their homes and realizing, "Okay," you know, "Day three. It's getting late in the afternoon, and I got a chance to get out." And they started walking out. Basically this was just the regular people walking out. I think there was a lot of people— I know there was a lot of people that could have left but didn't 'cause they were sick. One guy was sick with cancer. And an old guy who's wife was taking care of him. And one guy didn't want to leave 'cause his sister came to pick him up, and she didn't want the dog in her brand new car, so he stayed. He had nine feet of water. And there was a lot of young people that, to me, could have left.

Did you have problems trying to convince people to get out of the city?

Yeah. A lot of people just didn't wanna leave.

Did you transport anyone that was very ill?

Yeah. Yeah, we had a couple of guys from Delgado that were diabetic. And one of them was very, very sick. I mean, I think he was running out of medicine. And he was. When we got to the embankment, it took— he was a big man— about four people to almost just kinda drag him up the embankment. And we pointed out to the St. James Sheriff's Department that this guy was pretty sick. And they had told us before that they had a couple of diabetics. So, we kinda put the older people with the young, with the kids. And kinda put him there, and fortunately there was some people on the other side of the trestle in a boat: Mike Chachere and some of his people. I kinda knew some people to put them with.

Mike Chachere of the "Tony Chachere's"?

Yeah. Well, that was his uncle, yeah.

How were the "Cajun Navy?" How were all the Cajun men who came down there handling it?

Oh, they didn't have any problem with it. The worst part was just getting around and knowing where to go. I mean, it was frustrating for everybody, too, because it wasn't that you could just— I mean, when you got back to your car— like my neighbor went three times— you had to come all the way back to Lafayette. Then it wasn't like you could just go to your house like a job. You had to get back in and restock on fuel and water and do what you gotta do to get back over there.

What was the most difficult part of the whole experience?

Just probably getting the boats off the trailer 'cause you had to drag them off. I mean, when I tell you drag, I mean drag a seven hundred pound boat. 'Cause there wasn't enough water. We backed the truck into the water to the point where it almost killed the truck. It took four of us to drag it off. And then, I guess, the second-to-most difficult [thing] was leaving and watching all those people. Especially at the triage over there at Causeway and I-10. It was sad. I mean they just kept bringing them in, and bringing them in, and bringing them in. And they didn't have any transportation. That's what I didn't understand, was why there wasn't any transportation. Maybe they didn't think about it in advance, but in the pictures afterwards with all the buses... Our company, we lost eighteen vehicles, my company. I guess everybody was pretty much not thinking about worst-case scenario even though you hear about it.

Has this changed your outlook in any way of storms, New Orleans, or in general?

I guess I have a better appreciation for the city and the culture. The city's coming back, but it's going to be a very long and difficult road. I think that— I believe that out of something bad, something good can happen. But they're still having to deal with the awful criminal element, the displaced people, as well as the displaced criminal element. It seems like what was probably in one part of the city is spread all over the city. We were fortunate this year to be spared a storm. Very fortunate. I think if it had been hit again like that, I don't think the Feds would have been as prone to come in there. But the big thing now is to fix the levees, and the number one thing is, and this is way before that, is the coastal erosion. And if they don't fix that, they can't fix anything— you can only build the levees so high.

Would you do it again?

Hmmm. Went back out after Rita. We went back and— Rita went into Vermillion Parish, and that was different. New Orleans was contained. It was quiet. It was just a big pond. Now there was all that craziness in there, but when we went out in the boat during Rita, it was 50-60 mph winds through flooded sugarcane fields. But it's a different culture. There's a Cajun culture— and I remember asking people who were sitting there with water up to their houses— or a foot of water in their houses and saying, "Y'all need a ride?" And they were like, "Nope. We're good." They fine. They were on their shrimp boats tied up to their flooded house. And in New Orleans it was different. They didn't have that type of "I can do it by myself, I can stand on my own" [attitude]. Rita got so little play even though it was a catastrophic hurricane; it didn't hit a major metropolitan area. But it displaced a lot of people. It flooded, at some points, thirty miles inland. In some respects I think it was a stronger storm. It just hit a less populated area. I mean, the city of Lake Charles is probably thirty miles from the gulf. It flooded Lake Charles. [In]Lake Charles, up until a couple of months ago, sixty percent of the small businesses were closed. I mean, it closed every church and school on the coast from Grand Cheniere down through Cameron [Parish] from Pecan Island— now they're talking about Forked Island and Cow Island. The Iberia Parish school board has now closed three schools— only one got flooded— 'cause they know it could happen again. So, they're consolidating further inland. They know that any time there is a man-made channel, like the MRGO, or the Houma Navigational Canal, or even a small one like the Port of Iberia, or a big one like the Calcasieu Ship Channel— that's a conduit for water. It doesn't matter if it's forty miles inland. Once that bubble of water comes, it's not gonna stop until it runs out of steam.

What do you think of the lack of recognition the Feds gave to the "Cajun Navy?"

I don't even think they had a clue as to what went on. I think it would have happened anywhere. You didn't hear the people in Mississippi whining, people in Southwest Louisiana whining, the people who were whining was New Orleans. And I hate to say this, there's some of them who just shouldn't have whined. I don't think the federal government will ever be in a position where they can bring in 1,500 or 2,000 boats the next day. I don't think that's real world. Could they stage it better? Yeah. Could they have transportation out of there? Yeah. As far as putting people up, they put people up as far north, from what I understand, as Seattle. Houston took them in much to their detriment. They're complaining about it. I thought the stupidest thing was Blanco and Bush arguing over who was going to be in charge. And if it's true what they said, that she wanted 24 hours to think about it, then shame on her.

I think the biggest catalyst to get Bush off his ass [was] when Ray Nagin told him to get off his ass and get down there. You can like Nagin, and you can dislike him; it doesn't matter. But the truth be told— because, I mean— when you fly over in your big plane and make two circles over the city and see a big lake, things need to start happening. And yeah, they were moving already, and I think there's probably some misinformation that they didn't think there was that much help 'cause the news sensationalizes a lot of stuff. In this situation they kinda needed to because it was getting to be critical mass down there. I mean, they had hospitals with people in there for six days— dying on roof tops, respiring them by hand for four hours while doctors from another hospital could evacuate— stepping over the patients. There was some bad things going on down there. Federal government, under those circumstances, I don't know if they could've done any better. You're talking about response. That's staging the National Guard; that's setting up shelters; that's staging all the medical supplies, getting the fuel and the infrastructure.

I guess the answer to your question is... Baby, they could have brought cruise ships in sooner. I think they ought to figure out public transportation. I believe the government could have done that. I think that would have been maybe the most critical thing. You can't make people leave the city. I mean, you watch a video of a guy who decided to stay in a shrimp boat in the Empire Harbor with the strongest storm in fifty years coming on board. They gonna do what they gonna do.

Manning Billeaud: Interviewed by Shannon Billeaud

That's Got to be the River!

Erin Dowd
Interviewed by Nicole Pugh

Erin Dowd evacuated with family to Denham Springs, Louisiana, and listened as her brother, an air traffic controller, updated the family on the status of their parish.

On Friday, I was in meetings all day with the teachers, and my nerves were shot, so I picked up my puppy and went to the beach. I got a phone call letting me know that a hurricane was coming. Saturday morning, I secured my house in Bay St. Louis. I put everything high and closed everything down. My sister actually called me from New Mexico. She said, "Do you know there is a hurricane coming?" They were making it a much bigger deal on the national news. My sister in New Mexico and my brother in Texas were hearing more than we were hearing. I went home after packing up the Bay house and setting everything up high which was a waste of time. When I got back, I got a call from the [St. Bernard] school board. "Call the teachers and tell them there will be no school Monday, and we will let them know about Tuesday."

On Saturday, nobody was overly concerned about the storm. I think it had reached a Category 2 by that afternoon. I called the teachers. We made jokes about having an extra two-day vacation, thinking that nothing was going to happen. The principle of the school where I was stationed was out of town. She called to ask if I would go and pick her computer up off of the floor in her office, which I did. That was a waste of time as well. We secured the school and made sure that all the benches were pulled in case of high winds. We mopped up and made sure the alarm was set. Then I went home and put some stuff together and tried to decide what I was going to do. I called my mother who is 73 years old. I wanted to get her out. I didn't want to get stuck in traffic. I had done that twice before.

It took us from 4:00 p.m. in the afternoon until 10:00 p.m. to get to my dad's near Baton Rouge. By that time, it was a Category 3. I thought that if we got a couple of feet of water in the house, everything would be fine. We just put everything up high, but we didn't take things that we normally take— family pictures and things like that. My parents had just moved to St. Bernard when Betsy hit. My first three siblings have no pictures of themselves as babies. Now none of us do. That was something that we always pack up, but we decided it was up and high. They were things that were important to us, not monetarily, but things we'd remember and things that are connected to a holiday or something that we did. We'd always take those with us. My mom has fifty-some-odd Hummels. We'd always take that. We made some really poor decisions.

All of our pets came with us. There was no leaving any pet behind. My puppy is my baby. We went to my dad's house because my nephew and my nephew's wife were all going to my brother's house. So that there wouldn't be a lot of people at one place, it was just my mother, my sister, and myself at my dad's house in Denham Springs. Basically, we were thinking we were going to spend a few days there.

Of course, when it hit, it hit Denham Springs, too. We lost electricity. We lost everything. All we had was the radio to listen to. The news said that the levee was breached and that the water flooded the Ninth Ward and St. Bernard Parish, and that there was anywhere from ten to twenty feet of water in those areas. The levee breached on Betsy, but for Betsy, there was four feet of water tops. When they said this, my dad was saying, "Oh, there's no way. They are exaggerating." Of course, my aunt and my mom were like, "Why in the world would they be making this up?" He was just in total denial that anything like that could possibly happen.

Then my brother called. He is the most laid-back person in the world. A bomb could go off, and he'd be going, "What's that noise?" He's an air traffic controller, and he's got the perfect personality for it because nothing upsets him. I could hear it in his voice. They had gotten pictures at his work. He said, "I just kept looking at them. I was like, this must be upside down! That has got to be the river!" Then he saw the high school near my house. It's shaped like an "E," so it is really easy to pick it out from aerial views. He said, "I could only see the top of it, so I knew where mama's house was from there. At Maureen's house [her sister], you can't even see her subdivision. It's gone, Erin. There's just water. It's like looking at the river, but it's not. It's St. Bernard."

That's when I knew. He was seeing the government photos. He knew what the wave was like coming over on the 40 Harbor Canal. He said it looked like an ocean. I have since seen the pictures, and his description was correct. It looked like ocean waves. He said that he could not even believe what he was looking at.

Two of my sisters were calling because they were starting to see the images on TV, but they weren't seeing St. Bernard. St. Bernard was not shown for almost two weeks because no one had gotten in there. My brother, Jody, emailed them the pictures. Then the pictures started showing up on the Internet. In Denham Springs, we were without power for about a week. We wound up getting a generator. By Wednesday we could look at TV. We had to see the pictures. That was what we used the generator for. We didn't use it for the air conditioner or anything else. We all just wanted to see the TV. By the following week, the library in Denham Springs was open, and I could pull the pictures up on the Internet.

We went the first day they let us back in the parish and saw the destruction. My aunt put it in perspective. She said that it wasn't as upsetting as we thought it was going to be because you weren't looking at your house. The destruction was so massive. The houses didn't even look like it was your houses. You could kind of remove yourself from it. Of course, my mom has been in her house for close to forty years now, so she had forty years of us in that house.

It was destroyed. You couldn't pick out a whole lot of anything. It was pitch black. We saw more in the photos when we developed them than we could see in the house. All the rooms were jumbled around. Stuff definitely floated up through the attic and into other rooms. That was the only way we could see how stuff moved because some of the doors were shut. My mom's entire closet was emptied out— all of her clothing, all of our pictures, everything. The doors were ripped out. It was empty. I'm telling you, that closet had more stuff in it than could probably fit in a 1,200-square-foot house.

The Hummels— those were the most important to us— made it. We don't know how— somebody was coverin' 'em up. That was the only closet whose doors did not come off, and it was the only closet where the ceiling was still intact, and the shelves hadn't fallen. They were still sitting where we had left them, no worse for the wear. Not a one was broken.

My mom's china we had put up on the cabinets in the kitchen. All of that made it, too. Some of it was on the floor, but we figured it must have floated down in the water and settled easily. We were able to save the china and those Hummels. Also, one box of our Christmas ornaments, for some reason, had no water in it. The other ones were saturated. It just so happened that that entire box was Disney ornaments that I have been collecting for years. The big joke was: "No one's going to touch Disney. Walt has some power."

The furniture was in shreds. My grandmother's furniture that came over with her from Ireland was totally destroyed. She had pieces that had been in the family for years that actually furnished her house in the French Quarter. They were totally destroyed— just ripped apart. And this wasn't particleboard furniture. This was the real stuff, with marble tops and everything.

Getting into the houses was extremely difficult. In my house, you couldn't get into the back at all except for going through a window because everything in my kitchen fell. The refrigerator was balancing on one of my dining room chairs. We don't even know how, but it was. A lot of cars that were left were leaning up against trees, or they were on top of houses. A friend of mine's street was blocked by a two-story, 2,000-square-foot house, slab and all.

Pictures don't even convey the unbelievable power of nature. With some of the back houses by the canal, all that is left is the toilet. We have learned that if there is some kind of danger, hang on to the toilet. In my sister's house, the one that was afraid of flooding to begin with, she has about three feet of mud. Her breakfast bar was bolted to the ground. It was ripped up and smashed to pieces. My shed was four doors down in the backyard of one of the neighbors with the lawn mower and everything in it. My swing I had taken off and put inside my house. The A-frame was still outside. We found that on somebody's roof. My entire back fence and everything, all of that, it was gone. My house was split apart, so it was pretty destroyed.

They had a curfew, so you had to be out by six o'clock no matter what. When we did go back in [after Hurricane Rita], most of what I had left by the door had floated off. We were able to find it again, though.

St. Bernard is a small parish. There wasn't any school in the parish where I couldn't have walked in and known most of the faculty there, and they would have known me. I was based at Riley, but I worked throughout the parish on the curriculum. The faculty was a family. We are all separated now. We are all in different areas. We have been keeping in contact through email and text messaging. Occasionally we can get through to each other on the phone.

My mom, my oldest sister, and myself all lived within walking distance from each other. There were nineteen houses in my immediate family— brothers and sisters, aunts and uncles and cousins— that were destroyed. We are Irish and Catholic, so we do multiply. Most of my mom's family lost everything. My nephew— he's been married a year— they lost everything, their house and all the things that they got for their wedding gifts. He just opened a business, and it's under water. Most of us are teachers, so we all lost our jobs. We have three professions in our family: you're either a teacher, a lawyer, or an air traffic controller. The lawyers still have jobs, but all our schools were messed up, so a large portion of our family was out of work. Then my mom's younger sister's son was diagnosed with leukemia in the middle of all this. He is ten years old, so that kind of put things in perspective. He is going through his second round of treatment right now, which has been very difficult. They are in Dallas, and we can't help them. We can't be there for her. Right now, we have people in Houston, Dallas, Jackson, Mississippi, Jefferson, Denham Springs, Albuquerque, and Lafayette. We were a very close-knit family. Now we are spread out all over the place when we need each other the most.

It's one day at a time right now. It's not like we can go back to our neighborhoods and pick up the pieces. That's not going to happen. It's not just family. It's friends too. I know I can make new friends, but they are not the friends that I've grown up with and who have known everything that has gone on in my life.

Erin Dowd: Interviewed by Nicole Pugh

My mom and her sisters, they are older. My aunt is 69 and my mom is 73. They did a lot of things together. She is in Dallas now with her daughter. My neighbors are in New Mexico. I think I have talked to them more since the storm because they are lonely there. You knew everybody in your neighborhood [in St. Bernard]. It was still that kind of place. That's going to be hard to replace.

The people here have been wonderful. They have tried, and they have bent over backwards to be helpful. They even have offered to write my lesson plans! They have been very welcoming, but it is still not home.

I came from a place where I was higher up on the chain [professionally], and now I have gotten knocked back down. That doesn't bother me that much because no matter what I do, I'm going to do it. If anything, I think it has been awkward for Cahee and Boone [Gina Cahee and Tara Boone, principal and vice principal at Lindon Elementary]. They keep asking, "Are you okay about being back in the classroom?" That hasn't really been a problem for me. It is less stressful, actually. It is a less stressful school than where I was before. It has been probably the most settling thing for me. It's when you go home, and you try to call your friends, and you keep getting that stupid woman's voice telling you how the "PC phone you are trying to reach is no longer in service," and you know for darn well that it is. Those things have been hard. This has been the easiest thing to do every day— to come here to Lindon.

I think once they decide what they are going to do with St. Bernard, then we can finalize things. I know I can't go back right now. Breathing in that stuff, I've been getting strange sores all over my skin, which is highly unusual for me. My nephew's nose has bumps on it. That is not normal. When my sister came in from Albuquerque, the same thing happened to her. I think once they decide what they are going to do with St. Bernard, it would help.

Hubris and Two Gallons of Gas

Peter Syverson
In His Own Words

Peter Syverson tried to secure the windows in his home as his possessions blew past him in the storm. The nights in the abandoned city were quiet and beautiful, and then he heard the radio's announcement, "The levees have been breached, and people are dying."

We didn't leave until Tuesday afternoon, while the water was still rising and the city was just starting to eat itself. I somehow managed to convince two friends to stay with me and brave Katrina, and reluctantly they did, but after watching Wal-Mart get looted and hearing gunshots up on Napoleon and St. Charles [Avenues], it became quite clear that we needed to get the hell out of the city, and fast. Of course I had the only car that could make it out, and of course I had not filled it with gas because, of course, this hurricane they called Katrina wasn't going to hit my city, and it certainly wasn't going to kill a thousand people with floodwaters. Of course. So what I left with was a gallon or two of gas in my crappy Camry, two friends, and a cat with no tail. But that is the end of the story. That is the story of our evacuation.

Where it begins is mainly with my own hubris in thinking that Katrina was going to be an [Hurricane] Ivan, and nothing would happen, and so on Saturday with everyone leaving and people freaking out all around, I said I was going to stay. I'm a homeowner, so I figured I had every reason to stay. Basically a bunch of macho bull from a not-so-macho guy, but I said it and stuck by it. I called my family and lied. I said I was heading to Austin, and that I'd be fine and call them later, but of course I wasn't going anywhere.

A city of half a million gets real quiet when ninety percent of the people get the hell out of dodge, and all that is left is a bunch of scared, talkative people who half hope that the shit hits the fan and they get the chance to play hero. I know that's how I felt. But in the end none of us were heroes, just idiots. Not one of us, I am sure, imagined that something close to the worst could have happened.

I sat at Ms. Mae's on the corner of Magazine and Napoleon and drank High Life and talked to a shrimper who offered me his fridge full of frozen Gulf shrimp. I asked him why, and he told me that he was getting gone soon, that he had to go grab his mother in Slidell and that they were headed for Atlanta. He was dreading the drive.

The power went out at around 2:00 a.m. on Monday night. The whole house hummed and then just died. And it started to get really hot. Sticky. And the rain got worse. The wind came, and you could hear the slate tiles on the roof blow off and whistle through the air like throwing stars. Later, after the hurricane passed, we found a bunch of them sticking straight up out of the back garden, as if the earth had been stabbed to death.

The windows in an upstairs room blew open, and the bed flopped around inside like some sort of person coming down off heroin addiction was in there bouncing off the walls. When we opened the door to nail the windows shut, anything that wasn't heavy flew right out the windows. We had to shut the door behind us just so we wouldn't get knocked down. Gia grabbed a towel, and Jontie had a hammer, and I held the towel to the window as the two of them took turns with the hammer and nails. We were simply trying to keep the rain from getting in and doing more damage to the house. Gia cut a hole in the middle of the towel so that it would stay put. The house groaned, and the water rose outside. Trees fell over; branches snapped. It was like the end of the world. I've always thought Mother Nature had the upper hand. And in seeing all of this, her power is awesome.

I guess the adrenaline of being in such a powerful storm made time pass, and at around 10:00 a.m., we were able to go outside and watch as the water receded. It was still raining, but mostly drizzling. And we thought the worst was over. The power was out, so we cooked a huge feast of frozen foods that would go off otherwise, and we drank beer and Jontie's thirty-year-old Port. We sat on the front porch and listened to the dark and the silence of the city. It was beautiful. And it was scary. In the deep of the night you could hear screams and yelling, like a pack of wolves, except these were human voices, but they took on the sound of animals. We all thought the worst had passed until the next morning when Gia's radio picked up a signal that told us the water was coming. Get out while you can. The levees have been breached, and people are dying. Get out. The voice on the radio was deadly serious. I don't think I have ever been so scared.

We went to the Uptown Wal-Mart because we'd heard it was open for people to get supplies. But when we got there it was all chaos. Church ladies piling shopping carts of Oil of Olay and pots and pans into their big, old-lady Oldsmobiles. Mothers looting televisions with their children in tow holding video game systems and candy bars. Jontie took a picture of an NOPD officer loading his cop car with computer equipment and then going back inside for more. It made us all want to leave. It made us sick. Only a few people were taking food and water. One woman actually said that it was all free. I wonder if she still believes that.

In the end we got out just fine, though it was a bit nerve-wracking driving on empty from Gonzales to Baton Rouge. But it is not the storm nor the looting nor the destruction, but the radio announcer telling us to get out, that the water is rising, like he was the captain of a sinking ship. His voice was calm and deep but serious as anything I've ever heard. And I will never forget.

What the City Forgot

Lynn Morice and Robin Rodriguez
Interviewed by Zachary J. George

Robin Rodriguez and Lynn Morice worked as nurses at New Orleans hospitals during Hurricane Katrina and witnessed the human suffering and casualties caused by the lack of adequate staff, planning and supplies. More than three years later, neither Memorial Hospital nor Charity hospital had reopened.

Lynn Morice

Lynn Morice helped evacuate patients from Memorial hospital, where staff had to improvise while saving patients in a hospital that was without power or communication.

What day did you go in? Were you working a similar schedule to Robin, where she'd go in for four days straight and then have a week off?

I pretty much worked 36 hours a week. And I was on the schedule to work Monday, Tuesday, and Wednesday that week of the storm, so they were calling all employees that had to work within those few days to come in Sunday by noon. We had to pack all of our stuff and stay there starting Sunday.

So you brought all of your stuff with you?

Yeah, like just important papers, and my mom came with me. Just clothes, stuff like that.

Had you had to do that before?

Yeah, I did it once before, but I only spent the night there and went home the next morning.

What hurricane was that?

I don't remember the name. Ivan, maybe. I don't know.

How long have you worked at Memorial?

About 2 ½ years.

When you went in, how were people acting, or were people worried about this?

No. It seemed like everybody was in good spirits. People brought their families, their dogs. One girl brought— what was it? Two dogs and three cats. I mean, everybody just had their families and movies and food, and it seemed like a vacation almost.

How many total people would you say were in the hospital, patients and staff?

Well, I know our unit was pretty much full. I'm pretty sure we had thirteen, or almost thirteen, and we, combined with— I work in the SIC [Surgical Intensive Care]— we combined with the MIC [Medical Intensive Care], so we had... I don't know the exact number, but it's thirteen beds each unit, so maybe about twenty beds total.

What was it like inside on Monday morning when the hurricane actually hit? Did the electricity go out?

It flickered. Water. We moved to the eighth floor, which was the MRI, because the SIC building is separate from the hospital, and there was a walkway that they didn't want us to be jeopardized from getting across to work, so we moved all the patients over to the main building on the eighth floor. We had to move everybody over, all the patients over to the other building and get everybody in one unit, and then once we got there, glass starts breaking [in the unit]. Water started coming in the patients' rooms, and remember we had to... We were on a limited supply of linen. We were trying not to use that much linen, but we had to put towels and everything on the floor and then move the patients away from the windows because water was coming in from the rain.

At that time how were people reacting to that?

Everything was okay, but we were just scrambling to try and get the patients away from the room 'cause it was only a few rooms where that happened. It wasn't every room. We got that taken care of.

Tuesday morning is when we heard news that the levees were being blown up. There were rumors going around everywhere. I mean, we heard that the levees were being blown up on purpose and that they were trying to even out the city with Lake Pontchartrain. That's what we heard. And that it was going to be no more than, I guess, twelve or thirteen feet of water, even with the lake. And then, we… Everybody just kind of started crying and, you know…Some people started crying. Everybody was kind of waiting to see what was the truth because nobody really knew what was the truth and what wasn't 'cause we didn't really have phones. We had radios, but our power went out Tuesday night at midnight. I remember the power cut off. The transformers were in the basement.

What about people on machines or things like that?

Those all got out.

They got out beforehand?

Yeah. They all got out.

And where'd they take them?

They took them… Some went to Houston. We were calling different hospitals on Monday to get them out. I'm in ICU, so we got all the ICU patients out Monday and Tuesday. By Tuesday most of the

ICU, I mean, everybody that was on ventilators and stuff like that, were out.

You weren't accepting any more people trying to get in?

[No.] People were coming up by boat and stuff like that, trying to get in.

What was the water level around that area?

Well, Tuesday, throughout the day, you could see the water rising, and then by that night it was up to…What are the big, brown garbage bins like? I don't know, maybe, like, three feet or something.

Were there people that tried to leave, like nurses or doctors or anybody?

Some nurses did leave because they were worried that, like…One nurse left. Her shift was over, though. She'd only had to work Sunday, so Monday she ended up leaving because her husband— or Tuesday, I don't remember what day— her husband had ended up going back to check on their house and ended up getting stranded on a bridge, bridge I-10, somewhere, and he ended up saving a few people that were floating. Anyway, she was worried about him. She ended up picking him up on the side of the highway in Baton Rouge. He was hitchhiking. He had made it to Baton Rouge.

When did you actually get out of the hospital?

Thursday. Thursday afternoon.

What was it like from Tuesday to Thursday?

Mostly trying to get all the patients out. The Coast Guard landed at around 2:00 a.m. Tuesday, or Wednesday morning, and it was pitch black because the power had just went out, and everybody was pretty much sleeping, and the Coast Guard lands and says… I guess it

Lynn Morice & Robin Rodriguez: Interviewed by Zachary J. George   285

was [Coast Guard], I don't know, big orange suit, and he had a gun on him, and he's flashing around a flashlight, and he's saying that everybody needs to get one bag. We need to get out now. The water's rising. It's not getting any lower, and it's not going to get any better, and so everybody kind of... That started a kind of pandemonium because we were like, "What the hell?"

So, everybody's grabbing one bag, hurrying up, trying to get their things. Well, the Coast Guard guy never even talked to the administrator of the hospital, and well, there was no communication anyway, but our administrator went up and talked to him and was like, "Look, we're not getting anybody out of here right now. All you're doing is causing mass hysteria." 'Cause everybody was pushing and stuff like that, and it was pitch black.

The people were starting to freak out, and the Coast Guard left. It was... That was all. I can't believe they did that in the middle— at two o'clock in the morning. That was uncalled for.

We were just trying to get patients out, up until Thursday. I mean, it was just scrambling, and you never knew... There was helicopters landing, and you never knew when another one was going to come back, and they could only take one or two patients at a time, so we had patients waiting up on the ramp, up on the helicopter pad up until another helicopter came. And some patients were getting out by boat. So, we had a couple of different things we were doing.

Were you scared?

I was never scared for my life, but you started to get nervous. I guess around Wednesday, you started to get nervous about, okay, when are we getting out of here? You started getting nervous about when you were getting out. I was never scared for my life. We always had plenty of water, plenty of food.

What kind of food? Did you have MRE's?

We all brought food, and the hospital was still serving food, and we had juice packets, fruit, and we had watermelon. I mean, we all brought a lot of food, so we just pooled our food together.

How were you able to, in the dark and everything, take care of the patients?

People had flashlights. People had flashlights, and basically we just worked by that. Fanned the patients with cardboard. We tore apart cardboard boxes and fanned them. We had portable suction devices that were eventually dropped down to us on, I believe, around Tuesday.

What's that? Like to help breathe?

No, like, whenever anybody has a trach [tracheostomy tube] or something like that if you want to go down and suction them. And one person, I believe, died because they couldn't suction, and that just choked them 'cause there was no suction device, and eventually suction devices got dropped off to us.

You don't have to talk about this, of course, if you don't want to, but what about the patients who were supposedly killed or injected. Do you know anything about that?

Thank God, I wasn't anywhere around. I was on the helicopter pad.

When did that actually happen?

They're saying that happened Thursday when we were all getting out, but I was on the helicopter pad, so I wasn't around anything, thank God.

Do you know the ladies?

I worked with them, yeah. I worked with the two nurses... They were surgical ICU nurses. They were excellent nurses.

What do you think about all that?

Well, if it was my grandmother sitting there suffering, breathing three times a minute, I'd want her to be comfortable, you know. I don't think that anyone would want their family...I mean, you don't treat dogs like that, you know, much less treat humans like that.

It seems they did the best they could in the conditions they were in.

Exactly.

How did you finally get out? Was it Coast Guard came again?

No. We had Louisiana State Troopers, and then we had the Texas Wildlife and Fisheries.

Boats?

Boats. And a lot of volunteers were using their boats. We got out by boat.

You're talking about people that lived in the area?

Yeah. We got out by boat, my mom and I, with a bunch of the nurses, and we ended up getting dropped off at Prytania and... Was it Napoleon? Prytania and Napoleon, on that intersection.

They ended up boating us out, and we boated down some of the way, and then we had to get out before we got to St. Charles and walk to that intersection because that's where the buses were picking people up. We were intermixed with community.

Where is Memorial?

On the corner of Napoleon and Claiborne [Avenues].

What was that boat ride like? Were there people out? Was it during the day or at night?

It was during the day. It was afternoon. The boat ride was fine. It was… And then it started raining. Not raining heavily, but it started sprinkling on us. So we had a tarp over us, and then we had garbage bags on us as ponchos, but what sucked is they ended up dropping us off at I-10 and Causeway.

Oh, so you were just with—

With everybody. It was disgusting. I mean, it was, like, dirty diapers, needles everywhere. I mean, people that looked like… Had bandages with blood on them, I mean, I don't even know who was getting dropped off there, but everybody was there.

How many people were in that area would you say?

There were thousands. But they had it organized pretty nice, like right when you got dropped off there was a Salvation Army truck handing out food and stuff, and you would walk up, but the thing was that everybody was waiting for buses, and when the buses would pull up— they set up barricades— and when the bus would pull up everybody was pushing and fighting to get on the bus, and it was really sad 'cause they had three old people that were sitting in lawn chairs underneath the overpass, just away from everybody else, and they must have been in their seventies or eighties, just waiting, waiting. It was sad.

But we ended up getting out [from] I-10 and Causeway only because a nurse of ours was in the military, and she went up to the State Troopers, and she's like, "Look, we've done our time. You need to get us out of here." So they ended up moving us over on the other side of the barricades, and we kinda stood behind the ambulances.

What were the barricades for? Separating police and military from the people?

Yeah, because if something would've gone down, they wouldn't have been able to control that crowd. It's just ridiculous. So, they moved us, and they kinda hid us. A charter bus pulled up, and as the charter bus pulled up for us a whole bunch of buses started pulling up for them. So we got on, and we left.

Where did the charter bus take you to?

Baton Rouge. A nurse that worked with us, her brother owns the GI clinic, so we all went there, and they had McDonald's for us, and coffee. We washed our hands. I mean, we were filthy. We washed our hands.

How do you think this has changed you, or has it changed you? Do you look at your job differently? ·

I mean, not really. I would do it again. I think... I'm surprised at how poorly organized everything was, but it goes to show you how much... We rely too much on computers and all that nonsense. Like, there's no form of communication. Everything's done through that now, and when all that goes out... People are too dependent on that [communication systems]. They need to devise some kind of system where there's a method of getting people out or something 'cause it was mass confusion. Nobody knew what was going on. But has it changed? I feel more, I guess, more qualified now to take care in situations. I enjoyed the challenge of it. I enjoyed getting people up in the helicopter, and I enjoyed getting people out, and triage, and all that stuff. It was pretty cool, but....

It was a challenge.

Yeah.

How is your job different now? Memorial's back?

No, Memorial's not open yet.

Where are you working now?

I'm working agency now. I'm working at Tulane, East Jeff, and Meadowcrest hospital.

Is your job different?

No, I'm still doing ICU. What's different is I was doing surgical ICU. We don't have any of the means, like the heart surgeries and stuff in town anymore. We don't have our main— what we used to take care of, there's less than that. You see people coming in with pneumonia and heart disease, stuff like that, but no big heart surgeries or belly surgery, stuff like that. They're going to different hospitals, or they're going out of state now. The acuity is down.

What if another hurricane hit?

I think we'd be in trouble. I think we'd be in big trouble. Unless they get something better organized, but they need to focus on getting patients out a lot quicker than what... They didn't start getting them out 'til Monday. I knew it was gonna come... It was coming. I mean, everybody had said, you know, if a hurricane comes to the city, it's gonna be bad.

What the City Forgot (Continued)

Robin Rodriguez

Robin Rodriguez worked at Charity Hospital in downtown New Orleans. Unlike Memorial Hospital, Charity Hospital did not evacuate its intensive care patients before the storm. Charity Hospital was once a safe haven for the city's poor but now treats patients in an abandoned department store.

When [the hospital] told you that you needed to come in on the 28th, what were you thinking?

I was thinking that I was going to go for four days, and then I was gonna have a week off after.

You had no idea about the storm or you had...

I didn't think it was that bad because I was on the activation prior to this one, and we stayed for a couple days, and then we went home, and nothing happened.

For Hurricane Ivan?

Not Ivan; it was... I can't remember. I think it was like three years ago.

What about the others in your group, the people you work with?

Oh, they thought the exact same thing: we were gonna go home. We were gonna work for four days, you know. We get paid for 24/7. And then have a week off after. The recovery team's gonna come and work, and that's it.

When did that start to change?

That started to change when I saw the water rising, and it wasn't going down.

So that was after the levees had broken?

Yeah.

So once the hurricane hit, was the hospital still running with relative normalcy?

Yeah. We lost electricity, and after that we just waited to see what was going to happen. We thought everything was fine. We looked outside. We saw a lot of wind damage, but no water. I think Tuesday's when the levees broke. Was it Tuesday?

So, we waited out Monday. Everything was fine. We were just assessing the damage outside, and then we heard that the levees were breaking and that Lakeview was flooding. Then Chalmette. And that's when we started getting water. It was Tuesday afternoon. The water started rising.

We measured it by a fire hydrant that was right in front of the emergency room, and we could see how high it was getting.

It was getting higher and higher.

And higher and higher, and finally, it finally peaked at a certain area, but it would get high tide and low tide like it would at night... It would go up and down.

It would be moving?

Yeah.

Wow. Then how were people reacting?

Everybody starts freaking...

The electricity's out?

Yeah. Right. We're totally out.

Did they have generators to run?

We had generators.

What about people who were attached to equipment?

Well, that was the problem. We had certain people who were on vents. We had generators for the certain units— our ICU units. And we were working off of that until we could get our patients out. Some of them had to be manually bagged, by hand, for them to breathe.

Were they able to get patients out of there?

Yeah. We were carrying patients on spine boards up and down the flight of stairs. And then we started using cafeteria tables. We would unscrew the legs and use those as stretchers to carry patients downstairs.

You were doing this?

No, the guys were.

Once they got downstairs, where did they go from there?

Then we put them on a truck. It was Air National Guard that was helping us out at first, and we were using their big trucks, their armored trucks that was carrying the patients.

How many patients would be in one truck?

Four critical patients. And each patient had a doctor with them because you had to manually bag them.

Where did they take them?

We would go to Tulane teleport. Blackhawks would come down. But then there was times where Tulane's patients— not Tulane's patients— actually Tulane's employees were getting on the planes before these patients, before these critically ill patients were getting on the planes.

Weren't there people saying, "This is wrong," and how were they responding?

They just, you know… What is it, "feast or famine?" Everybody was looking out for themselves.

Everybody was scared. Wednesday when we saw the water rising, that's when everybody started panicking.

Did doctors or nurses take off?

No. Not our nurses. Not our ER doctors. We stayed together as a group. We worked as a group. But there was some people that were not taking it well and started freaking out and having anxiety attacks. Some of them had to be sedated. Which, some were nurses.

Can you give me an example?

There's a certain nurse that really freaked out, and we had to sedate her with some atavan.

What's that? Like a tranquilizer?

Yeah. It calms people down. And eventually we had to get her out of there, so she evacuated before any of us did.

We had a good day crew. I was on the day crew which was from 7:00 a.m. to 7:00 p.m. And then our night crew came on and took over.

What about food and water for everybody?

Food and water— generally during the day we had canned foods like raviolis. At first it was tuna fish, you know, and we had water. We had plenty of water. We had a large supply of water. And at night the nurses and the doctors had MRE's, and they were feeding the patients with that.

Were there any fights or anything like that? Big disruptions?

Not with the employees. Amongst ourselves we never argued. I mean, people were crying, upset, scared, and we were able to call our family members because we had phone lines.

So you knew your mother was all right?

Yeah. We got in touch with people.

Where did she go?

She went down to Houma. She stayed with my aunt in Houma.

Were there other people there that didn't know about certain family members?

No. Everybody eventually got in touch with their family members.

What about the patients?

A lot of these patients were either homeless or didn't have very many family members. A lot of people were dumped on us.

Who brought them there?

A lot of nursing homes brought patients. Some patients that were found out in the water. EMS brought them in, or they were boated in.

We were still accepting some patients, but eventually we had to turn down people because it was getting... We just didn't have enough room, enough space, to hold these patients that were walking up to the ramp.

What happened to them?

We'd just tell them to turn away and go to the Superdome.

Did you know if they had services at the Superdome?

Well, I heard they had some medical services, but it was quite dangerous there.

Have you left for hurricanes before? Have you evacuated before?

I did evacuate [before], but it was while I was not working in the hospital.

How long had you been working there?

I've actually been working a total of five years at Charity.

It's a little different now then before the storm?

Hell of a lot different. We're working out of a department store called Lord and Taylor, and it's like a makeshift hospital like a M.A.S.H. unit. We're working in cubicles now. We were in tents. Literally. Tents.

When it was over by the Convention Center?

[At the] Convention Center it was in tents, and as well as at Lord and Taylor, we were still in tents. They brought the tents to Lord and Taylor.

This is almost a year after the storm.

Yes. It is.

As an employee, what are you hearing about?

They're supposed to be renovating University Hospital and getting that all cleaned up, but we're supposed to be there in November [2006]. But from what I'm hearing, I doubt November. Possibly December, but I doubt December.

Were you scared at any time?

Yeah, I was scared. At one point I went on a caravan with some patients to go drop them off on the ramp with some of the doctors, and I just walked out on the ramp to get some fresh air, and they're like, "Can you help bring some patients?" And I'm like, "Sure, I'll ride along." 'Cause they wanted, you know, certain employees going with every patient to make sure they were okay. So I decide to go, and on our way back, we heard some gunshots, which we can't tell if they were shooting at us....

Was it dark or light at this time?

It was during the day, and we heard gunshots, but during that time you don't know if they were shooting at you or if they were shooting in a different area. You could just hear the echoing. So, I got kinda scared because by this time they had some shooters shooting at the helicopters and the people on the ramp at Tulane.

Why, do you think?

Because there was... I don't know. We were trying to help people, and they were trying to shoot at us. They were snipers.

What else did you see while you were on the streets moving the patients?

There were people walking around on Tulane Avenue. There were people just on the median, just sitting there. I don't know what they were gonna do. I was just amazed at what I saw. It was random... Like, you know, a block... We would pass by, and there's just people sitting on the median on garbage bags. They're holding a garbage bag, and they're just sitting there.

It was amazing. And then we got on a ramp. We transported all these patients out, and they were bringing them in pick-up trucks to the top where the heliport was. And then that's where the helicopters would pick them up and bring them off to destinations of unknown... I don't know. Some of them went to Lafayette; some of them went to Houston. Some of them went to the airport, and then from the airport they went to places.

Do you know of any casualties or anything like that?

I know that we lost— I don't know the exact numbers— but I know that we lost approximately about five patients or less than that. I'm not quite sure.

Was it clean [inside Charity]?

For some reason they brought Port-a-lets in there. We had Port-a-lets to use the bathroom. Course we had no plumbing, no water— no running water.

So nobody was showering?

I showered the first... I showered the first two nights.

How?

We had power, plus we had a shower, and we were still using the water until it was finally shut off. When it started flooding, and the water was high, that's when we decided not to use the water anymore. And we would use the staff bathrooms on the 15th floor. We'd go up there.

How'd you finally get out?

Well, the ER, we were the last people to leave besides some family. There was probably about approximately seventy people left....

How many were there in the beginning?

I'm not quite sure. I think maybe 300 people. Possibly. That's including faculty: staff, employees, family members. Approximately 300 people. Maybe more; I'm not sure. But, we were told— the day shift was working, and they were told that the ER people, all the ER nurses were getting out today, which was Friday. It was approximately maybe 12:00 p.m. So, our night shift were sleeping, so we had to go wake up the night shift people and tell them. They told us that we could bring one bag only. One knapsack, one little suitcase, whatever you can, and that's it. And they all put us on an 18-wheeler.

How many of you?

I don't know how many nurses. It was probably, maybe fifteen. Fifteen nurses, and we had patients on those 18-wheelers, as well, with us. And we we were brought to the airport.

What happened once you got to the airport?

Once we got to the airport there was mass confusion there, of course. We sat around for a little while, didn't know what we were supposed to do, then finally we talked to people that were over FEMA, not FEMA....

Were you inside or outside?

We were standing outside. People were just standing around. Bunch of buses coming through. People getting dropped off; these were charter buses. People coming on charter buses.

From where?

From just all over the place. Just wherever.

Like different states? Different cities?

Well, no. There were people coming in to help out, but there were evacuees they picked up, and they brought some of them to the airport, but mostly it was all hospital people. Hospital people from all different facilities. That's where the staging area was for all the Baptist... All the Meadowcrest people brought their staff, their sick people there.

The airport turned into a hospital.

A holding stage for people to get flown out.

Obviously, you're working out of a department store, but are the standards as good?

No. We have very sick people that come in, and we have... We don't have the capacity to take care of the sick people that we have now, so we just transfer a lot of patients out.

To where?

Different facilities.

Is there a problem now? Is there not enough room in the city for the amount of people who are sick?

No. There's not. There's so many sick people and not enough beds. There's people that are staying in the ER for days until they get a bed open up on the floor.

Would that happen before the storm?

Well, there was a lot of patients that stayed in the ER waiting for beds, but now it's just... The bed's have cut back. I mean, there's only, what? Maybe six major hospitals that are open, compared to God knows. They had maybe fifteen hospitals or less than that; I don't know. We used to have about 700 beds. Now there's probably 300 beds available in New Orleans open for sick patients.

How has your job changed?

Well, it's tiring, you know. You work, it's like you do all this work for these patients, and sometimes it's just not enough. I can only do as much as I'm capable of doing with the....

Resources?

Capacity. Resources that I have now, which is minimal. It's just tough.

Are the patients different?

It's my patients. It's not that they're worse. It's about the same that we were getting before; it's just that we don't have a hospital to take care of them. We still have our chest painers; we still have our diabetes patients coming in with high blood sugar, low blood sugar. We have our traumas that come in. So it's similar to what we were getting prior to Katrina, but the facility we work at has hardly any resources for us to take care of these patients.

There's a lot of other facilities that I hear about from other... I have a lot of girlfriends that are nurses, and they tell me their stories and... Granted it was a bad time, but I feel that we had enough— we had water. We had food. We had generators working. Granted it was a poor environment at the time, but I don't think it was any worse than any other place.

How is the city different?

Things have changed dramatically. You can't even go to Taco Bell anymore at twelve o'clock at night. Just the little things that you took for granted. Now, it's hard to go to the mall. We don't even have a mall on the West Bank anymore. We don't have a mall to go to. You have to drive across the river, which is no big deal, but still, it's a problem for people who don't have automobiles. They rely on the bus system. And there's still a lot of people here that don't have insurance, you know, the people that work for the school system, a lot of teachers that were laid off. 'Cause I take care of those type of people, too, not just the poor.

Is there anything that you would have done differently?

No. If I had to do it again, I would.

So you'll stay again if that happens?

I don't know about this time. We don't even have a facility. I don't even have a hospital to go to. So, no. If a hurricane comes this year, I'm not staying. I don't think we're liable this year. No hospitals.

Where are we gonna stay? At the Lord and Taylor— at the old department store that's leaking now on the 3rd floor?

I don't have the same job that I had before, [the job] that I loved. I'm still working for the same people, but it's not the same every day. I'm not working at a hospital. I'm working at a department store. I can't give the same care. I can give as much as I can, but I'm not doing what I was doing a year ago.

What were you doing a year ago?

We were a Level One trauma center. We dealt with multiple gunshots, motor vehicle accidents; we took just about eight parishes. In all eight parishes we took transfers that they weren't capable of handling… We had a wonderful ER that took care of a large part of our population, and now we can't even do that. We can't help those people. We had a large psych unit, which we don't have anymore, so all the people, all the mentally ill patients are out running around in the streets, and we don't even know about [them]. You can go to McDonald's, and probably there's someone there that you don't even realize literally has a mental problem. They're not getting help.

Scary, Scary, Scary

Steve Williams, Sr.
Interviewed by Mary Sparacello

Steve Williams, Sr. and his family rode out Hurricane Katrina in a Motel 6 in the New Orleans suburb of Kenner.

We left Sunday. The wife and the son in that truck. I had filled up with gas. It's something I always do before storms. We went to the Motel 6 at Loyola and Interstate 10 [in Kenner]. Just as soon as it passed over we had to take off because the side of the building... The windows started blowing out, and the water started rising around the hotel. It had you as nervous as a cat on a hot stove. The lights had went out. The building was shaking. Water was coming in, so it was very scary. We were on the 4th floor. We was in a room until the windows started blowing out. Then we went into the hallway. They didn't blow out in the room I was in, but on the room next door they did. The insulation started coming out of the walls, so it was time to cut out. Even the emergency generator wouldn't run in there. They had a generator there, but it didn't even run the emergency exit lights. Waters was coming in through the windows and walls as well. The hallway was crowded. They came out of their rooms. A lot of them came all the way from the bottom floor. The people who were on the bottom floors had their rooms destroyed.

We went by my niece's house in Baton Rouge. It was just about a little bit better than walking because of the traffic. It took three hours to get there; normally it would take you one hour. It was a good month we stayed there. We weren't able to get back here until the 7th of October for my daughter when she started teaching school. It was a couple weeks before we could come back. People came from St. Charles Parish and down the levee and snuck in to get a chance to see their house. Our only source of information was they had a guy who lived up there, and he stayed through the storm, and he was the only one who was giving us information because our cell phones wasn't working, and the phones in the house weren't working. He actually had come from downtown and came out here because his house was totaled, in the Ninth Ward on Piety [Street].

We had saw it, my house, one time before. They said come back at 6:00 [a.m.], and you had to leave by 5:00 [p.m.], but if you waited until 5:00 it would probably be 10:00 [p.m.] when you got to Baton Rouge. I can tell you this… It is hard to describe how you feel about it when you see everything. Furniture falling apart, beds and everything in mud. See how these bricks should be red, but they have that film on them? Then we came back and got in touch with insurance company.

Next time? I think I'd leave instead of going to a hotel here. I'd go straight out of town in the first place. But all the other times they had storms, I went to a hotel, and I would go back after. I bought a new generator, and it went under. That's what I had planned on doing: using the generator and come back and start cleaning up. Look at all my wife's plants. Whatever it was, I guess that saltwater, it just killed them all. I'm staying with my daughter over on Clay Street [in Kenner]. They didn't get any water on her street in the houses. I come home during the day to clean. That's what I've been doing. Cleaning up, tearing out the old sheetrock. I had to dispose of all the furniture.

The Lucky Thirteen

Margie Stoughton-Pyburn
Interviewed by Missy Bowen

Forty-three-year-old Margie Stoughton-Pyburn and her husband Tom chose not to evacuate and remained in their home with their eleven-year-old son and seven-year-old dog Caruso.

We survived hurricane Katrina. Our SUV was parked in our driveway while we waited for the twelve-inch floodwaters to recede. New Orleans residents and visitors would know our street because of the landmarks. We are on Pritchard Place, across from the Notre Dame Seminary on Carrollton Avenue, near the stone lions. We survived Hurricane Katrina and had plans of driving out of the city. Then, the 17th Street Canal breached, and the flood waters rose four feet within a day. We were trapped in four and a half to five feet of water in our driveway. Some places were over our heads in the low spots of the street.

Our home is a raised basement style of architecture with a cypress foundation that was built in 1917. It has survived all the hurricanes of the twentieth century, including Katrina. When asked why we chose to stay, we can barely remember. Maybe because the news media sensationalizes so many things, maybe because evacuating becomes more of an inconvenience than a convenience, maybe because we have a dog, a snake, fish, and were babysitting three cats, maybe because we wanted to protect our belongings, maybe because our house is built like a tank, and we felt safe. All of it is moot.

The storm was humbling. We stood on our back porch and watched forty-foot trees snap like toothpicks. We felt our house shake, and saw the toilet-bowl water shift. We heard in the darkness the low rumble of the tornado winds, high above our roof. After the storm, we had hopes of driving out, until the flood waters rose, trapping us in the relative comfort of our home.

Within a few days we came to the realization that although we could survive for a week or two on our provisions, the deteriorating security and sanitary situation meant that we would have to evacuate. The city was lawless, and the water that surrounded our neighborhood was becoming more contaminated by the hour.

One of our neighbors was a Vietnam vet, and he made us realize that we were safe in what we knew. It was the unknown that was dangerous. Several of our other neighbors stayed. We conversed over flooded yards, built rafts, gathered supplies from other homes, fed neighbors' pets, and vowed to stick together. We had ample water and food, running gas, and flushing toilets. Our cell phones weren't working, but we could receive calls on the land line. In actuality, it was more comfortable than many fishing camps.

We tried to enjoy the millions of stars that were visible at night and the chorus of frogs. By carefully limiting how often we opened the refrigerator and freezer, we were able to enjoy fresh food for the first two days. We had to eat things as they thawed, so of course we consumed the best things we had first. We ate Omaha steaks, wild mushroom rice, drank French champagne. At night we played cards by flashlight. We were safe and relatively comfortable until we left the security of our home.

Our only connection to the outside world was the local AM radio station, WWL. We were glued to it, listening carefully for bits of information regarding flooding, looting, conditions in the Superdome, etc. Our family consists of my husband, 46, our 11-year old son, and me, 43. We also have a big dog, a snake, and fish. We felt the city was deteriorating and lawless, and soon we would be in peril. Because we were surrounded by so much water, we had been relatively safe. We knew our home was more comfortable than the Superdome, and that the "system" wouldn't tolerate a dog. We told our son that we would do whatever we could to save his dog, although in the back of our minds, we knew we were not going to jeopardize a human life because of a dog.

Our dear friends that had evacuated called and were willing to pick us up in La Place. It was the closest to New Orleans that they could get. They would transport us to Baton Rouge, and our relatives would pick us up and drive us to Memphis. Then we would rent a car and drive to relatives in Orlando. We had a plan. If we were totally self-sufficient, we could get out and save our dog, Caruso.

Our neighbors, two doors down, and their nine-year-old daughter wanted to depart with us. We decided to stick together and make it work. We built four rafts out of air mattresses, blanketed them and laid the sturdy pieces of plywood, with which we had boarded up our homes, on them. On the third day after the storm, two families of three set out with six mountain bikes, dry clothes, water, food, sunscreen, bug spray, tweezers, clippers, Swiss army knife, Band-Aids, Neosporin, chapstick, pliers, four ropes, flashlight, monocular, two radios, batteries, Vaseline, a map, a sharpie, ace bandage, sunglasses, personal documents, one cat, and one dog.

We thought defensively, trying to anticipate every angle of the unknown. We stashed our credit cards in a deck of cards. We wrapped cash around gift cards. We hid our check books under my shirt, flat against my shoulder blades and covered by my long hair. We mingled our wedding rings on a key chain with a handful of keys. No diamonds, no glitter, nothing to attract attention to our possessions. Everything was triple bagged to prepare for our wet journey. We decided not to carry a gun. If we were to be accosted by thieves, we decided it was safer to simply give them our belongings rather than engage in a gun battle where we would definitely have the disadvantage. We opted to travel together with a baseball bat and our eighty-pound dog for protection.

We started our journey on Thursday, the third day after Katrina ravaged our city. We waded through three miles of flooded streets chest-high to knee-high in water, down Carrollton Avenue from the Notre Dame Seminary to the River bend area by the Camellia Grill. The water was disgusting with visible chemicals pooling on the surface, dead worms and rats, and all kinds of debris.

We wore old soccer socks to protect our shins from underwater debris. The three-mile trek took three hours. We banded with other families as we trudged to the levee at the Riverbend area, hauling belongings, pets, elderly, and children on rafts. The Notre Dame Seminary is on Carrollton Avenue, a natural ridge, and higher ground. It was also under water, about thigh-high in the street.

We encountered many lost and desperate people but luckily no thieves. There were many people with no supplies, confused about what to do, not knowing where to go, standing in the middle of the water on Carrollton, resting on dry land, hanging out of buildings. They seemed to be wandering aimlessly. Utter confusion, lack of direction and self-preservation wore heavily upon their faces.

We passed our son's new middle school, Lusher. That is where the water ended. We soaped our bodies with antibacterial soap, changed into dry clothes, and disposed of any excess weight. We gave some of our water to a diabetic and some to an elderly woman. Our neighbors' cat escaped after biting his owner.

The transition from rafting to biking was dangerous. We felt vulnerable because we had water, and food, and means to get out. We quickly changed and walked two blocks to the levee. Each person had a backpack and a small pack on the handlebars of their mountain bike for the next leg of the journey. We tied the ropes together to make a long leash for the dog. We were clean, dry, and relatively safe from desperate people. We had parted from the wonderful families that we had met along the three-mile trek down Carrollton, promising to send them help, since they were not as mobile. We were headed toward our friends in La Place. Our dog was with us. The breeze on the levee was refreshing. We felt good as we trotted thirteen miles of the thirty-five mile journey.

We fell short of our goal by about twenty miles. Our eleven-year old son is very athletic, but the neighbors' daughter was having a hard time, as was our seven-year-old dog.

It was beginning to rain, and it was getting later in the day. We toyed with the idea of spending the night in the Dansk/Scandanavian furniture store on the corner of Airline Highway and Clearview Parkway. One side of the building had been ripped off by the storm and the plush furniture inside looked mighty inviting. We knew, however, that it was too dangerous. Because of the situation and the hour we had to turn ourselves in to the system. We were still relatively self-sufficient. We had food for all of us and water, supplies. We backtracked five miles more and turned ourselves in to the FEMA evacuation site at the Causeway Blvd. overpass at I-10.

Our first feelings upon arrival were those of relief. There were lots of National Guard and State Troopers around, so we felt safe and out of harm's way. We were excited at the thought of getting out and uniting with our friends and relatives. It didn't matter that we threw away six mountain bikes without a second thought. Material things other than food and water became unimportant. We were concerned about the practicality of having our dog, but hadn't given up hope as of yet. We reunited with our new friends from the Carrollton

Avenue water trek, as we waited for the buses to arrive at the FEMA camp.

We began sharing our stories, and our web of connection became visible. Unbeknownst to us at the time of the water trek, our sons attended the same school. They actually had had a flag football practice together. A woman amongst us was a karate sparring partner of one of the sons about three years back, as well as an acquaintance of my husband's co-worker. We began to unravel our connections, which is typical of New Orleans: a large town with a small town feel. A year ago we had been at the same crawfish boil. We remembered prior conversations. It was curious that we would be brought together under these conditions and find that our paths had crossed before.

Our second and lasting impression of the FEMA camp was disgust. The buses trickled in. There were 1,200 to 2,500 people at the site at any given time, with only eight Portolets. Many of the people had come from the Superdome. We were put in a grassy field under an overpass by I-10. It continued to rain, which got things damp and cold. We were standing in muddy water. With time, the wet ground became more and more saturated with urine and human waste. We were wet. We were cold. We were among the lucky few that were able to secure cots, which allowed us to rest off of the ground, dry our drenched feet, and give the dog some much needed sleep.

Five to seven buses would show up every six or seven hours. Only 250 to 300 people could get on the buses. In the meantime, there was a constant arrival of rescue helicopters dropping off refugees, which would again swell the ranks. The crowd was ready to riot because the conditions were so deplorable. If you were old, if you were young, if you were ill of health, your chances of survival were slim. Our son witnessed things that he did not know existed. We passed people we felt certain were going to die. We saw people collapse. We heard stories of mothers watching their children who could not swim being swept away, of daughters watching their mothers die, of family members being separated, great loss, and horrible behavior.

We tried to surround ourselves with people who had the same values. We didn't care if they were white, black, Mexican, or Vietnamese. It didn't matter what they looked or smelled like. We only cared if they were the type of person who would offer their cot to a stranger in need, if they chose not to use foul language, if they were caring, considerate, compassionate, and most importantly, calm. We tried to keep the spirits of our children high. We saw fighting over cots, people in the crowd carrying guns, people smoking cigarettes laced with drugs, verbal and physical abuse toward toddlers, and other deplorable behavior. We felt animosity from some of the crowd toward our dog. Our neighbor went to get medical help because he was bitten by his cat. He was only able to receive ice for the swelling, which by now had his hand looking like Popeye's. People were dying around us, and the medics had to triage the more critical cases.

Amongst this madness we saw the heroes of mankind: heroes who maintained their composure, who shared their food and water, who genuinely cared for another in need, who spoke to each other respectfully with kindness, and comforted those in moments of despair. Strangers came up to me when I cried and put their arm around me. We helped a woman weighted down by sleeping babies quench her thirst and hunger. We brought supplies to the elderly who couldn't reach the trucks. We had no hope of getting out.

The clock was ticking regarding our dog. How do we to explain to our child what may become of his dog? We smelled of urine and feces. It was degrading. The stench was nauseating. We were preparing ourselves for the worst— leaving the dog behind. He had provided us with safety and warmth, yet he most likely would not be permitted to get on the bus.

Tom talked to police or military security people, and they said that it was possible that the dog would be allowed, but not likely because of his size. Tom asked if they would please shoot the dog because they couldn't stand to see it suffer, but the police assured him they would get the animal to the SPCA. Tom said that that broke his heart, but he could see no other choice.

Would the bus ever come? We hadn't seen one in almost twelve hours.

How did we get out? We relied on the kindness of family, friends, and strangers. Our neighbor had been trying for days to get a message to her brother who might possibly be able to help. Eventually the message was relayed, and after more than 22 hours at the FEMA camp, with no end in sight, her brother found us and ended our ordeal. As an employee of Entergy, he had access to a service truck and was able to transport us to a feeding station.

We were treated to cold water and fresh food. The Entergy workers and volunteers embraced us with tears, even though they were strangers and we smelled of waste. We spoke to many workers, who hadn't had an opportunity to return to their flooded homes and gave them information about what we had seen.

Entergy then took us to a Ramada Inn. We were able to take turns going upstairs in small groups to a room to shower. While waiting our turns on the sidewalk, we were just glad to be dry and safe. The concrete in the shade was luxurious compared to the conditions that we had been in.

Entergy then transported us to Dougie V's, a restaurant in Luling, Louisiana, just upriver from New Orleans. Volunteers there were cooking three meals a day to feed approximately 500 Entergy workers. We were treated with that loving southern hospitality that we adore about New Orleans. Our neighbors' daughter was having her birthday Saturday, and it was Friday night. We were sat in a separate room with our group. The staff sang "Happy Birthday" to Jena, who was soon to be ten years old. The volunteers presented Jena with candled cupcakes and gifts of brand new tennis shoes and a full box of rice crispy treats.

Our neighbor's brother then drove us to Baton Rouge where our loved ones were waiting to drive us to the next part of our journey [to Memphis]. Our group consisted of seven adults, an 85-year-old Creole couple, four children, one cat, one rabbit, and one dog. We hugged and said our goodbyes. The connection we feel is strong. We call ourselves the "Lucky Thirteen."

One of my brothers asked me about all of the things that we had lost. I said, "If I focus on that my glass will overflow with tears. Material things are unimportant. We are good. We are alive. Many are not." It saddens me to hear that people are placing blame and implying that this is a racist issue. I was there. This was a tragedy. I have no energy for blame. I have barely enough energy to pick up the pieces of my life and rebuild a home for my son. I am thankful every day that we were three of the "Lucky Thirteen."

Life in a Van

Benny and Millie Reine
Interviewed by Mary Sparacello

Kenner resident Benny Reine evacuated with his wife Millie to a hotel. When they were unable to return to their home, they went to various shelters before returning to Kenner to live in their van, which they moved between various parking lots that were near bathrooms.

Benny Reine

When we left, we went through Texas. We stopped at Prairieville at a hotel. It was what you call a no-tell motel. It was pretty torn up, but that's all you could get at that time. Nothing worked at that hotel. The curtains were busted. The air conditioner was bad. The electricity went out, so we headed back to New Orleans. We got stopped about two miles away from the bridge. The state police turned us back. The police said the levee broke, and this is going to be flooded. They brought us to Home Depot. We stayed there that night in the parking lot. They came by asking for people with special needs. We went to the hospital. Then we got into Lamar-Dixon Expo Center. We stayed a little over two weeks there. They had about 2,000 people there. They had so many people. A lady was having a baby right here. They couldn't get a stretcher to her, so she had the baby before they could get her a stretcher. A lady was on a cot way in the middle. She had a diabetic stroke.

Then we got in touch with [Millie's] cousin in Texas. They had a lady, a volunteer, there who got in touch with him over the computer. We called him on his cell phone. They lent us a cell phone, and we called him. He invited us over. We had our own room. We loved to stay there. She wanted to go there, so we went. It was nice to go to somebody's house, but I think staying in the shelter would have gotten us more.

When we were coming back they told us [at the shelter] we could come back for one or two days and then leave. When we got home, we had a tree on the roof. The telephone poles fell and pulled all the electrical work in the house. The insurance company called me and said, "Your claim has been paid." I called her Monday, and she said, "I didn't tell you that, I told you this: it's going to take about two more weeks."

We slept in the van because we didn't have anywhere else. There happened to be a pay phone, so we called every 800 number we could find. Even Red Cross said they could do nothing for you. Eighty dollars a day to stay in a hotel. We went one day to a flea-bag hotel. Then FEMA sent us to a place for $10 a month. That was a crack house.

Millie Reine

They said where a spider bit me. Trisha, his daughter, came to the shelter. She was outside smoking. I was sitting by a tree with her. The tree was full of spider webs. The doctor cut into my leg. He showed me, under the microscope, part of the body of the spider.

They brought clothes, baby junk. Wal-Mart would come every day. Helicopters dropped food and water. There were kids. Anger over football. Some of my medicines got stolen. A man who was at the Superdome when a piece of roof came off was in Gonzales. He was hit on the head, and they helicoptered him out of there. They stole his wallet. I've got diabetes, thrombosis, pains in the leg. They let us use the phones there. I finally got my daughter-in-law. She's a computer nut.

Blanco came there, and what's her name? That blond. Mary Landrieu. The police chief came in from over there and told us all that stuff about getting raped, people breaking into homes, wasn't true. He lied because people broke into the first three houses on this block. That's so low to take advantage. He was telling us it wasn't true. I guess to try and keep panic and stuff down.

My cousin, his wife had died a year before from breast cancer. We finally ended up at his house in College State. He's eighty years old. He gets around better than me or [Benny]. He's a professor at A&M.

When we got back to Kenner, in the beginning we were down the street at the Winn-Dixie at the grill. We go there and get sandwiches, go to the bathroom. Police officers came over, and they said some of the patrons complained about us. They asked, "What are you doing?" I said, "Living."

Seeking Refuge

Debbie Baxter
Interviewed by Peter Syverson

Debbie Baxter and her family sought shelter at local Bonnabel High School before leaving New Orleans.

Since Hurricane Katrina my life and the lives of my family have been turned upside down. Before Katrina I had decided to stop working full time and concentrate on going to school to pursue my nursing degree. I was in school for only one week before this catastrophe took place. My fiancé and I debated about evacuating because his mom refused to leave. We decided to stay because I didn't want to leave her behind. We went out, fueled up, stocked up on water, candles, food, and other necessities needed to ride out the storm. We figured everything would be okay considering we had a two-story home. How bad could it get?

But as Hurricane Katrina made landfall we started to get scared. It was about 2:00 a.m. when the winds began to blow really hard, and the rain began to fall harder. The noise was so loud it woke my fiancé up, and he woke me up and asked if I thought we should leave. I asked him what he thought, and his response to me was, "We better go now." We had already loaded his truck with things we would need just in case the situation got worse and we were forced to leave. We woke our two boys up, and my mother-in-law, and got in the truck. As we were leaving, the rain was pouring down and the wind blew so hard it moved the truck from side to side. We passed a building that was on fire. We could feel the heat from the fire on the window of the truck. It was incredible that fire could break out with all that rain coming down. We made it to Bonnabel High School. By this time the water had started to rise and was about two and a half to three feet high. We unloaded the kids and our belongings and went inside. The power was out at the shelter, and there were about 150 people already there. We set up inside and just waited for the storm to pass.

The time in the shelter passed so slowly. It was horrible. We were there for three days. No power, no water, no food, and no sanitary restrooms. Thank God we packed enough supplies for our family, but I felt so sorry for the other people who didn't do the same. On the third day we decided that we had enough of the shelter, and we were determined to leave. The water had not resided because the pumps had not been activated thanks to our wonderful know-nothing parish president and mayor. They moved the pump operators to Slidell rather than have them man the pumps. We went out into the water, and it still was about four feet high. After going over different ideas, we decided to go for it. My mother-in-law and I pushed the truck while my fiancé worked the steering wheel. We pushed for about five blocks until we were on the on-ramp at Power Blvd., clear of all the standing water. After making it to the I-10, we started the truck, and we were headed to Baton Rouge. It felt so good to be out of that horrible place.

Once we made it to Baton Rouge, we searched for hours for a hotel, but everything in the area was booked. We finally got word of a shelter that had power, running water, and sanitary restrooms. After traveling for four hours, we finally made it to the shelter. It was a beautiful place considering what we had come from. We had hot meals, pillows, blankets, toiletries, and water, things we would all take for granted before the storm. We slept there that night and prepared for our next journey to begin early the next morning.

We were rested enough to start the long journey to McDonough, Georgia.

Because the twin spans in Slidell were totally gone, we had to take the long way to Georgia. The trip took us thirteen hours compared to eight hours before the storm. But we knew that we had no other choice. Gas was scarce, as well as food and drinking water, as we traveled through Mississippi and Alabama, but with the help of God, we finally made it.

I never thought in my wildest dreams that this could ever happen. I lost my home and my children's school. My fiancé is displaced from his employment that he has had for over seven years. I even lost contact with my mom for five days. I have never experienced anything so horrendous in my entire life. I can't say what the future will hold for my family and me. I do know that I love Louisiana, but this whole ordeal has taken a lot from me. It is good to talk about all of this. It feels kind of like therapy.

A Place Found Us

Nicole Pugh
In Her Own Words

Nicole Pugh was about to embark on a new journey in her life when Katrina turned her aspirations of a new bohemian lifestyle into a miserable reality.

By the end of July 2005, my fiancé Jeremy and I had quit our jobs and were about to start brand new lives. We would soon become fulltime students again— me at UNO and he at Loyola studying music therapy. It had been almost a decade since either of us set foot on a university campus. The month of August 2005 was filled with giddy banter about our much-anticipated, soon-to-be bohemian student lifestyle. We daydreamed about how we would sip espresso together and study in the middle of the afternoon, buy matching rolly-backpacks (a must for our almost middle-aged backs), meet new friends, take the streetcar and bus to our respective campuses, maybe even buy one of those beaded doorway dividers just for the heck of it. Life would be a canvas on which we would paint a groovy little life of creativity and self-expression. Finally, we thought, after three tough years in the Crescent City, during which we endured death, financial troubles, heartbreaks, sickness, it looks like things are about to turn around.

Then came Katrina. Beautiful, powerful, awesome, terrifying woman roaring towards shore. Her name means "to cleanse or purify." She came in undercover, and I imagine she must have been pissed about something. In my day-to-day life before the storm, I didn't even know she existed. I went to my restaurant job at Taqueros/Coyocan on St. Charles on Saturday evening and sat around the bar with the other employees watching the weather channel. By Sunday midday, Jeremy, myself, his sister Cambria, her two kids, and Milkshake the family dog were stuck in traffic with 10,000+ other frantic citizens crawling slowly north. Cambria's son, D'mitri, noticed the first wave of thick gray clouds move into Slidell as we sat on the freeway. I noticed how the strange currents of the pre-hurricane winds made birds fly in every direction like scampering fleas.

It took us eighteen hours to get to Chatanooga, eleven of which were spent in Slidell. Once there, we stayed with a gracious friend and her one-year-old child who had a spare bedroom for us to sleep in. It was in Chattanooga, on a tiny T.V. in her sparsely furnished living room, where we first watched images of the levee breaches and of tired, angry faces out in front of the Superdome. We sat in that living room watching in disbelief at images of spewing water, of random folks being plucked off rooftops, of a pale-looking Governor Blanco and a weary Mayor Nagin. And we were asking the questions that everyone was: Where is the National Guard, the federal government? Where is the water, the food? Why are the levees breaking? What is happening to our city? I am not sure that most people know the answers to these questions even now.

We stayed in Chattanooga for about a week. Most of our time there was spent in front of the T.V. or on our cell phones, text messaging Jeremy's sister and brother, Magenta and Capricho. Both of them elected to stay in the French Quarter instead of evacuate. Finally, we got word that his brother had gotten out on Tuesday as the water began covering the city. Magenta stayed until Thursday. She waded across Rampart St. on day two after the storm to get food and water from the Winn-Dixie. On day three, she was held up by gunpoint because she didn't want to buy the computer monitor the woman had stolen. On day four, she and three of her friends made it to the ninth floor of the Canal Place parking lot where Jeremy had parked his truck the weekend before. They walked up the parking lot ramp together in the pitch dark, passed looters who were smashing in windows of cars up to the fourth floor. No one in her group really knew how to drive, but somehow they managed to get out of the Quarter, past the CBD and a cloud of desperation at the Convention Center, across the highway to the West Bank and out of harm's way.

In Eunice, a week and a half after Katrina, our whole family reunited at the family home of a close friend. We had a "family meeting" to decide what our next step was going to be. It began to dawn on us all that we were not going home to the French Quarter and the Marigny any time soon. The levees were breached and water was spilling out by the millions of gallons, engulfing neighborhoods. What were we going to do? Where would we go? The kids felt the increased nervousness of the adults. In reaction, they were beginning to bounce off the walls, and their mom was on the verge of a nervous breakdown. We needed to make some decisions, and fast. Cambria and the two kids needed to be somewhere where they could settle down and get into a routine again.

We gathered together as the mid-afternoon sun shone down on Acadiana. After we settled around Micah's parents' living room coffee table, we held hands for a moment in silence then each of us spoke in turn. Soon it was clear we all were being pulled in different directions. Cambria decided she would go back to Roslyn, Washington, where the family had lived before, and where friends were waiting with a trailer and a little cash gathered from the locals. Magenta would go to Shreveport where her evacuee buddies had already secured an apartment. Michael, Jeremy's dad, would go to California with Micah. Micah and Michael had just returned from San Diego, where Micah had discovered his alter ego as a Cajun surfer and Michael had discovered an old friend who owned a newspaper in need of an ad-man.

As for Jeremy and I, we would give Magenta a lift to Shreveport, then head down to Lafayette to see where life would lead us next and if there was anything we could do to help. Practically speaking, it made sense for someone to stay close to home so that the houses could be checked, and cats, hopefully, found when the time came. As for me, I was not ready to leave my newfound home. New Orleans and Louisiana had mysteriously nudged their way into my heart. Jeremy, as it turned out, couldn't bare the thought of leaving me, and he also had a desire to help other evacuees. We chose Lafayette because it was fascinating to us as the home of Zydeco and Cajun culture.

When D'mitri, who was sitting on the floor next to Cambria, realized that the family was splitting up for a while, he began to cry for the first time since we evacuated. For a moment, his ten-year-old "tough-guy" persona was shattered as he clung to his mom and wept.

"What do you want to do, D'mitri?" his mom asked gently as she held him in her arms.

"I want to go home. I want to go back to New Orleans. I want to see my friends!" His pleas brought tears to our eyes as well. It was what we all wanted to do. Yet it was the one option that was not available to us.

In Shreveport, Jeremy and I dropped Magenta off at a run-down little apartment in a not-so-nice part of town.

"Are you sure you are going to be okay?" we asked.

"I'll be fine," she said. Her voice was less than reassuring.

With family members now traveling, or already settled into their various destinations, Jeremy and I were on our own for the first time in over two weeks. As luck would have it, we found a nice hotel room in a casino/resort in Shreveport for the night. Our plan was to have a good meal, get some much-needed rest and be on the road to Lafayette by midday.

Instead, we were awakened at seven the next morning to a call on Jeremy's cell phone. It was Magenta.

"Hi...uh, can you pick me up?"

"When?"

"How about in an hour?"

After a half a day at the apartment, Magenta was convinced that Shreveport was not for her. She was unsure, however, if she wanted to go back to Lafayette with us or take a Greyhound to Washington to be with Cambria and the kids. In retrospect, I think that her indecisiveness was a product of too much trauma, too fast. Through the stories she told us, four extra days in New Orleans after the storm would be enough to put anyone on stress leave for a while. Resolved to the fact that we were going to stay in Shreveport until she could get some rest, settle her nerves, and figure out the next step, we decided to use the time to get some assistance. We heard rumors that somebody (the Feds? the state?) was giving out food stamps. We decided to check it out.

Shreveport is a fairly small town. And far enough away from the Gulf that it wasn't saturated at the time with evacuees like us. It turned out to be the best place in the state to sign up for the stuff that us evacuees need to survive in the post-Katrina world—FEMA, food stamps, unemployment, Red Cross. When we arrived at the Shreveport Social Security Administration, there were only a handful of people in the waiting room. Jeremy dropped me off to fill out the forms while he made his way across town to pick up Magenta.

It was in the waiting room where I met Chip. Before the storm, he lived in Lakeview with his wife and two kids and worked at the Hilton on Canal Street. Their house was completely destroyed. Chip and his wife sent their children out of the city two days before the storm hit, but they stayed for work. They camped out at their respective hotels of employment, the Hilton and the Holiday Inn, and tried to wait out the storm. Chip described the smell of dog and cat shit in the lobby of his hotel.

"It's amazing how fast the whole thing can break down, you know? People began coming in from the street. A lot of them had pets. There wasn't any other place for them to go, so they just let them do it right there in the lobby. No bother about cleaning it up. After a day and a half, boy did it start to stink."

He described how he waded through waist-deep sewage water to get to his wife's car so they could make their escape. Chip told the story like it happened to someone else– flippant, nonchalant– but I could tell it all happened to him. A small bead of sweat began to form on his upper lip as he talked about the escape, as he called it, and how much he and his wife missed their kids during those few fateful days. Before too long, a woman wearing a Red Cross Volunteer sticker on her jacket came out to the lobby, called his name, and he was gone.

We found a place to stay that night— or, I should say, a place found us— as we bought supplies at a Walgreens in the middle of town. We were trying to figure out how to use the food stamp card with little success ("Slide it across just like a credit card, dearie." The lady behind the counter was instructing me). A tall, thin man in a white shirt and a funny-looking bowtie came over to us. That tie should have been a red flag from the get-go.

"Are you evacuees?" he asked

"Yes, we are."

"Looking for a place to stay?"

When we answered yes, he gave us his card. "Broadmoor Community Church," it said.

We stayed at Broadmoor for three nights. The food was starchy but life-sustaining. The noise was bearable with only 75 people staying there and a handful of children. The neon lights that switched on at 7:00 a.m. sharp were harsh but tolerable for the time being. What was the most difficult for us to swallow was the preaching. And boy did they preach. Before supper. Upon waking up. Before going to bed. They even cornered us when we stepped outside to get a breath of fresh air or have a smoke.

"How are you doing today? Do you need to talk?" they asked. "Can I give you this mini-Bible to read? The Lord can help, you know."

"No, thank you," we said repeatedly. "We have our own faith. No, we're not really Christian. No, we don't need a copy of the Bible. Thank you anyway. You all have been so generous."

How were we going to tell them that we found their form of "assistance through salvation" offensive when we were relying on their generosity for our well being at the time? Come on, Magenta, I secretly prayed to my own set of universal powers, make up your mind so we can get the hell out of here, no pun intended.

There are two things that happened at Broadmoor that I am truly grateful for. First of all, I got to meet Ms. Shirley. She approached me right after dinner on the first night we arrived. She was wearing thick glasses, a dark blue mum, and she demanded a hug right there and then. She said she had lost everything to Katrina— the home she had lived in for the last thirty years, all of her photos, her position as perpetual grandmother for countless children in her St. Bernard Parish neighborhood throughout the years.

"As you can see, I ain't got nothing but this hug, so I'm not gonna take no for an answer!"

The other thing I am grateful for happened the last night we were at the shelter. Magenta had decided the day before that she would take a bus the following weekend to Washington to meet up with Cambria and the kids. The early hours of our last evening together were spent outside, standing by Jeremy's truck, chatting, smoking, and singing songs. Magenta's voice is like Ella Fitzgerald and Bessie Smith rolled into one. She sang "Summertime" as a serenade to another shelter resident from Kenner who came to Shreveport searching out his two dogs. He heard a rumor that his neighbor had them and was heading up the state. As Magenta's voice thundered through the church parking lot, folks began to come out of the shelter. Soon there was a mini-audience gathered around us, and a chorus of would-be singers joined in. It didn't take long before the whole thing turned to gospel, but that seemed okay as well. That night, we sang under the same southern moon that hung over the great, underwater city of New Orleans. The smell of cigarette smoke, sweat, and redemption swirled around us. It almost felt like home.

From Shreveport, Jeremy and I (alone again) made our way to Kaplan, LA, where Jeremy had arranged a bed for us that night. The Kaplan American Legions Center was also a FEMA site where we could sign up for whatever assistance may be available. At the shelter, which is about forty minutes from Lafayette, we met Mr. Henry. He was a bear of a man in his late sixties with a VFW cap on his head and an uncanny capacity to do at least five things at once. Rumor had it that Mr. Henry single-handedly placed over four hundred individuals with host-families around the Kaplan area. Would we consider doing the same? Hmm, staying in a real home where we could experience Louisiana culture, eat real gumbo, gather our thoughts and get to know folks in the area? Sounded good to us. Besides, at that point, rental options were next to nil, all the hotels were booked up, and the actual existence of the infamous "FEMA trailers" was largely up for debate.

So entered Pam, Bozo, and the various members of their extended family into our lives. We lived in a small room in their house for about two weeks. Pam and Bozo were as Cajun as it gets. The first weekend we were there, they took us crabbing and garfish fishing. We got to see Bozo's son, Kyle, smash in the side of the garfish's head with a baseball bat. ("It's the only way to kill 'em," Bozo said. "They're tough as nails.") We toured the rice factory where Bozo used to work as a foreman before he got lung cancer and went on disability. We ate a lot of real Cajun food— boiled, broiled and, of course, fried. We had a crab boil with those crabs we caught and ate okra gumbo until it was coming out of our ears.

Just about the time Rita rolled into the Gulf, we began to get to know more about our host family than we were prepared for. The word "nigger" began to pop up here and there in discussions around the kitchen table. Soon, the topic of black people, especially those "black niggers from New Orleans" began to dominate many a conversation between members of the extended family and friends, over pots of gumbo and in front of CNN playing on the wide-screen TV. Pam was apologetic when Bozo and his friends began their tirades against African-Americans. Still, it continued.

"A good nigger is a dead nigger," a cousin of the family said once while the others nodded in agreement. Pam sat on the sofa, blushing uncontrollably.

In retrospect, I am ashamed to say that we never said anything to Bozo about how these comments made us feel. We never spoke our minds about how angry it made us. We never expressed to them how sick to our stomachs we felt that, as non-black people (Jeremy is from New Zealand, and I am half Chinese and half Mexican), we were given space, food, even clothing from their family while our friends Terry and Dow, back in the Kaplan shelter, had been waiting for two weeks to be placed with a host family or some other form of housing in the area. We knew that Pam and Bozo would never show them the hospitality they showed us, and this was based on the color of their skin. We were in conflict with regard to our feelings for this family who had befriended us. They had been kind, had fed us and shown us so much of their culture that was unique, beautiful, and warm. We felt real affection for Bozo and admired his zest for life after the cancer almost killed him. We saw his passion for the okra patch he tended with such care and the devotion he showed to his son and daughter. At the same time, it was difficult to look past his racist views. We came to this part of the state through a set of unforeseen circumstances. Once here, we decided that we wanted to learn as much as we could while here. We have not been disappointed.

Hurricane Rita, little sister to Katrina, headed straight for Kaplan and points west during our second week living with Pam and Bozo. It was also my second week on the job at Green T. Lindon Elementary School in Youngsville. I was hired as an "evacuee teacher" shortly after we came to the area. When evacuation from Vermillion parish became mandatory, we convoyed with Bozo, Pam, and Kyle to their friend's house in Lafayette. Freddie and his family are from Columbia. Freddie is as dark as any light-skinned black person, and according to Bozo, one of his best buddies. Go figure.

To our surprise, we had a great time staying at Freddie's. As the wind howled outside the house, Bozo made a mean gumbo, Jeremy made a friend out of John (a.k.a. Sebastian), Freddie's nine-year-old son and a budding guitarist. I made bead necklaces with Freddie's thirteen year-old daughter and got to practice my Spanish with Ella, Freddie's wife.

The morning after the storm, Pam stuck her head in the door of John's room, where we were sleeping.

"We're fixin' to leave. Alicia just called. They lost everything in Forked Island. Eight feet of water in the house. They're on their way to Kaplan with the RV. You all comin'?"

We did not go back to Kaplan with Pam, Bozo, and Kyle. As I heard their Chevy truck pull out of the driveway, I felt a sinking feeling in my stomach. It was a here-we-go-again kind of dread that lodged itself in my upper chest. Jeremy was sleeping beside me. He opened his eyes at the sound of the truck's departure.

"There they go," he stated simply, looking at me through the fog of just waking up. Then his gaze shifted towards the window. Outside, trees swayed back and forth like sea grass, and leaves were blowing in every direction. As partners sometimes do, we were both thinking the same thing. What would we do next? One thing was for certain. With the coming and going of Rita, we at least knew that it was time for us to move on.

There have been times in my life when I have chosen homelessness and the vagabond ways of the traveler. Yet, as I hitchhiked with other ragamuffin twenty-somethings out for adventure, I always knew that I did so by choice. I could go back to the straight life (job, school, apartment) at any time. The difference with this situation, obviously, is that this was no one's choice. Not those in shelters, not those staying with families, not those who fled or were transported to the other side of the country, not for Jeremy and me.

I know that we are among the fortunate ones. We have a vehicle, jobs, and each other. Everyone we know and care about has survived without injury, yet the fear and anxiety for the future remains. We still look for housing in a market that is saturated with thousands of evacuees like ourselves. We still wrestle with the reality that, because of my health issues and the toxicity in the city right now, we may not be able to return to New Orleans permanently. Then there are the big questions in our little lives to consider, those that we avoid until they bubble over in us like sores that have turned blue. Where do we go from here? Will the city ever be the same? How long will it take before our lives, all of our lives, return to "normal" again? What do we do with this longing to return home that comes over us in waves? The smells of the French Quarter, the sounds of Mardi Gras, our tiny apartment on Dauphine and St. Ann with its little pond of fish— we miss all of it so. Question upon question with no clear answers.

Life is different in many ways here in Lafayette than it was in New Orleans. Still, the clock keeps ticking. We do better together, and individually, if we don't plan too much into the future. To me, this makes sense when I remember how fragile our plans were to begin with. We never planned in a million years that all the things that happened over the last two months would happen, that here we would be in the Fall of 2005, a part of the wave of transient lives, each of us trying to put the pieces of our lives back together. Sometime it is like a puzzle that doesn't quite fit. And other times, we recognize the flow and are amazed that we are part of an event that could very well signify a shift in the consciousness and circumstance of the United States as a whole. With that perspective, our lives seem, if not well planned for, at least worth living.

Cash and Water

Mary Funti
Interviewed by Virginia Corinne Akins

Mary Funti chose not to evacuate for Hurricane Katrina so that she could work at Tulane University Hospital. When it became clear that the city was unprepared for the disaster, Mary and her friends sought immediate shelter and rescue on their own.

Had you stayed in the city for the storm?

Yes. Working at the hospital, I was not on the hurricane crew, but I had to work the evening before the hurricane, which was Sunday, so Tulane put us up at the [Park Plaza Hotel of New Orleans] next to the hospital. I stayed there because I was to work Tuesday after the hurricane.

So that supposing nothing had happened…

This had happened before for one or two other hurricanes where I was at the hospital. I would stay at the hotel, and I would be able to work the next day after everything blew over, so to speak. This time it didn't. This time we were stuck.

Prior to working at the hospital in other hurricanes, had it been your habit to evacuate?

Evacuate, always. Mainly just the fear of the wind and the noise and the fear, actually. It was never a matter of flooding that I ever actually thought about. It was the hurricane itself, the wind, and I always got out. I always evacuated except for the times when I was working at the hospital.

What had you heard about this storm prior to its arrival?

That it was going to be a very bad storm. We heard Category 3, then Category 4. I can't remember when I heard Category 5. I don't believe I ever did realize it was Category 5, but I knew that it was going to be bad, and of course, we thought it was going to be a direct hit to the city. Which, it was not a direct hit to the city; actually it bypassed the city a little. It was the breaches in the levees that caused the flooding, which we had no clue about. We did have a radio after the electricity went out at the hotel, and we found out that it was flooding, and it was continuing to flood. It was getting higher and higher, and we were stuck at the hotel.

At what point did you hear that the levees had broken?

The morning after the hurricane had passed through, on Monday. That would have been, I guess, August the 30th, no, August 29th, when the hurricane came.

And you heard…

Right after that, on the radio.

And how long did you have the radio for?

The whole time. We had extra sets of batteries, and we had the radio. We stayed glued to the radio.

What news source was actually coming in?

It was local, on WWL radio. They did a wonderful job keeping everybody as informed as they could because, I believe, they had trouble, too, coordinating the news, not really knowing what was happening. At the hotel, I had my two friends along with me. We were on the 9th floor of the hotel, and we were watching the water rise on Canal Street as the day progressed. We kept thinking that the water was going to go down. We had certain places where we were measuring, cars and signs, and then we noticed that it wasn't going down.

In the course of one day, how much did you watch the water rise?

It was probably about three feet, four feet. Then I was to go back to work the following day, on Tuesday, and I was all ready to go to work at 7:00 a.m., and we could not get down to the 1st floor of the hotel. They were stopping everybody at the 2nd floor because of the water. Then I had no way to get in touch with the hospital. My cell phone was out, no electricity. The hospital was right there, and I just couldn't reach or talk to anyone, and it was very frustrating, I just wanted to get to be with my friends. I wanted to get out of the hotel.

Who was stopping you?

Well, the management of the hotel wouldn't let me out at that time. Then, after I'd thought about it, I'd heard from word of mouth through walking the corridors of the hotel that Tulane was not letting anyone in unless they had ID. My two friends didn't have ID, and there was no way I could leave them. And, in retrospect, I'm glad I didn't go back to the hospital.

We stayed at the hotel till Wednesday, and then they announced that they were running out of food and water. We were on the 9th floor; no electricity. We did have a flashlight, that was lucky, and sporadically the lights would go on, so you could see through the corridor to get to the stairs. And then we'd go down to the second floor for breakfast, lunch, and supper. Like a muffin and coffee, I mean, anything was just fabulous, anything to eat, and water. And when they announced that they were running out of everything, we knew we had to get out. I did not want to go to the Superdome, all the stories that we were hearing on the radio. It was like, no way were we going to the Superdome. Luckily, Beatrice Crane, a friend who I was with, had keys to a friend's apartment in the French Quarter. So, that was our plan, that if we got out of the hotel, we would walk to the French Quarter and go to her friend's condominium.

And where you were intending to walk, approximately how far to get to the next place?

Approximately twelve, thirteen blocks. But we had heard also that there was no water in the French Quarter. Not knowing where it ended or began or whatever. We finally left on that Wednesday. We had to leave our luggage. We had to leave everything at the hotel, not knowing whether we were ever going to get it back, but that wasn't the most important thing. We walked out the back door of the hotel into maybe about two feet of water, and then as we approached the block where we were to turn to go to Canal Street the water got up to our necks.

I had no fear; actually, I credit that to my prayers, to the Blessed Mother. I mean, I prayed, and I had no fear. And then we walked to Canal Street, and then the water started receding, got to maybe our knees, but [in the] meantime the purse or the backpack that we had was light, floating on the water, but once we got into the French Quarter it was heavy. It was hot, and the sun was beating down on us. My other friend, Alberto Gonzalez, had just finished chemo and radiation, and I was very concerned about him with the heat and the whole experience. And we would stop and wait and rest, and stop and rest and sit down, and we wound up on Burgundy Street in the French Quarter. We just kept plugging along. It was so hot, and we were so dirty and wet. Then we met up with three policemen, and that was wonderful because we felt like we were safe with the policemen.

Is this the first time you had seen a policeman during this "experience"?

Oh yeah. Yes, yes.

Even in the hotel, looking down, had you seen...

No. Well, we had seen some trucks passing on Canal Street, some police vehicles, but at that point in time, no, we hadn't really seen any police. We saw a lot of looting, from our window on Canal Street. Actually not... Well, [at a] carpet store. Two looters went into a carpet store and looted carpet. Now, we wonder what they were going to do with that carpet. Another reason we wanted to get out of the hotel [was] because the looters were coming back in, and they had the stuff that they had acquired, so we knew all that was going on, and we knew that [it] was time for us to get out.

How many people were in the hotel with you?

I'd say maybe about forty, fifty. I would occasionally see some of the hotel employees that I had known. Some faces were familiar. I might have known, seen... Of course, I was on the 9th floor, and so there were, maybe, fourteen floors to this hotel. We were quite separated. I didn't see any of my coworkers. Of course, a lot of people wound up going back to the hospital, which had a story in itself, the hospital running out of electricity. They suffered a lot, but they also saved a lot of lives at the hospital. But I didn't see too many people that I knew after. I wasn't able to get much information from any employees about what was going on at the hospital.

After you left, what were you doing?

We went to the French Quarter; we were very lucky that we were able to stay at a condominium. There were two other people that had gone there, and actually evacuated to this apartment. There was a French chef that lived in one of the apartments, and he had cleaned out everybody's refrigerator, knowing that it would go bad. We had some really good food he barbequed with charcoal. We were treated very well there in the French Quarter. We stayed there from Wednesday until Sunday. As luck would have it, I was walking down the street with the chef in the French Quarter, looking for a friend of his. We saw the National Guard standing around on a corner. A young guy asked if I needed water. I said, "Yes." He said that his brothers were coming in from Missouri with a van, and they would be able to give us a ride out at dusk on Sunday.

His brothers drove all the way from Missouri to get him?

They belonged to some church group. There were four men, four guys. They drove down here just to help out in any way, which they did. We had no idea what was going to happen. We couldn't walk to the 'Dome, the water was still up. This was on Sunday. I couldn't go get my car that was parked in the Tulane hospital parking lot. We were still stuck, so to speak. We tried to walk to the Convention Center, but [we] were stopped by the National Guard at Canal Street and told to go back into the French Quarter.

When was that?

Saturday. So, we couldn't get to the Convention Center. Two of us would go; the rest of us would stay at the apartment. Just to check things out. Just to see how we could get out. We even thought we could walk to the interstate and get up on the interstate because when we were at the hotel, we saw people slowly coming and walking on the interstate. We just thought of every imaginable way to get out. And when this boy said his brothers were coming, and to be there at 7:00, at dusk, it was like, we're there. We went back to the apartment and informed everybody that we had rides to Baton Rouge at dusk that we had to meet. That was around noon. At five o'clock, we were just on edge, waiting to walk down and meet the van. It was a huge van, and they were wonderful boys. Their family owns the Olivier House in the French Quarter. One of the boys lives there, one of the sons. The other two sons live in Missouri.

Did they know before they arrived here that they were going to be driving people out of town?

I would assume that they came with that big van, and I imagine they were going to try to get people out. As a matter of fact, it was the three of us. Myself and my two friends, Alberto and Bea, and then we picked up another young woman in the French Quarter who was going to Baton Rouge. They dropped us off Sunday night [September 4th] in Baton Rouge, at the airport, where we spent the night on the floor of the airport. Sunday night, we tried to sleep, but nobody slept at the airport in Baton Rouge. And then my daughter got the three of us a flight to Dallas, and we left that Monday, and got a flight out to Dallas. We did get some MREs at the airport, which were delicious. We hadn't eaten very much.

I was reunited with my family, who hadn't heard from me. It took about two days [before] they heard from me. There was only one phone in the French Quarter. There was no electricity. I could not use my cell phone. We would walk to this one payphone on the corner of Barracks and Royal and would get in line; I was able to call my children collect. My children hadn't heard from me since the hurricane for four days. They were beyond themselves. They were so thrilled. I was so thrilled. That was, I think, what I was worrying about the most, not being able to get in touch with my children, worrying about them worrying about me. That was the main thing. That was exciting. I think we were like zombies though, the three of us, just one minute to the next. Just keep going. A mind-boggling experience really.

You don't know, really— time— you really don't know the day. After all is said and done, hearing news, but it's mainly news about what they can get about what's happening, about evacuation, about what's happening with people. It was… "Surreal" is the only word that I can come up with or a lot of people can come up with. The French Quarter was totally empty, which I don't think had happened in, as far as in my whole lifetime. There was no activity at all, no lights. Total quiet except for, [now and] then, a few guns and then explosions.

What were the explosions?

We didn't know at first. One morning, it was about 3:00 a.m. or 4:00 a.m., early morning. It was this horrible explosion. We thought, everyone thought— jumped out of bed, where they were sleeping— thought that it was a war. We were scared. We thought bombs were going off. We saw a big flame. Because we were on a balcony, we had a view of the whole city. It was a huge fire in the Marigny area, Faubourg Marigny. It was a warehouse, as we found out later, with some type of chemical, which was not dangerous. I'm not sure exactly what it was. Then another thing that was on our minds, to get out of the city because of fires that were starting; you could see [them] all over the city. And helicopters started coming and putting the fires out; that was the only way they could. I believe they were getting the water from the river, the Mississippi River.

After that fire, were there other fires?

There were fires, some down off Canal Street, which we could see. There was a fire across the river, over in Algiers, at the Oakwood Shopping Center. That was started by arson for whatever reason. Then there were some fires on Carrolton Avenue, which was south of us. Like I said, we had a view of the whole city, which was magnificent except the fires. I was very concerned about the fires not being contained and then coming into the Quarter. Of course, that would have been a total disaster.

There were no services to put out the fire, except for helicopters?

None, yeah.

Of course, I'm not sure when that fire started, but it took three or four days to finally put the fire out. The fire kept going. We kept worrying that they wouldn't be able to put it out. It was a huge fire obviously. They finally put it out.

Were there reports on this on the radio?

Yes, that's how we found out that it was a warehouse; it was news on the radio. Then, meeting up with people who were using that telephone, people coming from that area and telling us exactly what was happening in that area where the fire was: looting, shooting etc. Besides the quiet, every once in a while there was a lot of shooting. We didn't know who was shooting. We didn't know; it was dangerous, but we didn't walk out at night even though it was empty. You just didn't know what was out there.

The storm itself eventually reached Category 5 and is considered the worst in decades. What was that like?

It was very strong; the wind was strong. We were on the 9th floor of the hotel, remember? The only way to gauge wind was to see things flying, or I was looking at the palm trees on Canal Street bending. That was mainly it. We didn't see the effects of the wind other than the palm trees that I was judging. We were so high in this room. Stuck. I never had any horrible experiences before. This one we couldn't go outside and see anything. We judged everything from the 9th floor.

Other hotels, their windows blew out. You guys were protected?

From the last storm, this was an old hotel. They informed us they had made the windows hurricane proof and installed hurricane proof windows in the hotel. It was a huge hotel, maybe thirteen, fourteen floors. I remembered from the year before the windows were hurricane-proof. That was really a relief, too, because if the windows would have broken— I can't even imagine— at hurricane force....

Your house is located Uptown, the older part of New Orleans. What were you expecting?

We understood... Yes, and of course, the French Quarter is the oldest part of the city, and it didn't flood because it is higher. From what I understood, all areas along the river were not affected because they were higher. Uptown areas, main parts of Uptown, close to the river, didn't flood. I was very, very lucky.

Did you know at the time?

No, there was really no way of knowing, except maybe that people would call into the radio station and inform the radio announcer that there was no water at certain streets. It was difficult. It wasn't until we got to Dallas that we saw a video on the computer, and we could see what areas of the city and what areas of the neighborhood were flooded, that I knew that my house had not gotten water.

Other people that were around you, do you remember their general attitude?

I think everyone was just worried or concerned to get out as soon as they could. The main topic of conversation was, "How are we going to get out?" No one, as far as I was associated with, had fear.

At what point did you begin seeing some National Guard members?

We started seeing the National Guard, I would say, it wasn't until about Friday that we saw the National Guard in the French Quarter. We did hear on the news that they were here, but besides that, it was probably Saturday, not until Saturday, that the helicopter, the Red Cross, well, the National Guard, too, was here in the French Quarter. Like Friday and Saturday after the hurricane.

When did you hear the news say that they had arrived?

They probably were saying that they arrived, maybe, by Thursday. The hurricane was Monday. I'm sure they must have gotten here sooner, but I mean, we didn't see any. I didn't see any until Thursday or Friday.

The Department of Homeland Security's stated motto is "when responding to a catastrophic incident, the Federal Government should start emergency operations in the absence of a clear assessment of the situation," which is why I'm curious as to when Federal officials actually arrived into the situation?

I don't believe they "arrived" right after. I saw them Thursday or Friday. Well, I take that back… Yeah, it was about Thursday or Friday because that's when we heard that they were on Canal Street; the National Guard were on Canal Street, and that's when we went and tried to get to the Convention Center. That would have been on Friday and Saturday, two different days. The other two people at the apartment tried to go, also. Twice we tried to cross Canal Street to get to the Convention Center and were stopped by the National Guard or someone.

When your friends were stopped at Canal Street and told to go no farther, what was the reason?

They weren't given a reason, just rumors of violence going on or too crowded. [They] were not given a reason. Told to go back, there was a gun put to their head. A gun was put to their heads, and they were told to go back. No questions asked, no reason given for why, and so they walked back to the French Quarter, back to the apartment. We heard the news and were stuck again.

Now, out of the situation, a gun to someone's head seems extreme, did these people who were walking, were they males or…

A man and a woman.

And you believe that the people stopping them were National Guard? Are you sure of this?

They were not New Orleans police. They assumed that they were National Guard. We didn't know what forms of armed services were there. [The people from the apartment] said National Guard, but I'm not sure.

Did they express any objections?

They expressed objections to having a gun put to their heads. That was not necessary, they thought, to have a gun put to their head. Nothing was a surprise for us anymore, [just another] day-to-day thing, just surreal. Most surreal part was in the French Quarter, the Francis Parkinson Keye's house, on Chartres Street.

I believe [her house] was rented out as a bed and breakfast. I'm not exactly sure, but from our balcony, we could see the balcony on that house, and they had a table and tablecloths and wine glasses. They were enjoying themselves. It was like, "Where are they getting this lovely meal?" As if nothing had happened, and everything was just okay with the world. I wish I'd had a camera. Especially with a helicopter going overhead and these people enjoying their breakfast and supper. Actually, at one point in time, [they waved at us] and asked [us] to join them for a croissant. It was like, where did they get this?

And did you?

No. Because, I think, at that point we were afraid to go out. It was getting to be dusk, and we were not supposed to go out at night.

Basically, by September 11th, Congress had allocated over 60 billion [dollars] in aid. What forms of assistance have you experienced [in terms of] assistance and aid from individuals and organizations?

When I got to Dallas, luckily, my daughter got on the computer, and we got in touch with FEMA, and I got a FEMA number. I received from FEMA $2,400, right off the bat. I didn't know the condition of my house at that point in time, but I received that. After [I spent a week] in Dallas, I was able to get a flight, through my daughter once again, to Fort Walton Beach. Once I was in Fort Walton Beach, I was able to get in touch with the Red Cross. Which— I got $600. That's mainly what I got from FEMA and Red Cross. Coming back to New Orleans, I had no damage to my home; I got nothing. I didn't need anything. Friends, actually relatives, gave me some money. One of the main things that helped a lot [was that when] we were going to the hotel, I had the presence of mind to grab some cash I had been saving for my property taxes. I had this cash at my house. I was so relieved that we had cash on us. [It's] the most important thing in an emergency, [when there's] no electricity, [you] can't use ATMs; you need money. [I] at least [had the] peace of mind of having a little cash. That was a wonderful thing that I had that extra cash.

Cash and water, right?

Cash and water, yes.

When did you return to your home in New Orleans?

I stayed in Florida about two months. I believe I got home a little before Thanksgiving in November. It was several, many weeks that I stayed in Florida.

You say you haven't experienced any damage to your home. Have you experienced any post-Katrina life changes or hardships?

Well, it's hard that my friends, a lot of my friends, still have not moved back into their homes. Life is not the same. My routine is not the same because so many people are not here. Life is not the same. All of the people still aren't here, especially my godchildren. They evacuated to Hot Springs, Arkansas. Their mother decided— they were in school, the thirteen-year-old was in school, so she decided [the child] was going to stay in school for the rest of year. So she bought a house in Hot Springs, Arkansas, and they're living there. Life is a lot different. Everyone has their own story. It still hangs over your head. A lot of forgetfulness. People really— I'm surprised I'm still talking and remembering things because you forget, just little things. We call it the Katrina Syndrome. So far I haven't experienced any real depression, which is a blessing. So many people are still depressed, and that's understandable; losing their home, losing all their possessions. It's horrible. It's lingering... Unspeakable... Something that's still here, Katrina Syndrome.

Sadness over the city?

Yes, sadness. An underlying sadness for sure because things just are not the same and will not be the same for a long time. Might never go back to the way it was; may never go back.

I know the Center for Disease Control and other federal agencies had predicted that there would be health impacts from the storm, [as the result of] things like contaminated water, toxic spills,

garbage not being picked up. Are you, at the hospital, experiencing any different syndromes?

No, not really. I didn't start back at the hospital until February. They reopened the hospital, Tulane Hospital, downtown, reopened February 14th. As far as immediate illnesses [as a result of the] hurricane, I'm not aware of [any], and I haven't heard any statistics about diseases. As far as what's coming in now, I don't think that there have been any types of epidemic situations.

Any respiratory illnesses?

A lot of respiratory illnesses. A lot. That's been going on. That, I've been hearing from the very beginning. I believe a lot of respiratory illness is due to the fungus and the mold.

Will you stay in the city?

I will stay. I have all intentions of staying because this is my home.

Thought I Was Gonna Die Out There

Jesse Hampton
   Interviewed by Zachary J. George

Jesse Hampton survived alone on his rooftop for two days before being evacuated to Iowa.

I guess if you'd just like to start with where you were on August 28th, the day before. What was going on, what you were thinking?

Well, August 28th, a majority of my family had already evacuated, and I was trying to evacuate, but the thing is that I had a dog. And my dog was trained. He would only take food from me, and if I put him in a kennel or sent him someplace he wouldn't eat. He would starve. And so I said, well, I best keep him with me, but I lived on Michoud Boulevard in New Orleans East.

And the storm, it had tracked to hit downtown New Orleans. It was heading toward New Orleans at, what? Thirty something miles from New Orleans, so I knew I was going to be without power, I knew I was going to get some water. But, so we just— I met with a group of friends that were staying because they figured, you know, they— we dodged so many bullets before that they didn't think it was gonna be all that big. So, they were like me, and they waited around, but most of the people in my neighborhood had already left. But these were friends that lived in other neighborhoods and stuff like that. We had a hurricane party where we drank a bunch of hurricanes, mixing 'em up ourselves. And I got damn blitzed, and a lot of the stuff I don't remember from that night, but obviously somebody brought me home.

As far as feeding the dog, I must've fed him because it looked like I just ripped open the bag of dog food and dumped it all over the kitchen. But I had slept, and I had slept. In the wee hours of the morning, the storm had changed direction and turned a different path, and it went through St. Bernard Parish. My dog, it was like— the sun was just starting to come up. My dog was pulling me out of the bed, and I thought he just wanted to play or something, but he bit me really hard, and he actually pulled me out of the bed and made me bleed, and I jumped up. I put my little slippers on. I saw that I was bleeding, and I started chasing him around the house with a broom. I was gonna beat him, and by the time I got in the living room, I'm like, "What in the hell?" The glass... All the windows were broken. I had, like, maybe four inches of water in the living room.

I'm like, "What in the hell?!" And I kept hearing this noise. I said, "What in the hell was that?" Then I looked out the window. Damn, I could see it coming. It was not like heavy rain; this was a big-ass wall of water. I'm like, "Holy shit." I grabbed my dog, and I tucked him under my arm, and at the time it was a wooden house. There's a brick house now that sits on that foundation, but back then it was probably the only wooden house on Michoud Boulevard at the time, and my Vietnamese friends owned it, but they had left. They lived on one side. I lived on the other.

First thing I did was pull down the attic stairs. I tucked Rommel under my arm, and Rommel was a big dog. He was half-rottweiler, half-German shepherd, and I tucked him under my arm, and I went up those stairs so fast. Before I could pull the stairs all the way up, the water had hit the house. It sat on these stoop things and knocked it clean off, and we were up in the attic, and I could— I didn't have time— if I knew... I had tools and stuff in the attic at the time, but I just didn't have that much time. I'm talking three minutes maybe from the time— not even three, more like two— from the time I saw the water. The bottom part of the house had filled with it, but this big wave, when it hit, it just tore it off the foundation, and the house swimming down the street with me in the attic.

You were moving?

I was. The house was moving, and it was— the attic was full of water, and I had forgot all about Rommel. I was worried about saving my own ass at the time because I— the house wasn't upright; it was on its side. And when the water got up to my nose I freaked, and I just went to kicking. The first couple of kicks I got— thank God I had shoes on. The roofing nails went through my feet, went through my shoes. It hurt like hell. But when the water got over my head, and I went to kicking even harder, I didn't feel shit. I didn't feel anything. It was like survival mode, and I was finally able to kick the panel through. Because of all the shingles and stuff that were on the roof, I had finally kicked out a portion of where the water was actually going out, and it obviously created an air pocket, and the house started to tilt a little bit, but it wasn't laying flat anymore, and then once it straightened up, and the house was still moving down the street... By the time I had pushed the rest of the plywood out— the roof where the shingles were, I finally pushed it out— I looked, and I could see the roller coaster by Six Flags. This was, like, six, seven blocks.

What, through the hole?

Yeah, through the hole in the roof. And I said, "Damn." And I went looking for my dog. He was in the far corner, like, right where the... at the top, where you could see the fence from outside. He was dead. I was so sick. And when I went out to look around there, I thought— I cried for quite some time because I loved my dog to death, and he was dead. I crawled up on the roof, and I start looking around, seeing if there was anyone around, seeing if anyone could help me because— Jesus, the water was almost up to the gables. I'm like,

"Jesus Christ." It was flowing like a river. And then maybe three or four hours later I started seeing the bodies floating by. Scared the shit out of me. And I sat there. I didn't have any— then I tried to go back into the house. The food that I could find, it was all contaminated with filthy water. I opened up the fridge. I found an orange that I found in my refrigerator. That's all I had to eat. Nothing else I could touch because of the filthy water. Then the sun came out a few hours later, and it got so fucking hot. It was so hot, and all I could do to escape the sun was to go back and forth into the attic. There was still water in the attic, and my feet, you know, with the open wounds. They just got so infected. I kept my shoes on 'cause I figured that would protect me a little bit. Lotta good it did. And I had nothing to drink, and after the first day, sitting out in the hot sun, my eyes started to dry out, and I had problems seeing.

I was in the Marine Corps. I'd done jungle survival training, desert training, all that shit. And as hard as it was for me— the only way I was going to stay alive— I had to drink my own piss to keep fluids in me, and that was hard. But I had to. And the second day came. Any noise I heard I would poke my head out, thinking it was close by. I heard choppers, but I never saw them in the immediate air, but I could hear 'em. And I sat out there... I mean, that's the lowest I felt in my whole life. I thought I was gonna die out there 'cause I thought I was the only one left. And the second day, right before....

You couldn't see any people on other roofs?

No. No. None of my neighbors. Everyone was smart enough to leave. And I sat on that roof. I didn't know what I was going to do. And right before sun went down, I looked up, and I heard it, and I started screaming, but my mouth was so parched because I couldn't drink my piss anymore because you can only do it so long before you start to poison your body. My lips were so... They were cracked;

they were bleeding, and, I mean, I didn't have any more fluids in me. And I just waved and waved, and finally the chopper came by, and they lowered a basket. I climbed in.

And this is on Tuesday?

I forget what day that was. Not the 29th, but it was, like, the 30th. I think it was like the 30th or 31st. When that chopper finally came, they brought me to Baton Rouge first, but with me not being able to walk, they couldn't handle anybody non-ambulatory. When they saw how infected my feet were, they didn't want to deal [with me] because they couldn't treat me.

And so they took me to the VA. They had to pretty much slice my feet open because the pus was so bad, and they let it drain, and they pumped me full of antibiotics, and they would wrap my feet up. They said, "Don't walk. Don't walk." But, I mean, I don't want nobody to take me to the bathroom. I can go to the bathroom by myself. But, that's how it had to be. When I got to Gonzales, it got to the point where I was crawling on all fours just to get to the bathroom with all of those people in there. And when…She was a pastor from a Lutheran Church in Des Moines. She came in with a group, to Gonzales, and says, "We're taking you guys outta here. Who wants to go to Des Moines?" I was— I had been sleeping on a hard, on a gymnasium floor. It was some kind of Civic Center or something, but the floor was so hard, and all I had was a little blanket, maybe a quarter-inch thick. They gave me some clothes, and I would roll up the clothes as a pillow. I was really hungry, but there was so many people that they were trying to feed, you know. The food we got was better than nothing. And they brought me to— they brought me on a plane. They brought me to the plane, lowered me on the plane, and the next thing you know, I was landing in Des Moines, Iowa. And they put a lot of us up in the Embassy Suites hotel.

What was it like when the helicopters came, I mean, what was going through your mind? What were you thinking?

I was saved. I'm gonna live.

And there were guys, girls?

What? You mean the Coast Guard and all that?

Yeah, when they first came to the roof.

Oh, no. They didn't come to the roof. They were in a chopper. They lowered a basket. And once the basket…it's on a…it's a wench. They wenched me up, and they pulled me out of the basket.

Then what was it like?

They had a pilot, co-pilot, and a medic. They just loaded me with fluids. They had tons of bottled water. I must have had eight granola bars. Close to eight. Jesus Christ, I must've ate like eight of them. I was so… I was starving. They were feeding me on a regular basis, but they kept pumping me with water. That's one thing— I had plenty of water. There was food at the first evacuee station I went to. There was plenty of water, and with me being as dehydrated as I was, it was hard to eat, too— my lips cracked and bleeding. Then my feet are hurting. I tried to walk, but it hurt like hell. I was waiting for somebody to do something for me. I mean, there were lines everywhere, and I was scared I was going to miss out because they were like animals in this place. And I said, "I gotta get something to eat." So I went walking, standing in line, and it hurt like hell, and then the nurses were getting pissed off at me because I was leaving bloody footprints all over the damn place. And so they made sure that I ate first. The elderly. They would take care of the elderly and the disabled first. Once I arrived in Des Moines, life got a whole lot better.

What was the reception like? Were there people there waiting for you at the airport?

Oh, man. They treated me like— as soon as we got out of the airport there were charter buses there waiting for us.

I got carried out because they didn't want me walking. Put me in a wheelchair. Straight to the Embassy Suites, and I had to register with the Red Cross. I was already registered with the Red Cross in Gonzales, but I had to do all the paperwork all over again. And I was really hurting because they gave me antibiotics, but they didn't give me anything for the pain. Just a bunch of Ibuprofen and stuff, but all the nerves in my feet were exposed. Hurt like hell. They put me in the hotel. They put us in there for six weeks, like six, eight weeks, but once my wounds on my feet healed where I could actually walk around normally— it took a good three weeks before I could walk. My feet still hurt, but they weren't bleeding anymore, and they were no longer infected. I was losing my mind sitting in there, so a Red Cross worker came in there and talked to me, gave me my little debit card. Next thing, WOI radio came in there. They were talking to different evacuees.

How many evacuees were there in the Embassy Suites?

Tons. There were tons. And Mike LaValle came running up there and, he says, "I heard your story. Could you come down to the Embassy Club?" And I said, "My feet are feeling better, but, I mean, I don't have any uniforms or anything like that." He said, "Don't worry, I'll take care of it." And I went there. I met him. I met the executive chef and all of the sous chefs. We got there, and there were TV cameras everywhere, and they said, "We have an authentic, Cajun, Creole chef from New Orleans on the premises." The chef stepped out of the way and said, "We have a big function coming up this weekend. I know your feet are hurting, but just show us what to do." Man, heck. Hell with showing. I don't show. I like to do. And they cut me loose. It had been so long since I held a knife in my hand. I went to work. They hired me right there. On the spot. But there was one thing I had to do before my first day of work. I did an eight course Cajun/Creole feast for 24 people at the American— at the Des Moines Red Cross because they did so much for us.

And, the Hubbell's let us use their house.

They own car dealerships and…

That, real estate. Hell, the governor's mansion's their old house. That's how much money they got. They donated their house for the governor to use as his mansion. They bought everything. My new uniforms. I had cooks and servants helping me prepare all this. They were running the courses. I did— well, I do— I like fusion cooking. I combine Asian with Cajun. I was doing crab-stuffed shrimp with like a Vietnamese/Cajun Sambol sauce. It's like a sweet and spicy sauce but with Sambol. Oh, they loved it. And I did jambalaya. I did gumbo. Crawfish etouffee. Shrimp creole. White chocolate bread pudding with a caramel espresso, espresso caramel sauce. I mean with rum, of course. And they had never eaten— for them— like I said, that's why people come from all over the world to eat in New Orleans. Because we're masters of fusion cooking.

Once I did that event— that was also televised by KCCI, the local radio station— that's where I met Michelle Parker. She's the senior reporter there. And we just ran for it from there. And then once I went to work at the Embassy Club, my first day of work I had to go through all kinds of shit, and then the Des Moines Business Record, they had photographers and reporters there while I'm trying to work and show the chefs there how to cook. They said, "You're going to have to write it down." I said, "I can't. I can't write anything down because in New Orleans, we don't write anything down. We go by taste, sight. We go by taste, smell, and consistency. That's it. And you're always adding; you have to add stuff gradually. You can't... When I'm making a hundred pounds of gumbo, I ain't got time to stop and see how many spoons of salt I threw in there, or how much roux I'm gonna make.

And I just went to work, and you should've saw the line. Now, these were all club members. When they would do their luncheons they would have a bunch of people in the club— never that many— but they'd pour in because they said the chef's in town. We got real food. And the people didn't know jambalaya from gumbo.

But once they got a taste for it, that's all they wanted. It was— set out prime rib, rack of lamb, all of that CIA [Culinary Institute of America], European stuff, you know, but when it came to some authentic New Orleans food, it was too hot for 'em. But I tell you, I seen a seventy-year-old lady sitting down, eating some jambalaya, and it was hot as I don't know what, and she— her face sweats— and I said, "Is that too much?" And she said, "Oh, it's hot, but it sure is delicious."

It was great. And then I had the greatest... Of course, this was the spring. I spent three years there. I did a New Orleans night for Nyemaster's law firm, which is the largest law firm in Des Moines. I did their associate's party. I did their intern party. Any event that they had coming up— Christmas party or company picnic, I mean firm picnic and all of that— they would call me exclusively, and one of the senior partners, this one senior partner, he bankrolled my catering business. I started working as a personal chef, and at the Embassy Club they kept trying to get my recipes from me. I said, "I can't help you. I can't help you. You got a chef here. He's been a chef longer than I have. He's a CIA graduate, you know, he's been a chef for 25 years. Not me. I can do what he can do, but he can't do what I can do. So, you know, what's the deal?" And they kept pressuring me and pressuring me. I said, man, heck with this. So, I had, like, fifteen events already lined up within a two-month period. I just went to work for myself. And Frank Hardy, him and his wife— his wife was the president of the Des Moines Ballet— and so, they kept me so busy during the spring. The first winter there wasn't so bad. It wasn't a whole lot of snow, but the last two winters I was there, it was just brutal. And I just couldn't take it. I got tired of shoveling snow. But this last one was really bad 'cause when I opened the door there was so much snow I had to shovel snow into my living room just to get outside.

Where were you staying?

I was staying in the 200 block of Grand Avenue, right across from the Civic Center in a studio apartment, but the thing is, I had— I couldn't invite nobody to my house because my house looked like a warehouse: chafing dishes, hot boxes, cambros...

You brought your work home with you.

Yeah. And I did... I helped a lot of people. Like when they did *The Lion King*, the play, at the Civic Center, I had cast members come over, ordering stuff for me to make for them, and the hotel would take it back to the Civic Center for them. I did great, but I just got so homesick.

What did you miss about New Orleans?

Oh, man. I hated missing all the Mardi Gras. It was my favorite time of year. Course, I was drinking like a fish. I got drunk one night, and I just passed out in a snow bank. I could've died, but my friends went looking for me. It was snowing really hard. I didn't know where I was 'cause I got mad at somebody, and I'm walking home. If it wasn't for, um... Joanne went looking for me in an SUV.

I would've froze to death. Her and her daughter scraped me up and brought me home. They made sure I wasn't dead. They loaded me up with blankets, and they wouldn't leave until they knew I was alright. And I said, heck with this, I'm coming home.

And then, since I come home, I got scammed bad. I paid— it cost me $2,700 dollars— I paid online for a place on the 1300 block of, yeah, the 1300 block of Camp. Right on the corner of Camp and Perrier. There used to be a house there.

Not anymore. But on the website they had the old house and this and that and this and that, so I said, ooh, that's not bad for nine hundred a month. They wanted first month rent, last month rent, and deposit. It cost them another $2,400 dollars to move all my belongings from Des Moines back to New Orleans. The guy even mailed me the keys. So, when I got to the airport, and I went to— I'm looking around going, "What the...what's going on?"And I didn't see a house. I'm sitting here with keys, and that's where the cab driver brought me. This is where it's supposed to be. Right here. But there was nothing there. There was a shell way back, looked like somebody was— like they just started rebuilding something, but it wasn't right on the corner where the old place used to be because there wasn't always a big lot there. There was always a house there. And they used... I don't know what the heck happened. And then five days later my belongings came from Des Moines, and they delivered 'em to the vacant lot, and the crackheads, the dope fiends, they started stealing stuff. I was losing it.

Then I ran into my old boss from the Orleans Café. Hired me on the spot. I slept in the storeroom at Orleans Café for the first few months until I landed the job as the executive chef at the 300 Club Bistro, and I had made enough money where I could afford a month's rent, but my apartment was empty over at Esplanade and

City Park. Paying $1,225 dollars for a one-bedroom apartment. Then the owner of the 300 Club Bistro gave me the money for the deposit, but I had to sign a contract. And for three months I worked for him. My drinking got really bad, and I lost that job. I really liked that job, too. I mean, I just gone downhill ever since I come home. Coming back to New Orleans was the worst thing I'd ever done because when I was in Des Moines I didn't drink every day. I just drank during certain events or if it was a party atmosphere. Once I come back to New Orleans, it was an every day thing after that. So, um, coming home was the biggest mistake of my life.

Blown Charts

Kirsten Stanton
Interviewed by Nicole Pugh

The storm forced Kirsten Stanton and her partner Craig out of their new Uptown home and their alternative medicine clinic.

It was Friday night, and we got a call from Craig's mom. She obsessively watches The Weather Channel. We had no idea that anything was going on. We tuned in to the television. We had left for Ivan last year and really didn't want to go through that again. However, we decided, "Okay, maybe we should go." That night we started calling around to reserve. Everything was booked. It was his mother who finally called us back the next morning and said that she found something online for that night.

Craig went to work at the office that Saturday. It was he who called me saying, "Maybe I should end early. I've already had two people cancel saying they are not coming." I just made a mad dash and grabbed stuff in the house, got the dog together, got the dog food, and drove out [to Metairie] to meet him. It was funny because something felt different to me, intuitively. I was scared in a way I hadn't been before, but I didn't think anything of this magnitude would happen. We went to Baton Rouge Saturday night. It took us about four and a half to five hours to get there, and it normally takes an hour.

[Once we got there] we pretty much became glued to the television between then and Monday. We went to the grocery store on Sunday, which we realized was too late. There was nothing on the shelves even in Baton Rouge. We got the few things that we could find and just hunkered down. It seemed interminably long until Monday rolled around, sitting in the motel room. Then, of course, being petrified. I think that on Sunday night, the more we watched the news, the more scared we became. I think that I was praying that it not hit New Orleans, but also that it would not come to Baton Rouge. They were saying that if it came to Baton Rouge, it could possibly be bad there as well.

I don't think I slept that much on Sunday night. I tossed and turned. I remember waking up and telling Craig that I just have to turn the TV on— at five in the morning, then at nine in the morning. We were so exhausted. There was so much dread and sadness already, even before knowing what happened.

Then the power went out in the motel. Nobody knew what was going on. The winds died down at around four in the afternoon. We went out. We didn't know what else to do. We sat in the car and listened to the radio. I think— like everybody else— people were reporting that New Orleans wasn't hit that hard and that everything was going to be okay.

That day went on, and I remember hearing on the news that there were broken levees but there wasn't all that water at that point. Of course, it wasn't until a day or two later when it all happened. It just seemed interminable. On Monday, I think we were hoping that in a couple of days we would be able to go back.

Then all of that changed. We were in the motel until about Thursday. That was when our friends from Morgan City called and said, "Please come stay with us." We had reservations because of our crazy dog, but they were really kind about it. That's when we realized that we would not be getting home anytime soon.

At this point, I think that Craig and I had made peace with the fact that maybe the house, even if it was there, would have water damage and that we might not have anything. But our office... We weren't even going to go in. We were just going to drive by. We weren't worried about it. I wanted to get in to see the house. I read reports on NOLA.com of people getting in [to New Orleans] on River Road and that you could kind of get by even though New Orleans wasn't suppose to be open at that point. My whole plan was, "Okay, let's just see if we can get in there and see the apartment." Of course, we were turned away by the National Guard. It was really harrowing going over the Huey P. Long— the plumes of smoke. You could see the fires still raging in downtown New Orleans.

The next day Jefferson Parish was opened. You could see the helicopters. It was more like a war zone. At this point, we were still seeing water, even in Metairie. You could see it as you were on the overpass on the Causeway. Also, there was garbage everywhere. We didn't even go into Lakeview. Since then, we have been to it, and it is horrendous.

It was random in Metairie— what was destroyed and what wasn't. We went to our office, and we were just blown away. The roof tore off, and the window blew out. Our office was just destroyed. It had water damage. I went in to try to salvage things, and my throat was hurting. I think I was breathing in fiberglass. I really shouldn't have been around it. I didn't have gloves, and I was trying to take things. Then I had cuts all over my hands because of all the insulation. That was a real blow to me to see that place destroyed.

Everything was in there. We had purchased furniture [for the office], and we didn't have insurance. That was something I was just about to get for the place. We bought some nice Japanese furniture, and I had equipment that I had brought to New Orleans from the acupuncture school: electric stimulators, PVP lamps, other equipment. Each of those things costs three to four hundred dollars. They were just destroyed. All my patients' files were blown everywhere. I couldn't even call people afterwards. I still don't have some people's numbers because all of my charts were just blown to kingdom come, and I didn't have a system where everyone was in in my computer. It was basically my charts. That has been very frustrating for me that I have not been able to contact everyone. I think that is still something I am processing. I wasn't expecting it. It was just such a weird thing. We were on the second floor, so that was why I never even thought anything would be wrong with the office.

We finally did get in before Orleans Parish was considered "open." They just waved us by. They asked for ID and asked, "Do you have any ammunition on you?" Then they said, "Okay, curfew is at six o'clock. You have to be out by then." It was so eerie because there were streets that we couldn't go on. They asked us where we lived, and they sort of watched you drive down to that section. This was at a point where all trees were still down and the power lines were down. I was telling Craig, "Look! We use to walk over there!"

We almost drove over a live power line. It was very scary. Honestly, it felt eerie to be there. We knew [that there had been no flooding] even before we got into the house because of those flood maps that they have online. We were relieved to know, but we didn't know if there was any wind damage that affected the roof. We saw that the house externally looked fine… A whole tree came down in front of our house, so it was hard to get in the front door. We just looked at it, went in, were in shock that it was all right, and got back out. I know it sounds weird, but we didn't even want to drive around. It just felt so eerie to be there, seeing the paint on every single house indicating whether someone was in there, whether no one had been found or whether there were pets in there.

When we eventually went in to the house, Craig and I were like, "What are we going to do with all this stuff?" It felt like a burden.

When it all came around, it just wasn't all that important. It bogs you down having all that.

The smell was horrific. This wasn't even an area where there was flooding or anything. Some people who had stayed had put fridges out. There may also have been dead animals rotting. It was really bad. There was so much debris in the streets that it seemed a little precarious to be driving around. And it was a ghost town. I think when we drove down there, we saw two people, and that was total.

The presence of the National Guard everywhere was strange. I know that it meant a return to safety for a lot people who had been there. Not having been there, it was weird. It created for me a feeling that there was something unsafe because they were there. We were really shaken driving in there, thinking, "What are we going to find?" I think that we had a lot of nervous adrenaline. To realize that it is okay, and then to have all of that around us... It was a lot to process.

I made the decision to not go back, and it took me two months to make that decision. Now I am processing the fact that I have left and that chapter of my life is over, including quite possibly my relationship with a man of six years. It's a lot that I am working out right now. The really good thing about all of this is that I am being given time thanks to my friend Jeremy, who works with an evacuee-relief organization and who knew about FEMA lodging. Since I graduated from school, I needed time for myself, and I never had it— just to get reconnected to who I am and what I really want. To me, that is invaluable... I am trying not to project and to be in the here and now. In my good moments, I do feel like things are going to work out, and I am going to be happier somewhere else than I ever was in New Orleans.

I Don't Own the Clothes I'm Wearing

Carol McCarthy
In Her Own Words

Carol McCarthy and her husband moved to New Orleans from her hometown of Chicago just five weeks before Katrina.

This was our first hurricane experience, and we wanted to do everything right. Mike and I just closed on our first home five weeks before. Being from Chicago and generally terrified about hurricanes, we talked about staying for hurricanes, definitely a Category 1 or 2. But anything higher than a two, we said we'd evacuate. And so we began the task of evacuating. It all seemed to go so smooth. Katrina was predicted to hit Monday morning. So, here it was, Saturday morning, when we woke up, brewed a pot of coffee, and hopped into the Subaru, bound for Lowe's on Elysian Fields to buy plywood for the windows. There were no lines at Lowe's. I thought that this was all so silly. No one else seemed to be frantic. It wasn't until we got to the Spur gas station on Magazine Street where it hit us. The lines were not that long, but the anxiety of those waiting was growing into a small panic. Horns were blaring at those who were taking too long. Inside, a man cut in front of me to pay, shoving me slightly to one side. I got nervous. "Here it is," I thought.

Mike was careful to measure and cut the boards properly. It was only nine o'clock in the morning, and his measurements were exact. We were to board up after he got off of work later. He left for the restaurant, and I said I'd get things prepared around the house. But instead, I did what any other person in denial would have done. I waited and watched TV, did a few loads of laundry, and took a nap. If I knew that we would be going for an extended period of time, I would have packed differently. But I didn't know.

The actual evacuation out of New Orleans seemed so easy. We waited until contraflow opened and left shortly thereafter, around 6:30 p.m. We didn't incur any traffic hassles until Baton Rouge, then it was bumper to bumper for about twenty miles. After that, we cruised west on I-10 in search of a hotel somewhere by the Texas border. It was late, and we were tired.

The funny thing about this hotel search in southwestern Louisiana is that there were no rooms available. It was as if hotels stopped taking reservations or people booked them in advance. So we kept driving until we reached our first destination of Orange, Texas. We forked up one-hundred dollars plus for a room, unloaded the car, and went to the bar, hoping to get up early in the morning to head to Houston.

And so the story goes: a few days in a Houston hotel, too much wine, too much CNN, too much time in a small car. And somewhere along the way, I realized that these aren't my clothes. I am wearing powder blue panties from Wal-Mart, Gold Toe label socks, royal blue snowboarding pants (Mossimo brand), a pink knitted sweater (labeled Liz Claiborne), and I smell of sugar body scrub. But because I left New Orleans, bound for Houston, with three outfits suited for ninety-degree-plus temperatures, complete with two pairs of sandals, I have accepted the donations from my wonderful friends back in Chicago where we finally landed.

Mike and I returned to the Windy City almost ten days after we evacuated. When we boarded up and left the Saturday before Katrina hit, we intended this to be a long weekend away in Houston. We didn't expect to be going back to Chicago. But we decided that staying close to home would bankrupt our checking accounts, and we needed to find a place we could stay that wouldn't cost us anything.

So, we returned to Chicago, a place that we just moved from five weeks before, to find shelter with family and friends.

Now we were there, and the climate was much cooler than we were used to, much less humid, with temperatures soaring only up to the seventy-degree mark during the day, much different than the climate we were slowly getting used to. We were gladly going to accept the donated clothing that our good friends had gathered from their closets. When we were en route to Chicago, days after the storm, friends kept asking the proverbial "What can I do?" My answer was simply to borrow some clothes, a small request of "Do you have anything in your closet you can spare?"

There is something different about accepting gifts on occasions such as birthdays or other holidays than accepting donations. I have always been keen to keeping tradition with our annual "Girls' Night Out," acronym GNO, celebrations. We celebrate the birthday of each friend for each month. As we grew older and new events shaped our lives, we began throwing elaborate bachelorette parties at various locations/states. Weddings crept up and time was spent throwing numerous showers and attending receptions, all with gifts in hand. Then came the babies, even more reason to celebrate, because buying baby clothes and toys for baby showers was the best. Then, of course, the delivery day, and more presents. And even more as Christenings happen, first birthdays, you get the point. These gifts, these moments, were special, and giving was all there was to do.

But for me, this was different, or so I assumed. The denial of accepting anything was getting out of hand. All we had seen of our city under water told us that we lost everything. There were no other clothes to return home to, probably washed away in the gulf. That was probably the truth, but for me, I just wanted to borrow a few items until I could get my own clothes out of my closet and on my back. And so it was, the day at Chris's bar outside of Chicago city limits, where we met up with some of the GNO girls, hands clasping black bags of clothes, handing off offerings of cards with gift cards, cash, checks, toiletries, makeup, you name it.

It was all too much, and it all came crashing down on me at that point. Between the hours spent in my Honda from New Orleans to Houston, then up Highway 59 to interstate after interstate going east, then north back to Chicago, and the hours dumped into CNN, MSNBC, and FOX, I was numb. There was nothing pumping in my blood up to this point, no emotion connecting myself to what was happening in New Orleans, even though I was connected. I had cried only once since, and that was the day that, after watching yet another newscast on CNN four days after Katrina hit, we decided to leave Houston and head up to Chicago. I cried then because I realized that I would not be going home anytime soon. I cried at the thought that home was no longer a place I could return to.

But somehow, through the gifts and donations from the girls, I had a breakdown, a much needed one. I carefully noted the tender looks in my friends' eyes as they were generally concerned about my life and us. I realized, in that moment, that I was a part of this whole mess, and under those circumstances, the people I loved were also a part, in an indirect way.

New Orleans is People

Niyi Osundare
Interviewed by Rebeca Antoine

Niyi Osundare, a Nigerian poet and professor, was teaching at the University of New Orleans at the time of Katrina. He and his wife were forced into their attic by the rising waters and were eventually rescued by a neighbor.

This interview is dedicated to my wife, Kemi, whose strength and courage made it possible for us to survive that terrible sojourn in the attic.

When did you first hear about Hurricane Katrina?

Like all the others in New Orleans, about four days before it actually hit. I think that was when it was still lingering on the Atlantic, before it entered the Gulf. Of course the warnings and announcements became intensified once it was in the Gulf barrelling towards New Orleans. And about two days before it landed, both the mayor and the governor were talking about evacuation. But it wasn't 'til a couple hours before the hurricane that they started talking about mandatory evacuation. So, like all the others in New Orleans, we, too, were glued to our television. We knew it was coming.

Were you worried about it?

Absolutely. Oh, yes. Nobody could have seen— could have heard— that that kind of storm was coming without getting worried, especially considering the havoc it wrought in Cuba, Jamaica, and some Caribbean Islands that it passed through. So, we were worried. I'm sure that your next question will be, "Why didn't you evacuate?"

Did you think about evacuating?

We did, but my wife and I had a daughter with us. She's our deaf girl. We wanted to get her out first. She was going back to Gallaudet University in Washington. So, Saturday morning, very early, my wife took her— tried to get her to the airport. There was such a massive traffic backup that she missed her flight. We couldn't even get to the airport. We had to return home. So, Sunday morning at three my wife took her out, and eventually she left that day. By the time she left, it was already too late for us to evacuate. And then, my wife also worked at Charity Hospital, and she thought she might be called because she was put on— I don't know what they call it— some kind of emergency. And if she was called, and if she had to leave, that I would go with her and shelter at Charity. So, that was why; we were waiting for the call, and then the wind started getting stronger and stronger.

When was that?

The hurricane came on Monday. That was Sunday before the hurricane came. It became impossible for us to leave the house, really, when the winds kept coming.

Where's your home?

5317 Wickfield Drive. Very close to the campus [UNO] here. That's between Filmore and Prentiss. Or something like that. It's quite close to this place. That's where we were. That's how it met us at home. When the wind came, it was very furious. Bit it onlyremoved a few shingles from our roof. It wasn't until about nine o'clock, ninethirty, on the 29th. That's Monday, when the water started coming.

Is that in the morning?

In the morning, yes. My wife looked through the window and said, "Oh, my God, what kind of water is this?" Before we knew what was happening, it was on our driveway. Before we knew where we were, it was under the house, and it started lifting the carpet, you know.

So, we were looking for all kinds of places to put our things. Normally, my wife and I had books, things, all over the place. The shelf couldn't take everything, and I'm not a terribly tidy person as far as keeping books and papers is concerned because I always like to see the books I'm reading. I like to see them physically. So, I have so many— I had so many books— close to, I mean, by my bedside. All those ones were the first to go.

And then: One foot. Two feet. Three feet. Four feet. And it was so rapid. And the current was also rapid, what we had in our house.

It was at that point we were trying to rescue all we could, trying to put all those things on the lower shelves right onto the higher shelves. That didn't work because the shelves started falling into the water. It was at that point my wife then said, "Niyi, we are going to drown."

I don't know why it didn't occur to me. I was so consumed by the anxiety to rescue as many of my books and documents as possible; of course I couldn't really rescue them. I began to wonder, "Where do we go from here?"

So my wife said, "Attic. Let's go to the attic." We had never opened the attic ourselves. It was the Terminix man who usually came, and I watched him one or two times when he had to go up the attic, so I tried to do what I saw him do, you know, it took quite some time. The stairwell fell into the river, and so we climbed up the ladder. There were about eight rungs to the ladder. The water went up as far as the sixth. So, we were sitting there near the edge, and our feet were in the water. We were watching the water rise on the 29th, afternoon, evening, and then night. Night was terrible. It was dark, and I was able to go up the attic with a torch, a flashlight, and my wife also was able to save her cell phone, put it between her teeth as we went up. And then, my small transistor radio. We also had my small transistor radio, and we could at least hear what was happening. Many of the radio stations were broadcasting. On it we heard people shouting "Oh, the water is rising. My uncle has drowned." My wife and I took turns, at night, to fix the light on the water. It was rising. We were so scared that it might rise, swallow us where we were, and choke us. It was a really scary night.

And about 5:30 that morning, the torch [flashlight] went out. I think it just burnt out. But it had served us. Now, we were able to make it through the night. Of course, no food, no water… Nothing.

And then we began to wonder, what's going to happen today? We were hungry. We were thirsty. We were tired. But even beyond that: can we survive another night in this kind of place? No.

And, of course, all along we were calling 911. And getting all kinds of responses, you know. I think we called five times.

The fifth time a lady picked up the phone and asked where we were. I told her where we were.

She said, "How old are you?"

I don't know what that has to do with our plight. We told her how old we were, and she said, "Go out in a boat."

And I told her, "There is no boat here. None at all."

I asked her in utter desperation: "How can we get one?"

"I don't know," she answered.

So I asked her, "A whole city is underwater? And there is no boat?"

This was at 2:30 in the night. And she said, "Okay. You stand on your roof and the helicopter might see you."

I said, "How can a helicopter see me at 2:30 in the night? And how many helicopters anyway?"

One or two was hovering above our head. Maybe, we heard their rumbling once every two hours. Something like that. And besides, we couldn't cut a hole through the roof. There was nothing to use, you know. We had no hatchet. And why wasn't there a hatchet in the attic? Because we had never been in that kind of situation before.

The fifth time we didn't actually complete the phone call when everything just went silent. "Brmp." I think it was at that time that the telephone system in New Orleans gave up. So, from that time on, we had no contact at all with the outside world. No contact at all. It was scary. I mean, everywhere around us was water. We didn't know what was happening out there. And I don't know what kept us going. Somehow we kept hoping that something might happen. Nothing happened for a long, long time. My wife and I were shouting occasionally, "Help. Help!" But as time went on, our strength diminished, and we couldn't even shout. There was a hammer. Some little hammer there in the attic. And I looked for a metal object. I hit the hammer on the object so as to produce some noise, some SOS sound, at least to let people know we were there. We don't know whether there was anybody around anyway. About four or five o'clock the following day... that was, oh God...

Wednesday or Tuesday?

No, on Tuesday. The hurricane was, the 29th? Tuesday, yes, on Tuesday afternoon. It was hot in the attic. Extremely hot. And the attic is where you keep all these insulation materials and so on. Yes, these materials were soaking up every bit of oxygen around and releasing heat. So we couldn't breathe. And my wife started running out of breath and gasping. I, too, started gasping. It was at that point I really got scared because I thought we were going to choke to death.

At this point, the water had stopped rising, but we had between eight and nine feet of water in our house. Now we had no air. No oxygen.

Miraculously, my wife said she heard a sound on the roof. I thought it was hallucination. But it wasn't. It was Placido Sabalo, our Cuban-American neighbor. He came to his house to see if he could rescue anything but discovered he couldn't because the whole place was taken up by water. He was on his way back when he heard our sound. So he traced us to our place. He rescued us. My wife and I owe our lives to this kind neighbor.

On Monday morning, when the water had just started rising, and was about two feet or so in our house, Placido and I kept on talking on the phone, and he told me if we needed anything we should let him know. About an hour later ,when the water had risen by about six inches, he came over to our house to see how things were going.

He came back again and said, "This is very bad water. A very bad storm."

And then it was raining. He gave my wife and me two life jackets. I almost said, "Oh, no, don't worry. I don't think this is necessary." Reluctantly, we took the two life jackets, and he put on the third. With a sword in his hand, and looking like a warrior, he jumped into the rapidly rising flood, waded off, and disappeared We didn't see him until the day after, and that was when he came on a rescue mission. When he came back the following day, the water in our house was between eight and nine feet high. Those jackets proved extremely useful.

From the roof, Placido shouted, "Professor, you are here?"

I said, "Yes."

"Come out. Go into boat. Go into boat. Small, small," he said. "You still have life jacket?"

And I said, "Yes."

I fitted the jacket. I fitted one for my wife. I told my wife, "You wait first. Let me go. Let me go first." So, I jumped into the water. Of course, my sofa, my— all our things were bouncing around in the... I had to make my way through.

Then I got to the door and discovered I couldn't open it because of the water pressure, and Placido and another guy in the boat were very anxious. "Get out! Get out! You know, uh, if gas finish, we die." Somehow I was able to force the door, but I could only get it open to a certain extent. When I was trying to crawl out of this small space the only shirt I had got torn. Happened to my wife, too. So, both of us left our house in a short and shirt. No shoes. None at all. They got us on the boat. We looked all around. Where do we go? The whole of New Orleans was underwater anyway.

We were boated off to St. Raphael's Catholic mission on Elysian Fields. It was impossible to recognize our neighborhood. I couldn't see a thing. We couldn't believe it. This was the same place where three days ago the children were playing.

There were so many other evacuees there. The place was crowded. Nothing to eat. Nothing to drink. Well, at least we were there, and we had people to talk to.

How many people do you think were there?

Must have been up to two hundred. That's a small place. In a small room. It was tragic. Children. Men. Women. Old people.

The following morning, a few boats came and took us out of the place. First, they landed us at Save-A-Center on Leon Simon. As we rowed by, I discovered that the University of New Orleans was dry— a happy surprise. The irony is that I had thought the university would be vulnerable because of its closeness to the lake; so I transferred my valuable literary documents and materials from there to my house. Of course, the water found them there and destroyed them. I was so happy the university was safe. Then I kept on wondering about water's logic. It went by this university that was so close to it and came right down to those of us that were far.

We were in front of Sav-A-Center for a couple of hours. Then one or two members of the National Guard came. And they took us to the new Kirschman building. When we got there we saw hundreds and hundreds of people. I couldn't recognize that hall, the way it was used. I said, my God, almost another tragic irony. Now I'm a shirtless, nameless, penniless evacuee on the same university where I used to be a professor. So, we're there. Nothing to eat.

So you still haven't eaten in…?

No. Nothing to eat. At about nine o'clock. That was September. I don't remember the date now. September 1st or 2nd. They started dropping MRE's. It took some time before we knew how to handle them. They had the water, and they set it down. That was on the third day after the storm hit.

Then we kept wondering, "Are we going to be here forever?" And we were told no, no, no; they were coming to take us to higher ground— that the helicopters were coming. It wasn't until the fourth day that the helicopters started coming. By then they would make one or two sorties and disappear. They would come at nine in the morning and tell you, "Oh, yeah, we're coming at eleven." We would never see them, you know. And we— we were all made to line up. Fifteen to each line, because the helicopter could only take fifteen. We waited and waited. Eventually, the helicopter came. We were packed in like sardines.

When you were here at UNO, you said you didn't have any food until they started bringing the MRE's. Was there any place to lie down, sit down?

The fields. The fields. That was where we slept. Oh yeah, one evening we slept in the corridor. Everywhere was taken. Everywhere! Lecture halls. Don't talk about the restrooms. Oh, no, no, no, no. I don't want to remember their state. Oh my god, it was terrible. I mean, the smell. The stench everywhere. And of course, after people had fouled up the restrooms they started fouling up their surroundings. People were reduced to the state of nature. You would see people as you were passing, especially when it was fairly dark. You would see them pull down their pants and do it— right there— on the field. Right there in the back of the Kirschman building.

It was terrible. Really, really, terrible. So, the helicopter took us— maybe on the fourth day— to Causeway in Metairie. You know, higher ground. We spent the whole day there. It was there we saw the evacuees from other parts of New Orleans. We spent the whole day there, and the buses started coming. We didn't know where they would be taking us. But eventually my wife and I got on a bus which took us to the airport: New Orleans Airport. We spent another night at the airport. Nowhere to sleep, you know. Nowhere to even sit. You had to struggle to find a place on the floor where you could even sit and rest your back against the wall. I had never seen that kind of crowd at the airport before. The following morning the police came, and they started to do crowd control. C30 airplanes, the green one came, and they started batch by batch. We got onto one of the planes.

And I asked, "Where are we going?"

"You just sit. We take you wherever we find space."

About one and a half hours later, the plane landed. I looked around, and I said, "This is Birmingham, Alabama;" I told my wife because I had been there two times before for reading and speaking engagements. I said, "It's Birmingham, for goodness sake." And, indeed, it was Birmingham, Alabama.

From there I was so weak they had to take me in an ambulance to the the University of Alabama Teaching Hospital where I was treated for dehydration. They gave me water, something to eat. My wife and I went to the Red Cross Center. Hundreds and hundreds and hundreds of people. At the Red Cross Center we all had to line up. We were processed. We were given bands to tie around our wrists. Identification tags. There were hundreds of cot beds. And who were we to complain? At least we had something to sleep on, a rare luxury. It was there we had our first hot meal in days. And a real good shower. The first time in about a week that we could brush our teeth. We also had access to TV in the hall, and we saw other evacuees on the screen. And we kept wondering, "How long are we going to be here?"

While all this was happening, e-mails were flying all over the place from people who cared about our welfare and wondered about our whereabouts. Hotel accommodations in different cities had been arranged; flight bookings had been done. But no one knew where we were, and we never knew of these generous gestures from friends and high school alumni, particularly Christ's School Alumni, until much later.

After two days at the Red Cross Center, a young couple named Autumn White and Scott Neuman— plus their boy Noah— came to us and said they would like to adopt us. They said they had a house and plenty of room. We said, "Okay, we'll think about it. Let's meet tomorrow." The following day they came back. My wife and I had made up our minds: we would go with them because they were very genuine. So we went with them. They gave us a place in their basement. Occasionally we went to the Red Cross Center to eat, and then we would come back. Now, for the first time in about 10 days I had access to a laptop. It was when I opened my email box that I saw so many messages. About 1,500 messages from all over the world. There were people that were anxious to know where I was.

The Nigerian community in Mississippi, Alabama, and Tennessee got to know what was happening, and they started coming and sending messages and so on. Many Nigerians in Birmingham traced us to where we were, and took care of us in several ways. There was an attempt to make us feel at home. But we had no identity. Nobody knew who we were, so we could not enjoy some of the facilities they were providing other evacuees. We couldn't even get the food stamps because we were like imposters. One afternoon, a young man, Rev. Korubo, and his wife, Bola, both Nigerians, came and saw what was happening. The man left, went to the library in Birmingham, Googled me, and came back with about eight pages. When he showed those at the registeation desk, everybody was like, "Why didn't you tell us you are a poet? Why didn't you tell us you are a professor? Why didn't you…" And I said, "What? I mean, I can't have it written on my forehead." Those papers became our ID. With them we were able to get food stamps. We were able to receive some kind of allowance, some kind of token, usable only at Wal-Mart. So, that was Birmingham.

Oh, while we were still in Birmingham, the Wole Soyinka Society advertised the OSUNDARE RELIEF FUND on their listserv for people to send in their widow's mites. Christ's School Alumni also rallied round with valuable support. Help came from many people in different parts of the world. Constantly people were being informed of what was happening to us, people on that listserv. So, it was they who told the rest of the world that indeed we were safe. And, of course I did a short note, which I sent to them, which they then passed on to other parts of the world. Eventually all Nigerian newspapers carried the story, and at last people at home knew my wife and I were safe. And then I kept on wondering, where do we go from here? No job. No house. No ID. Then a letter came from Franklin Pierce College (now University), very heart-warming, offering me a position as Visiting Professor and Poet in Residence for the Katrina semester, and promising some comfort for me and my wife, away from the eye of the storm. Three years earlier the university had awarded me an honorary doctorate, so I had some kind of relationship with the college. It was called college, then. The friend that facilitated my relationship with the university is Don Burness. He's a poet and an academic. He's retired now. We got that letter, and it was such a relief. But, how do we get to New Hampshire? We had no ID, and in post 9/11 America, you couldn't pass through the airports without a solid ID. We wrote back, and they made arrangements with the airline. The airline allowed us free passage; that was how we left Birmingham for Rindge in New Hampshire, where we were very warmly received. The university provided us a car. We used it for the three months we were there. Then, a couple, Peter and Jean Lemay contacted the university and offered us their house by the lake. We didn't pay a penny, you know. They didn't only give us a place to live.

They provided a lot of warmth, a lot of friendship. We got to know their family.

Peter Lemay is a business man, very articulate, and the wife, the wife is a great lover of literature, especially poetry. They made life really comfortable for us. It was quite painful when we had to leave. Some people felt I should have stayed on, but I couldn't abandon the University of New Orleans to the post-Katrina trauma because the university didn't abandon me in my hour of need in 1997 when we had to bring our deaf daughter back to the US for educational reasons. A job offer from UNO made my family's relocation possible.

We came back in January 2006, and New Orleans was a swamp. A mighty, smelly swamp. I'd never seen something like that before. The trees were dead. The houses— there was the stench of death and decay everywhere. It took me quite some time before I got to our house— or our former house: a place where all we used to own lay buried. It was very difficult. But our story with the Lemays has not ended. Mr. Lemay and his son and his friend's son actually came, and they were in New Orleans for about one week getting out all the dirt and decaying things in the house. I couldn't believe it. He used his contacts to get others to come. Another group came. Yet another group came until the whole place was empty. And then when we had problems with our insurance company, Mr. Lemay also came from Massachusetts. He lives in Andover, in Massachusetts. He came down from there to broker an agreement, literally, between us and the insurance company. We were able to get some money from them because those guys were saying it was flood that damaged our house, not wind, whereas, we're insured for wind and water. So, it's amazing, the kind of friendship that we discovered, and the kind of hospitality, and the kind of good will that we enjoyed all over the place. This took some of the sting of Katrina away. Coming back here was a challenge, a big challenge. We had nowhere to live in New Orleans.

But two Nigerian friends, Rev. Sola Falodun and Phanuel Egejuru, a professor of English at Loyola University New Orleans, got us a trailer at the Episcopal Church on Canal Street where we stayed from mid-January until early February . The Church people were kind, caring, and generous. But the trailer was cold, and most times we ran out of gas. Gas-hunting became a task for my wife and me. Teaching and the reality of our Katrina losses confronted me with a rude bang. For the first time, I realized what it meant to be a professor without books. Difficult semester, very challenging. All my books, all my records, all my lecture notes gone. All my literary correspondences gone. I felt stripped and dispossessed. Many of my students also had similar experiences. We were a community of deprived survivors.

Would you say the university was really the impetus for you to come back to New Orleans? Do you think that if your job wasn't here that you would've returned?

I must say that it's a combination of my love for this city and a love for the university. There is no other city that I've been to in the U.S. that's been like New Orleans. This city has a certain passion about it. It generates its own passion, and it has a way of generating that passion in other people. It's unique, which is why I was surprised when some people were saying New Orleans was not salvageable, therefore, just forget New Orleans and tell New Orleanians to move to other places so that this place could go back to the swamp as it was in the beginning. This city is a very important part of U.S. history, a very important part of the world's cultural landscape. So I returned here— the two forces were the university and the city. On one side I must say that people rose to the challenge in different ways. It was also a very instructive experience for me. The English department, for example, is the largest department in the university. It was amazing how Peter Schock was able to run a whole department on a laptop from an abandoned warehouse in Illinois; how he was able to galvanize people and strengthen our storm-tossed spirits. This was symbolic of what happened at the general university level. It is to our eternal credit that the university never lost the Katrina semester. The challenge was tremendous, and the university met it bravely in many ways.

I wish the American government had been equally forthcoming. I'm somewhat disappointed at the federal government's response to Katrina, first, when it happened, and then the aftermath. It was extremely dispiriting seeing the different universities jumping over one another, eliminating academic programs, cutting jobs, downsizing in very hurtful ways, just managing to hang in there. It was multiple jeopardy for many of the Katrina victims. You lost everything you owned to Katrina, and now you also lost your job. I know how hard things were, but I was thinking some solid, comprehensive rescue plan should have been extended to educational institutions in New Orleans. America is capable of doing it. Money's not the issue. I put it down to lack of care. Afterall, Katrina was not a totally natural disaster. No. The water that took away everything we had, that nearly took our lives, came from a broken levee. That is the London Avenue Canal. I didn't even know this until months later, that that was where the levee broke and soaked us all in water. So, they should have built a stronger levee and prevented that catastrophe. The government failed in one of its cardinal responsibilities— the protection of human lives and property. It should have made up for this with a salvage plan for the universities. Compulsory downsizing did a lot of damage that would take the institutions years to recover from. It's all very painful.

It seems all the universities here, especially the University of New Orleans, of course, are still recovering from that and from the loss of enrollment.

It's going to take a long time. In fact, I'm surprised at the way we've been able to heal. UNO was lucky that we didn't get water. I mean if you go to SUNO now or to Dillard, those people were soaked. You know what it means for the first floor of a university library or the computer section to go? The losses were devastating, which is why I also feel that more help should have been extended to us here. We needed it.

The city as a whole has lost a lot. Just see the ragged, boarded-up houses, the empty streets, the silent boulevards. For example, the African, especially Nigerian, community in New Orleans has literally disappeared. Makes me so lonesome most times. Yes, this city should have received more help. It deserves it.

It's not just the French Quarter that is New Orleans. No. Not just the tourist areas. New Orleans is people.

And it seems that prior to Gustav there was a lot of anxiety amongst, obviously, the population itself. It seems like there's a lot of anxiety that another Katrina could happen.

Oh, yes. Once it has happened to you and it has scarred you so deeply, it's natural for you to feel like, "Oh, well, I hope another one is not coming." Every potential hurricane or every potential storm gathering on the Atlantic now is more or less a potential Katrina until it proves otherwise. I believe that this city needs to be secured. It really needs to be secured. Just see all the steel and metal pylons now being driven into the earth to replace the mud and earth levees of the past. In the immediate period after Katrina, there was noise all over the place, the "ba dung, ba dung, ba dung" sound of heavy machinery. You wonder: why was all his not done before now? Why did it take an apocalyptic catastrophe of Katrina's magnitude to remind government about the necessity of a flood-control wall and metal levee around the UNO side of the Lake? I have never stopped asking myself, "Why wasn't this done fifty years ago or one hundred years ago?" Or whatever. New Orleans has been exposed, so dangerously exposed to the elements; we were lucky that the casualties were not more. This is a city that needs to be protected, and America can do it. A country that puts men and women on the moon should be able to secure the rest of us on earth. Flood walls. Solid. Impregnable. High levees. In the past, people put mounds and mounds of earth at the edge of the lake, and they called it a levee, you know. I think the government underestimated the fury of water, and also the anger of water. Water doesn't like to be underestimated. No. It doesn't like to be disdained. And I think that was what happened. We need the levees to be stronger; they will need to be higher. What we have at the moment can't go beyond a Category 2. Anyway, a strong Category 2 will top this and hit the city again. I believe that we should not succumb to a false sense of security. The yearly lull, when November has come and the hurricane season is gone, we tend to forget that June is on its way back again. I have been to Holland, and I know that most of that country is below sea level. You know, after taking two or three devastating hits, it perfected the art and science of flood control. America has one or two things to learn from the Dutch experience, without damaging the environment in the process.

Were you able to salvage anything from your home?

This is a paper here, and you know what it means to get two pages of a sixty-page essay? What are you going to do with those two pages, smell it? I lost my computer. I lost all my records, vital documents, manuscripts, literary correspondence, and rare books. I had just returned from Nigeria, and I had my box full of rare books, books I was going to use for my teaching and research. I hadn't even opened the box before the storm came. It was by my bedside. Katrina took them all away. I'm not talking about clothes or whatever; those ones can be replaced. I particularly miss my literary correspondence, two or three files of them, including the latest exchanges between me and high school students in the UK who had one of my poems on their syllabus, and who kept sending me ask-the-author questions and comments to which I responded. I lost all those, and also my works-in-progress files. It's as if Katrina took away my memory. For months and months after the storm I couldn't sleep. Nor are my nights free of Katrina nightmares, even right up to this moment. Which is why I have found it so difficult so far to write about the experience. But I surely will. Eventually.

We're Not Here to Protect You

Joel Fisher Rapp
Interviewed by April Martin

Joel Fisher Rapp's daughter had given birth prematurely the week before the storm, and since the baby was still in the hospital, the family chose to stay in New Orleans. As they searched for rescue, the family wondered where and when they would be reunited with the new baby.

What's the name of your stores?

Meraux Food Stores.

And did they all open back up after the storm?

I opened one up fairly fast in November, December of 2005. The second one we just opened up about two months ago. And, the third one will probably not open up. It was my original one, it was the biggest one, we had big sporting goods and all in it. And, the two, the one we reopened only had about twenty inches of water from the flood, and the other two had water up to the rafters. Probably between, the— just that the parish is coming back slowly and the magnitude of the damage— we probably won't open that one, if at all, any time soon.

The one that's not opening back up at all, you said that was the first one?

Yeah.

How long had that been open?

Since 1981.

And you started the business, or was it a family business?

Yeah, it is a family business. My brothers— I have two brothers— my brothers and I started it in 1981.

I know that you guys decided not to evacuate. Tell me about why.

My parents have always lived in St. Bernard Parish. We were supposed to be on high ground down there, and they never did— my father never did evacuate. But the storm had such a magnitude that we thought we needed to do something. My daughter had a premature baby, born a week before the storm, and it, the baby, had to stay in the hospital. The Saturday night before the storm, my daughter had to see her baby for the last time until the emergency would be over. So, her in-laws, her husband's mother and father, had hotel rooms downtown on Canal Street. And we were asked to go down there. My mother and my father, my daughter, and her husband, Stephen (my daughter's name is Julie, her husband's name is Steve). We, all eight of us, evacuated down there to the hotel room on Canal Street. And we did that instead of leaving because we thought usually a hurricane would be two or three days, and you can get back in and things like that. And everybody you talked to said "Oh, when I evacuated, oh, I took three days of clothes, and that's all I had with us." And that seems to have been the trend. So, we thought that we would be close downtown because Touro wouldn't be too far away, and after the storm passed, we could get my daughter back to Touro Hospital to take care of and see her newborn baby.

The hotel you guys stayed at, that was the Crowne Plaza?

Yes.

And you said your parents went with you. And, your daughter's husband's parents were there as well?

Yeah. My life partner is Max Shaneyfelt, and he went with me.

Okay, so you guys were there, you were at the Crowne Plaza for three days?

We went to the Crowne Plaza on Sunday morning, and we also took— we were allowed to bring our pets. So, we had three dogs and a cat. Like I said, it was the eight of us that were there. And, we got there Sunday and everything was, you know, fine on Sunday. Sunday night, early Monday morning, the storm came through. We were fine, there were no major problems with the hotel. It was still kind of blowing, so we decided not to leave the hotel because it was still pretty nasty Monday evening. We thought by Tuesday morning we would be able to get up and leave. Tuesday morning was when we found out about the breakages of the [17th] Street Canal. So, we decided we could stay one more day, and then maybe we could get it under control, which was not a good move. Our car, where the Crowne Plaza is right there on the corner of Canal Street, is right by the French Quarter. The French Quarter didn't have damage; they didn't have major water. Like I say, like a couple of inches in, on the streets all around the hotel. They didn't have deep water or anything. Our cars were all parked down at the other end of Canal Street where the old Krause building parking lot was. So, Wednesday, when things weren't coming too good and all that, we thought we could get out through the Crescent City Connection. My son-in-law and his father walked down to try to get our cars out. They got halfway down there, and the water was two or three feet in the streets around where the parking lot was, and there was no way to get the cars out. So we came back. They came back.

Later on, on that Wednesday, the hotel deteriorated. I mean, when you look down on the Canal Street from the windows that you could see— we were on the 8th floor— it was almost like a surreal thing, you could see some of the looting going on; you could see the police coming with their guns, and actually some of the looters came back up through the hotel. I don't know if they were staying there, if they were members of the workers' families, or what. It was pretty scary just being in the hotel. They had generators, but they would only work the elevators part-time so you couldn't go up and down. We had lights coming in through daylight, but there was very little light at night. Just some kind of little tiny lights in the hallway. And there was no, you were kind of in a closed-in room with no air conditioning, no water. We had to walk up because we were on the eighth floor, and, plus, there was a mezzanine. So, we had to walk up and down the stairs to get water, to use the— to go get garbage cans full of water and things like that to use the facilities. To get water and to go get food.

They had nice food, buffets and all, but it got down to where the food was going, too, so we had peanut butter and jelly sandwiches and some little things like that, which wasn't really a big issue because no one was all that hungry. So, Wednesday, we all kind of went downstairs because it was really hot upstairs. We all made our way downstairs because there was hope that buses were coming. There was all these rumors that buses and things were coming to get us and evacuate us. And, at that time, you could see on Canal Street, I think it was the old Gus Mayer building, was on fire. And you could see the fire trucks were there with just a little spout of water coming out and trying to handle it. And I'm thinking, "Gee, if we don't drown then we're going to burn to death now." But the hotel offered buses; the Monteleone that was just down the street ordered ten commercial buses to come in, and I think it was forty to fifty dollars a piece, which we paid, and we could go and get on the bus. Well, at first, we sent four, and then— because my mom and dad didn't want to leave their dog, I was going to stay with them and things were deteriorating so nastily in the hotel that I decided that the animals might just have to fend for themselves. We could only take one little bag and that was it. No animals would be allowed. So, we leave the hotel through the back door and we had to walk through about a foot and a half of water on that back street. We sat on cement, you know, cement doorways and things like that on Royal Street right across the street from the Monteleone Hotel, from about seven— I'm confused about the time, but it was daylight, getting late, but it was still daylight — until about ten o'clock that night. And, the buses never did come. And, the word was that FEMA or the government confiscated the buses to start, to still help people evacuate from the Superdome.

At that point, they sent us all back to the hotel. Well, we packed our little bags, so most of the stuff we had in our bags were wet at this time. Our clothes were getting a little thin. And, we went back to the hotel, and they let us back in. When we got back to the hotel, there was a young couple that was there. My daughter had her English bulldog with her. This young couple wasn't going. They seemed to be animal lovers, so I gave them some money to take care of the dogs and gave them my name and all that. And when, if they get through with the dogs, I would come pick them up and give them a reward at that time. Well, when we got back to the hotel, my daughter's English bulldog had died. We had to figure out that situation and try to figure out what to do. We had to take all the mattresses, the mattress thing off where the dog died. That happened Wednesday night, so there were a lot of emotions going on Wednesday.

Thursday morning, when we woke up, the hotel said that the hotel was closing down. They said that they had word that all the employees were… They couldn't keep the employees there, and there was no security there, and the hotel was closing down, but they had word that the Convention Center was secure and that they were going to have buses at the Convention Center, and that if we walked down to the end of the Convention Center up to the Crescent

City Connection, and at the top of the bridge there would be buses waiting for us. So, we're leaving; it was almost like a relief.

Thursday morning some time, I told my parents, "Just pack what we need. Don't bring—" because if we get to walk up the Crescent City Connection that was going to be hard enough for me, plus my parents are 83 and 84 years old; it was going to be hard enough to walk up the Crescent City Connection without us carrying anything. So, we had bare minimum. We had two sacks of medicines and things like that, and I had my purse. I had a canvas sack that I had my little cat [in], my cat that I've been having a long time; I put my little cat in a sack. And, we left the dogs. The other two dogs, we didn't think we had a carrier, or something that we could take the dogs [in], or sneak the dogs by. We left a note and let them know the dogs were left in the room and all. You know, it was a hard decision to make, but like I told my mother, the same as I told my mother the night before about the animals, you know, it's down to our life or theirs, at this point. Between the fires and all the, some of the looting going on Canal Street, the city was... There was no information. There was just hard decisions you had to make and, we did. So, we left the two dogs.

We had to go out the back door. By this time, the water was gone out the back door of the hotel. It had water the day before. I have a picture of us. We're walking, and like my daughter says, I wonder what we were thinking because we have all these smiles on our faces. When you actually got out there, it was a beautiful day; it was cool and a little bit overcast. It was almost like a breath of fresh air because we hadn't had a bath since Sunday when we got there. It was hot.

It was like a breath of fresh air. So, we walked down the street behind the hotel. We walked toward the river, and we finally got to the end of Canal Street and started walking up to the Convention Center.

I think we were right there by, I'm not sure what the building was there at the end, I don't know if it's part of the casino that's there, but there was some kind of big steps that we sat on when we were there. Well, at that point, you could see the National Guard; they wouldn't even talk to you. All they would do was turn their heads.

This was at the Convention Center?

No, this is on Canal Street. At the end, like right toward the entrance. You had to still walk down that street. I think we were at the casino. You had to walk down there to get to the Convention Center. So, it was right in that area. I'm a little bit fuzzy on exactly where , but there's a big building right at the end of Canal Street at the river, diagonally across from the aquarium.

Yeah, that's Harrah's, I think.

I think so. But like I said, I'm not sure.

But anyway, we all sat on the steps to rest for a little while. The National Guard wouldn't talk to you. The police were trying to be helpful, but I don't think they had information to give us.

They had a few police that tried to talk to us because we were looking for information. We just wanted to know just what should we do. We were looking for information, give us some guidance, what was going on, and what to do. And, you're thinking, the National Guard and the New Orleans Police would be it. The New Orleans Police did try to help us. The gentlemen, the two I talked to— but I think they were sketchy, they weren't really sure what was going on. Later on, not only were our cell phones not working, it seems like their communications were down, too. At this point, an elderly couple came out, pulling like a little cart and all, the elderly couple coming out of the French Quarter. He [the man] was an artist down in the French Quarter. So, we talked to them, and we told them to go ahead and stay with us. The gentleman, he was a little bit sick. I think he was on some kind of self-dialysis thing. He was pulling this cart. So, this couple stayed with us. Then two other men were down there. One lived in the French Quarter. I think he was a retired fireman or something, and he worked as a pizza delivery person in the French Quarter. He was coming out... I think the people were coming out of the French Quarter because they were told they needed to start evacuating; they were trying to evacuate the whole city. The other gentleman was from New Orleans East, who got flooded out somehow or another from that. He wound up down there. We're all kind of teamed... Oh, we had an extra couple from the hotel that was with us. So, we were eight, nine, ten, eleven, twelve. We were fourteen of us that kind of got in a little gang.

We found some kind of cart, must have been out of one of the hotels or something. We put all our bags on it and things. The two gentlemen that teamed up with us helped push the cart. So, we walked down Convention Center Boulevard, and it was almost like people waiting for a parade. I mean, it was a big crowd, and people offered you orange juice and big buckets of apples and things like that. People were giving you things along the way. I didn't even think about where it was coming from or what was going on. I was thinking it was the hotels' or the things that were along there, the businesses, could've been stolen food or whatever. But they offered it to me, and I didn't have nothing else better. Probably we were eating looters' food. We had an apple and some orange juice and kept walking. We walked down, and like I said, we walked to where the entrance was, down Convention Center Boulevard; we went up the Crescent City Connection like we were told. Well, we got all the way up to where it was ready to go straight on that curved entrance. And at that point, people were coming back down the Crescent City Connection.

They told us not to go, that we weren't allowed to go across the Crescent City Connection, and there were no buses. And, if we went across it, we were liable to be shot, that there were guards. So we didn't go check it out for ourselves, we just took their word, and we came back down. Well, as we came back down, we got there to the Convention Center, and kind of walked toward the Convention Center. We had been on the right-hand side going toward the Crescent City Connection. Well, this time, we were on the Convention Center side, on the left-hand side. So, this little short lady— I'll never forget her, she was a little short lady, kind of stocky, and she had a dark green polo shirt on and a long black skirt— she had a big tray of some juices or something. And, she looks at us, at our group, and she says, "What are y'all doing here?" We kind of tell her our tale of woe. She says, "Y'all shouldn't be out here; y'all going to get hurt. Y'all need to go inside." We were in the corridor, the entranceway, the inside of the Convention Center at this time. She says, "Well, go in there, and go down that way, and you'll see the Red Cross." So I'm thinking the Red Cross is there.

We walked down, and by this time we were looking for some bathrooms, which was hard to find anything to use in there because the bathroom facilities were horrible. We decided we may pick up some of these chairs; the guys said that. They set up some of the folding chairs they use in the Convention Center. We actually had a chair for each of us that was on this cart kind of thing; it was a big cart. We walk down where the lady told us to go. This time we get down toward the middle and stop. When she was saying go by the Red Cross, it wasn't really the Red Cross at all. It must have been where they had all the medical supplies for the Convention Center, and they had all these white carts like golfcart type of things that they must use for emergencies. They were all painted white with big red crosses on them.

All the kids were actually all around on them, sitting on them and playing on them down there. We stopped and kind of regrouped. We were trying to find the bathroom facilities. These two families come up and wanted to know what we were doing. They were black families. There was a little black lady and two black families that came up. We told them what we were doing, told them our little tale of woe. She said, "Y'all need to stay here with us. We're going to help you." So, they came by and immediately they got us one of a little, like maybe a twelve by twelve piece of carpet that they use for all the conventions. The guys put all the chairs around. They found a little table, and we had, like, a little campground. They got all kind of little things; they put them around it like a barricade around where our little group was. This was Thursday sometime, so we stayed there all Thursday.

They would come down with a little bucket of potato salad or a container of cheese. They would come down with a hot drink in a can and gave us all kind of stuff. And, we had a few little bottles of water. We didn't have a lot but what we were carrying around, a little bottle of water or something that we had brought with us from the hotel. So, we were there Thursday. Like I said, it was families that were in there, everybody was just as nice as they could be right there. We got really close, especially with those two families. At that time, we would try to move inside the Convention Center. There were some plugs, so we would try to charge our cell phones and different things like that. Another little kid was there; he came by us and stayed with us. We wound up being fifteen people total. Well, that night, my mama was just kind of talking to everybody. She was standing outside of our little group. All the sudden, one of the guys, one of the family members, or one of the gentlemen that was helping us out, said, "Tell mama to come in here. She needs to come in here now." So I told my mom, and she said, "Oh, I'm just talking; I'm not doing nothing wrong, Joel." And, I said, "Mama, Don said for you to come in here." She says, "Okay." So, she came in at that time. We're kind of taking turns laying on a little pallet. But there's not too much sleep going on.

A couple things happened. I guess I jumped ahead a little bit. First of all, Max was with me. He tried to go to the men's bathroom. And, right when he got in there, this woman with the loudest mouth I ever heard— it was late— and she screams out, "My daughter's missing, my seven-year-old daughter, I can't find her. Maybe she was raped or stolen and raped like the girl the night before." And then she screams about, "Oh, goodness, look in all the bathrooms, maybe they dragged her in there." So, Max, I thought he was going to have a heart attack because he was in there. He said he put the light around him to make sure nobody was in there. He said he wasn't going to come out alive if that... But all that worked out. But, all the sudden, it was like gang members that came through. They walked down the corridor. There were people against the walls of the area with pallets like we had. It was like a hallway between all the people where people would walk. And these gang guys came through. They all had on those baggy pants, and they all either had golf clubs or pipes from, I guess they picked them up from the Convention Center, from all the displays. Some of them had these women that walked around like they were these gang leaders, too, with them. They would walk up and down, and you would think, "Oh, Lord," and they were looking for the little girl. Finally, a little while after that, they found the little girl. She was by another family, and she fell asleep with her friend. So that simmered down. But, in between, it would settle down, and all the sudden you were thinking, "Oh, Lord, here they come again." That happened two or three times during the night. They would all come marching down that middle aisle, and they had their demonstration things going on.

Were they young people, or were they all ages? Could you tell?

They were young, probably their twenties or so, I would say. I'm going to tell you, I would tell you I examined them, but I wasn't [going to] because that's what the guy told us: "Don't pay attention to them, don't look at them, just stay out of the way."

I couldn't pick one out of a lineup. All I can remember is they would come through, and they had pipes and the golf clubs and that type of stuff.

The other thing that happened that night when we were inside the corridor of Convention Center, you could hear the helicopters going, and then all of a sudden— I don't know if they got lower or something— you hear a big thing go like "Ssshhhh," [dropping hand motion] like water or something. All the people outside, in the entrance way outside, there was all kind of people with their chairs. They were sitting there, and all these people started coming into the Convention Center. So, "Oh, Lord, now we're going to be trampled to death." I didn't really know what was happening 'cause they thought, "Oh, Lord, maybe the other levee broke, maybe by the river, and water was going to come from there." They all were getting nervous and coming in, but nothing happened. And then they all went back to where their little spots were on the outside of the Convention Center. I think what that was, from the news and things I got, I think helicopters did come, and they dropped water. I don't think they actually landed and unloaded the water. I think they hovered and just threw the water out. The swoosh we were hearing was the bottles of water breaking and swooshing. That was Thursday and Thursday night.

Friday morning we were there again, and one of the things was… I guess I keep going back to the bathroom facilities because they were so bad I couldn't take it anymore. I went through the Convention

Center, I found this rack, and I made... It was three sides, and I thought, "Oh, Jesus, maybe we could make our own port-a-pot," so I dragged that back and found some garbage cans. All the ladies thought, "Oh yeah, we got something going here." Then we found those curtains that they use as displays, and they put the curtains up by the time I came back with the buckets, and we had us a port-a-pot. Everybody was thrilled to have that.

Some of the people had TVs and things like that, and come to find out later that evening, we hear there's going to be an Army operation to come rescue us, that President Bush was coming through, and that after he comes through there would be an Army operation and that we would be rescued. I think it was about two or three o'clock that evening. We all pack up our stuff. I don't know who decided, but [they said] let's go outside so we could be waiting in line or whatever. I didn't care if I was the last person out; I would've waited in line to be last so I wouldn't be trampled or anything. I just wanted to go. We go outside, and we were by the Holiday Inn Select that was across the street. I think it was the Texas National Guard came through like a parade. They came through from the bridge area down toward... They went by the, what was that, into that Riverwalk parking lot and all came down. It was a big parade, and everybody waved and clapped for them. Nobody was being— nobody did anything wrong. The people were well behaved. The only time you had people not behaving, or not being helpful, was these groups that came out at night.

The other people were just victims; they were trying to help each other. They were nice to you; they tried to help you. When the National Guard came through, I can't tell you, I saw anything going wrong. This time, in the Holiday Inn Select, I guess, we brought our chairs with us and all of that. We were just kind of sitting there in one of the little corridor things in the entrance. And we go in; we're sitting there, and we're waiting. We see a big helicopter; it had to be Bush passing over and seeing, or some of that group, just checking out what was going on because it was a huge, huge helicopter. We were thinking that must have been his pass-by, and a few minutes later all that was gone, and we think, "Okay." Well, at that point you could go walk down to where the parking lot was, and they had all the National Guard. You walk down there, and for every person that went, they gave you a bottle of water and an MRE.

The National Guard gave you those?

Yes. They had a big display of all these MRE and water.

As you walk through, you tell everybody thank you and all that. We went back and had a little water. If you wanted anything you had to walk. Like I said, nobody was doing a lot of eating, so the little bottles of water we got, we all— the ones of us that could walk; like, my daughter had just had surgery, and my parents didn't go— we brought what we could back. So, that was fine. It got dark. And we're thinking maybe they'll do it at night. After everybody got fed, the next thing you know, the National Guard packs up, and the big parade that came in, they went out. We thought, well let's wait, maybe they're going to load down there and come through. We kept thinking that maybe buses were going to come, and we were going to go out. We waited and waited, and it was dark, and nothing had happened. No National Guard stayed there. So we're thinking that it must be going to happen in the morning.

We sat, and we decided we better camp down. Now we're camping outside. They went and found a little piece of rug, and we all made the best we could do right there. We spent the night there. And, about two or three times that night about four police cars came through. It would be more than four police cars if anybody was going to do anything. They just made their quick little pass; I don't know what they were doing. The next morning we were up again bright and early, with the sunlight, and here comes the same parade. Here comes the National Guard back through, and they went and set up their thing. Again we walked down that way, and they had MREs and the water out. We find out that if we brought somebody else's driver's license, I could get extra food or extra water. So everybody gave us their driver's licenses, and we carried as much food and water as we could. We go back. We went down there, and I told the National Guard, I said, "Thank you, what's the agenda, what should we expect about the buses?" And the National Guard looked at me and said, "Ma'am, we're here; we're not here to protect you, and we're not here to give you transportation. We're only here to give you food and water. And, with food and water, you should be safe because everybody will be fed and have water." By that point my heart just dropped. I felt like it went through the cement.

So, Max and I decided— supposedly there were helicopters down at the other end, down by the entrance to the Crescent City Connection, and the helicopters were supposedly helicoptering out sick people. I went down there to find out what we had to do to get anybody helicopted out. I was thinking maybe my parents and my daughter could be helicopted out because... So, they told us, "If you can walk, you can't be helicopted out." Now, I don't know if that's true or not because I'd seen some people walking to get on the helicopters; I don't know what their situation was, but that's what I was told. So, again, we walk back down.

To backtrack a little... The first day we were there, Thursday, we saw all kind of foreign press come through and talk to us. They would stop and talk to us and interview us and things like that. That Saturday, I think it was that Saturday, somebody came through, and I talked to them. We told them we had older people that had diabetes and somebody who'd just had surgery. Well, it started to get hot.

Our gang built some kind of sheet overhang because it was getting hot; it was beautiful weather, but it was getting a little hot being there. Actually we were right across… On the neutral ground right there was a body, a dead body covered by a sheet, I mean a yellow quilt type of thing that we were across from. About, I don't know, it must've been getting toward noon because the sun was going up and getting kind of warm, it just so happened, my son-in-law and his daddy had just walked to go get some food. Max and I had just gone to go find out about the medical helicopters and things. An angel must have been with us because a car came by and told us that there were buses three blocks over, I think it was on Tchoupitoulas Street. Just pick up your stuff, and walk over there calmly, and you should be able to catch a bus. Well, all of us was right there. Ten minutes before, one of us might have been someplace else and wouldn't have known where the person was. We would've been a nervous wreck. How do you leave and not take everybody with you?

We picked up our stuff, we walked up, and sure enough, there were buses. We got on the buses, and it was the first time we were in air conditioning in a week, so it really felt good. Finally, we all got up and across the Crescent City Connection, we left across the river some kind of way. So, someplace we stopped in— I think it's St. Martin— and they had a weigh station, and they had food, and they had all kinds of… They gave you bags of toothpaste and soaps and combs and different little things in plastic bags, plenty big bottles of water, and it was cold water, which was nice. They also had clothes all laid out on the grass, and they had them by ladies' and men's sizes and children's. Actually, a couple of us picked up a few little things off the grass, and I went to the back of the bus to change. By that time, I didn't really even have my own clothes on, and I'd put on clothes that were dirty and wet from the night before. I picked up clothes off the grass in St. Martin Parish and changed in the back of the bus.

We're on the bus, and we're going toward the north. First of all, they told us we were going to Houston. And I was okay with Houston. I forgot to tell you one thing. My daughter's baby, we didn't know from Monday until late Wednesday night where my grandbaby was, my daughter's baby. Late Wednesday night, while we were waiting in that line for the buses, the only cell phone usage we would get would be out-of-town people. My step daughter-in-law, who is like my, who is my family, she was on the phone every night like a Trojan. She was calling every hospital; she was in Birmingham, Alabama.

Sonja, Sonja Shaney Felt, and she's more like my stepdaughter; that's what I feel like. She's on the phone all night long trying to find the baby for us, what happened to the baby. Because we'd hear things that babies were being evacuated, horror stories about what was going on in some of the hospitals. We were quite nervous about what was going on with our baby; we had no earthly clue what had happened to her, whether she was alive or dead or what. All night long that's all she did; she found— I think it was in Lafayette, you might check your notes for what she told you— [that] the babies were evacuated from Touro Hospital. The baby was in Lafayette and was going to be transferred to Texas, and the baby would become a ward of the state of Texas until one of her parents, or somebody, would show up to make medical decisions, or [decide] how to take care of her, which I'm sure she did alright because I think all babies did good. But still, it was a scary thought.

She had five or ten minutes to find a neonatologist to accept the baby as a patient. They would fly the babies, some of the babies were going to go to Houston— I'm sorry— to Alabama. She found one [neonatologist], and they transferred my grandbaby to the UAB Hospital in Birmingham, Alabama.

Which is where Sonja lives?

Yeah, she was there constantly with the baby and had the baby taken care of until we could get there. We got the baby in Birmingham, Alabama. So, now we need to get out of New Orleans and get there. In between, my daughter was trying to breast-pump the milk. At first she was trying to save, and that went to the wayside. And then she just kept trying to keep her breasts going, she pumped the milk, and then we would just throw it away so that she could actually breastfeed the baby when we got there, which was also successful. Back to the bus thing, they told us at first we were going to Houston, and I was pretty calm with that.

We were back on the bus, and then they said Dallas, Texas, and I said, "Well, Dallas shouldn't be too bad; it's a big city, and maybe we can get out of it." Then they said, "No, you're not going to Dallas; we're taking you to Oklahoma." I thought, "Oh, Lord," you know, Oklahoma's over here [motions toward far right], and I have to be all the way over here [motions far left]. At that time, I said, "Max, I can't go to Oklahoma, we have got to get off; tell them to drop me off. After all we've been through, I'll walk to the nearest... Drop me near an exit, and we'll walk." So they dropped us off. They had a little bit of protesting about some of the people on the bus. They dropped us off in Shreveport, Louisiana. My daughter's mother-in-law's family was there, and the next day we were on those Angel Flights or Giving Flights. These little planes came and picked us up and flew us from Shreveport to Birmingham, Alabama, where we were reunited with our family and the baby. Yeah.

The other note is that we lost everything in St. Bernard Parish. I had five and a half feet of water in my house. My daughter had about eight feet. So, we had nurseries and all that, and the baby never got to see, do, stay. We started off with zero since the storm. To even take a shower, we had to go buy clothes.

Were you able to salvage anything from your homes?

We got some dishes, a few little things like that; most of our pictures are gone. I have a big attic room upstairs. It's mostly junk up there, so you sort through the junk, and I had a few little boxes of pictures. We have a few things like that. We lost our clothes, our furniture, you know, all our memories.

The sad thing that I think that they need to note is that I'm from St. Bernard, and St. Bernard was a really bedroom community. It was families and friends living there close-knit. And now everybody is scattered. Our whole way of life, our whole family connection... I've got friends that moved to Alabama. Others moved to Texas.

I'm in Slidell. Families, people, used to live within a mile of each other, and now I'm the perfect case because my daughter lives in Metairie, and I live in Slidell. So, where we [once] lived next door, or within a mile, [now] everybody's scattered, and you lost the close-knitness of your family and friends.

You can replace your things, and you get over your stuff. But, I don't think you get over losing the contact of your loved ones and your family. That [was] easy contact. I had friends that I met with; we painted a couple nights a week, and now that's gone. And going to see my daughter now is an effort, where it was just a run-of-the-mill thing.

Also Available from UNO Press:

William Christenberry: Art & Family by J. Richard Gruber (2000)
The El Cholo Feeling Passes by Fredrick Barton (2003)
A House Divided by Fredrick Barton (2003)
Coming Out the Door for the Ninth Ward edited by Rachel Breunlin
    from The Neighborhood Story Project series (2006)
The Change Cycle Handbook by Will Lannes (2008)
Cornerstones: Celebrating the Everyday Monuments & Gathering Places of New Orleans
    edited by Rachel Breunlin, from The Neighborhood Story Project series (2008)
A Gallery of Ghosts by John Gery (2008)
Hearing Your Story: Songs of History and Life for Sand Roses by Nabile Farès
    translated by Peter Thompson, from The Engaged Writers Series (2008)
The Imagist Poem: Modern Poetry in Miniature edited by William Pratt
    from The Ezra Pound Center for Literature series (2008)
The Katrina Papers: A Journal of Trauma and Recovery by Jerry W. Ward, Jr.
    from The Engaged Writers Series (2008)
On Higher Ground: The University of New Orleans at Fifty by Dr. Robert Dupont (2008)
Us Four Plus Four: Eight Russian Poets Conversing translated by Don Mager (2008)
Voices Rising: Stories from the Katrina Narrative Project edited by Rebeca Antoine (2008)
Gravestones (Lápidas) by Antonio Gamoneda, translated by Donald Wellman
    from The Engaged Writers Series (2009)
The House of Dance and Feathers: A Museum by Ronald W. Lewis by Rachel Breunlin
    & Ronald W. Lewis, from The Neighborhood Story Project series (2009)
I hope it's not over, and good-by: Selected Poems of Everette Maddox by Everette Maddox (2009)
Portraits: Photographs in New Orleans 1998-2009 by Jonathan Traviesa (2009)
Theoretical Killings: Essays & Accidents by Steven Church (2009)
Rowing to Sweden: Essays on Faith, Love, Politics, and Movies by Fredrick Barton (2010)
Dogs in My Life: The New Orleans Photographs of John Tibule Mendes (2010)
Understanding the Music Business: A Comprehensive View edited by Harmon Greenblatt
    & Irwin Steinberg (2010)
The Fox's Window by Naoko Awa, translated by Toshiya Kamei (2010)
A Passenger from the West by Nabile Farès, translated by Peter Thompson
    from The Engaged Writers Series (2010)
The Schüssel Era in Austria: Contemporary Austrian Studies, Volume 18
    edited by Günter Bischof & Fritz Plasser (2010)
The Gravedigger by Rob Magnuson Smith (2010)
Everybody Knows What Time It Is by Reginald Martin (2010)
When the Water Came: Evacuees of Hurricane Katrina by Cynthia Hogue & Rebecca Ross
    from The Engaged Writers Series (2010)
Aunt Alice Vs. Bob Marley by Kareem Kennedy, from The Neighborhood Story Project series (2010)
Houses of Beauty: From Englishtown to the Seventh Ward by Susan Henry
    from The Neighborhood Story Project series (2010)
Signed, The President by Kenneth Phillips, from The Neighborhood Story Project series (2010)
Beyond the Bricks by Daron Crawford & Pernell Russell
    from The Neighborhood Story Project series (2010)
Green Fields: Crime, Punishment, & a Boyhood Between by Bob Cowser, Jr.,
    from the Engaged Writers Series (2010)
New Orleans: The Underground Guide by Michael Patrick Welch & Alison Fensterstock (2010)

unopress.org